Ribbons of Green

New Century Gardens and Landscapes of the American Southwest

Baker H. Morrow, SERIES EDITOR

Whether practical gardening guides, best plant guides, landscape architecture showcases, or blueprints for urban ecology, books in the New Century Gardens and Landscapes of the American Southwest series address the challenges novice gardeners and skilled practitioners alike face with prolonged droughts, limited water supplies, high-altitude climes, and growing urbanization. Books in this series not only provide practical landscaping advice for backyard gardeners, they dive deep into ecology, built environments, agricultural history, and the emerging discipline of urban ecology. The New Century Gardens and Landscapes of the American Southwest series tackles the environmental questions that many communities in the American West confront as we all work to create healthy, dynamic, and inviting outdoor spaces.

Also available in the New Century Gardens and Landscapes of the American Southwest:

Ancient Women Gardeners: Prelude to the Chacoan World by David E. Stuart

The Design Competition in Landscape Architecture: Pedagogy and Practice by Kathleen Kambic and Katya Crawford

Growing a Sensational Garden in the Southern Rocky Mountains: A Monthly Guide by Nan Fischer

Feeding a Divided America: Reflections of a Western Rancher in the Era of Climate Change by Gilles Stockton

The Gardens of Los Poblanos by Judith Phillips

Water for the People: The Acequia Heritage of New Mexico in a Global Context edited by Enrique R. Lamadrid and José A. Rivera

A Natural History of Unloved Trees edited by Margaret Grady Ménache

RIBBONS of GREEN

The Rio Grande and the Making of Modern Albuquerque

John Fleck and
Robert P. Berrens

Printed in the United States of America

ISBN 978-0-8263-6968-0 (paper)
ISBN 978-0-8263-6969-7 (ePub)

Library of Congress Control Number: 2025054244

Founded in 1889, the University of New Mexico sits on the traditional homelands of the Pueblo of Sandia. The original peoples of New Mexico—Pueblo, Navajo, and Apache—since time immemorial have deep connections to the land and have made significant contributions to the broader community statewide. We honor the land itself and those who remain stewards of this land throughout the generations and also acknowledge our committed relationship to Indigenous peoples. We gratefully recognize our history.

Cover illustration: Fourth panel of *We Trust in the Loyalty of Old Firends,* Rob Rikoon, egg tempera, 6' x 24', on display at the Santa Fe Capitol Building.
Designed by Isaac Morris
Composed in Acumin, Atrament, and Meno,

Contents

Preface

RIBBONS OF GREEN

It was warm, with a hint of rain in the air on June 13, 1919.[1] When more than one hundred and fifty people gathered at the Commercial Club in Albuquerque's New Town to talk about their community's struggle with the Rio Grande, it was no less than a conversation about Albuquerque's future. Built of stone in 1891, the Commercial Club was an imposing, church-like four-story structure, a monument to a new city's ambitions.[2] Those ambitions were floundering a quarter century after its construction, swamped by an increasingly unmanageable Rio Grande.

Alternately flooding, swamping, and running dry, the Rio Grande had long posed challenges to the communities living astride the primary source of water flowing through a vast, arid landscape of western North America. From time immemorial small self-sustaining villages had straddled the river from its headwaters in the Rocky Mountains to the Gulf of Mexico, a string of pearls clinging to the long, fragile thread of water through the desert landscape.

As the communities grew beyond their Indigenous roots, first with Spanish colonization beginning in the 1500s and then Anglo settlement as the region was subsumed into the United States in the 1800s, they threatened to break the thread—or have the thread break them. One of the largest such communities was what was then known as Albuquerque's New Town, which by 1919 was well on its way to becoming the economic capital of New Mexico, a railroad stop in the center of the state.

The Commercial Club building, born of civic pride and city-building ambition, epitomized the challenge. It lay at the heart of modern economic

Figure 1. (*above*) Commercial Club, 1893. Courtesy of the Albuquerque Museum, PA1990.013.057.A.

Figure 2. (*below*) Looking north up Fourth Street from the north tower as the Commercial Club was being built, 1891. Courtesy of the Albuquerque Museum, PA1990.013.103.A.

power, within a short walk of the railroad that had kicked off Albuquerque's transition. By the early twentieth century the wool processors, banks, insurance companies, and warehouses in the blocks surrounding it had become the tools of New Mexico's entrance into a national economy. But from the time it was built in the 1890s, if you looked north from the windows in the building's steeple-like tower up the growing city's newly built Fourth Street, you were looking straight up an old Rio Grande floodway.[3] In high-flow years, valley residents would nervously work to reinforce a dike eight miles upstream as the river rose in the spring. When they lost the battle—as they often did—the Rio Grande would spill into the old flood channel where they had built Fourth Street, spreading water across the valley they were trying to turn into a city. When it wasn't flooding, the Rio Grande had left much of the valley in all directions a swampland, ill-suited for their urban ambitions.

It was a river doing what rivers do in a meandering flood plain like the Middle Rio Grande Valley—spreading out during high flows, depositing sediment, and leaving the low wetlands known in such river valleys the world over as *back swamps*. By the twentieth century the river, its flooding, and the back swamps increasingly clashed with the desires of a growing city.

The one hundred and fifty people gathered were grappling with these challenges that June day at the Commercial Club in downtown Albuquerque. How would they manage the flooding and drain the swamps to create the city they dreamed of?

The Commercial Club's membership was dominated by the most recent arrivals—the Anglo immigrants from the East.[4] But members of two other groups joined them: descendants of the Spanish settlers who had been living on the valley floor since the 1600s and Indigenous Pueblo people—*Pueblo* being the name given to them by the Spanish—who still lived in many of the riverside villages they had occupied since first contact with Spanish colonization.

Among those who organized the meeting and were on the agenda to speak were three men whose lives epitomize the threads of community coming together:

- The Chamber of Commerce Secretary Aldo Leopold,[5] who would go on to become one of the icons of modern American environmentalism, but who in 1919 was an able civic activist for the city-building work of drainage and flood control
- Bernalillo County Commissioner Max Gutierrez, descended from an old Hispanic North Valley ranching and farming family, an advocate of roadbuilding, drainage, and city building
- Isleta Pueblo leader Pablo Abeita,[6] masterful defender of Pueblo sovereignty and the legal and political bargains needed to preserve that sovereignty amid a growing city

The Rio Grande

In his epic book *Great River*, Paul Horgan described the Rio Grande as "an adequate though never a voluminous river except in flood tide."[7] It flows 2,000 miles from its headwaters in the Rocky Mountains to the Gulf of Mexico, passing through high mountain valleys and rocky gorges before spreading out through the desert on its way to the sea. For more than eight hundred miles, it makes up the border between the United States and Mexico, two nations that have given the river two different names: *Rio Grande* on the US side of the border and *Rio Bravo* in Mexico.

From Brownsville and Matamoros at the river's mouth on the Gulf of Mexico to Alamosa high in the San Luis Valley of Colorado, the Rio Bravo/Rio Grande is home to human communities large and small, and it shapes each one. The largest is the massive sprawling urbanity of the El Paso-Juarez metropolitan area, 2.5 million people on the Texas-Chihuahua

Map 1. Albuquerque and New Mexico's Middle Rio Grande Valley. Map by John Fleck.

border. Defining its smallest is an open question. The river's main stem and tributaries are lined with clusters of humanity, some as small as a few homes. Each has a story about its relationship with the river that can help explain how the community came to be.

We focus here on one such region and one such story: the one hundred and fifty miles of the river that New Mexicans call the Middle Rio Grande. The valley, long and narrow, is home in the twenty-first century to Albuquerque and the million people in its greater metropolitan area. Sitting astride the Rio Grande, Albuquerque is the political and economic center of the US state of New Mexico. The Spanish Villa de *Alburquerque* (the extra "r" from the villa's original name lost in the city's rush to modernity) is much older—dating to 1706. But our time frame is loosely taken as starting in 1880 in Territorial New Mexico, when the railroad first arrived in Albuquerque, and the ambitions of a modern city began taking shape.

The Making of Cities

Cities are one of humanity's great inventions.[8] People come together to share the social and economic benefits that flow from acting collectively at ever-larger scales. They are a tool for what the Bengali-born, Nobel Prize–winning economist and ethical philosopher Amartya Sen calls "capabilities"—the conditions that enable people to achieve what they have reason to value.[9] Things like roads, food supply systems, and schools provide those collective capabilities, and all of them are enabled when people gather and share the cost of delivering them and the responsibility of guiding them toward the community's desired future.

Sen writes eloquently about the ancient urbanity of the Ganga (the Ganges), the river of his childhood. The river spread through a vast delta thick with human communities on its way to meet the Bay of Bengal. "Our lives in east Bengal, which is now Bangladesh," he wrote, "were woven around these rivers."[10]

It is a story repeated throughout humanity's history, a river at each city's heart. The Tigris and Euphrates of Babylon's Fertile Crescent, the mouth of Sen's Ganges flowing into the Bay of Bengal, the Mississippian cities of precontact North America, the Yellow River on China's northern plains, the Thames of London, the Seine of Paris—humans gathering around their rivers. Before rails and modern roads, which are almost the entirety of human history, rivers often provided a central transportation corridor. They provided water and a way to dispose of waste. As communities grew they enjoyed their rivers' benefits and suffered their harms.

Each of these places, these cities, these stories, represents the sum of the hopes and dreams of a multitude of individuals, each striving for a better life, coming together to act collectively to make those hopes and dreams real. At the heart of each of those stories is a river.

Our River, and This Book

This book is our attempt to make sense of our city, what we call *modern Albuquerque*—an emergent collection of humanity barely a century and a half old—by studying it through the lens of the community's relationship with its river. In that relationship, in our need to solve the problems of life on a river valley floor, we argue, we *became* a community, finding ways to act collectively at the scales necessary to make a modern American city. We built roads, too, and schools, and the other tools of collective betterment. But first and foremost, we had to come together to manage the Rio Grande.

Our starting point is the arrival in 1880 of the railroad in New Mexico's Middle Rio Grande Valley. The deeper past provides our foundation—the Native American Pueblos, the villages of the Spanish colonizers, and the first wave of northern Europeans who came before. However, 1880 marks a turning point, as we began transitioning from a collection of villages and cultures to attempting to create a modern American city. That it bears the name "Albuquerque," attached to one of those villages, is more geographic accident than legitimate lineage. What came after 1880 was a new creation, emerging from the sometimes-uncomfortable joining of the old; communities increasingly connected socially, culturally, economically, and physically by the river flowing down the Middle Rio Grande Valley. A whole that became greater than the simple sum of its parts, and the story of managing its relationship with the river—the creation of an interconnected system of flood control, drainage, and irrigation—was central to that endeavor. By Albuquerque, we thus mean the greater metropolitan area beyond the city limits of Albuquerque itself, including all the urban-rural and cross-cultural tensions that come with that. Like the river, the story is winding, not linear. But we hope it gets us somewhere.

Our objective in writing this book was to investigate the evolution of a set of institutional arrangements—the created rules, both formal and informal—that shaped the city's relationships with the Rio Grande. In coming together to manage their relationship with the river, the separate cultures and communities that dotted the river valley floor became one. We hope that doing so contributes to the continuing evolution of those relationships and helps respond to changing conditions so that we better adapt to a changing climate and a river with less water.

At the heart of the story lies the Middle Rio Grande Conservancy District, a local government agency created in the 1920s to carry out the essential city-building task of managing the Rio Grande. Its formation—the writing of the rules by which the communities of the valley would help carry out the task of city building—was a tangle of conflicts over who would have a say in the city's formation, and who would have to pay for the work to be done. There was political power held by the largely (but not entirely) Anglo city builders writing those rules, represented by Aldo

Leopold. There was resistance from the small farmers, represented by Max Gutierrez, once a supporter of the project turned opponent as he saw his community taxed beyond its ability to pay without being given a direct say. There was even greater tension between Native American communities, represented by Pablo Abeita, swept up in the project of colonization and city building. But in their defense of their sovereignty, the Native American Pueblos lent their political and financial support to the project of river management and city building in a bargain that would ensure their futures as sovereign communities surrounded by the larger Albuquerque whole.

The injustices persisted, as many small-scale farmers living on the valley floor lived for decades under the shadow of tax delinquency and the potential dispossession of their land because of the flawed assumptions at the heart of the rules first written to create the Conservancy District, and because they were given no political say in the processes needed to change those rules. From that tension between power and resistance, a synthesis emerged over the next half century that left those land ownership rights largely intact but now embedded in growing urban pressures. We still see the evolving set of rules that persist in the river management and resulting urban structure today. The answers to those ever-present questions—who has a say, and who has to pay—are at the heart of what modern Albuquerque became.

The city builders' political power also led to a dark tragedy borne by a particular community. The construction of a flood-control dam was deemed essential to Albuquerque's future, which left a deep scar on the cultural heritage of Cochiti Pueblo, the northernmost community on the valley floor, where the dam was built, and, by extension, on all the Pueblo communities of the valley.

We celebrate what Albuquerque, the city we love, has become, but we must simultaneously acknowledge the injustices, sacrifices, and harms caused by our city's creation.

Gardens

This book grew from more than a dozen years the authors have co-taught *Water Resources: Contemporary Issues*, the introductory course in the University of New Mexico's graduate-level Water Resources Program. At the heart of the course is the idea of *institutions*, by which we mean the rules we write to manage the collective action of living with the shared water resource. The word institution more colloquially can mean the government agencies created to carry those rules out. But the rules matter most in our approach, providing the foundation.

A crucial piece of the puzzle came when Baker Morrow and Sonia Dickey at the University of New Mexico Press invited the inclusion of our book in the press's New Century Gardens and Landscapes of the American Southwest series. That word—gardens—has been crucial in clarifying our ideas about what Albuquerque's founders were trying to accomplish with the project of Rio Grande management that gave rise to our modern city. There is a distinction between managing and pursuing economic development through the metaphor of a carefully designed engine of growth versus seeing it as the tending of a garden—planting what you want to grow, pulling weeds and adapting as you learn from nature's responses to your best intentions. To borrow the deeply important *Nuevo Mexicano* word, we describe a trajectory rooted in a loving care of place—*querencia*.[11]

We see this deeply in Aldo Leopold's role in the development of modern Albuquerque. Long before his rise to national prominence as an environmental writer and thinker, a young Leopold was a central figure in the critical development of our growing city's Rio Grande–management institutions. Leopold's city-building role might seem odd to those more familiar with his later role as an environmental ethicist and champion of wilderness. But both then and throughout his career, Leopold centered the human in the ethical foundations of his ideas. He was not a booster of the city-as-an-engine-of-growth narrative but rather a booster of the let's-tend-to-our-own-garden-and-make-our-city-better-for-the-people-who-live-here narrative.

Pablo Abeita and Max Gutierrez represented the communities that had been gardening the Middle Rio Grande Valley for centuries—enduring the floods, swamps, and droughts, pursuing their hopes for their people's futures. Both acted to try to ensure their communities' place in the Middle Rio Grande Valley's changing future.

Public Entrepreneurs

The intellectual foundation for this book can be found in the work of 2009 Nobel laureate Elinor Ostrom. In her 1965 doctoral thesis, Ostrom turned a traditional approach to the analysis of water management on its head. Before Ostrom, scholars tended to treat government agencies as a given, a fixed unit of analysis for understanding water management. But they are never a given. Where do they come from? In a masterwork of narrative storytelling, Ostrom's thesis chronicles the stops and starts, the false directions and failures, and the success as a group of communities in Southern California collectively came together to manage their shrinking groundwater supply.

Borrowing from the business management and economics literature, Ostrom called the people behind the effort "public entrepreneurs." Like their private sector counterparts, public entrepreneurs first must recognize unmet needs and make the often-difficult conceptual leap to realize that the existing structures of government agencies and private firms are ill-suited to meet those unmet needs. They must take risks to form new organizations to do new things. In contrast to private entrepreneurs, public entrepreneurs, in Ostrom's formulation, are harnessing resources to pursue not private gain but public benefit. They must first write the rules—through the political processes of writing legislation—that enable the creation of the new tools the community needs. They must organize and manage the organizations and be forever innovating in the face of change.

> By using the orientation of public entrepreneurship to pursue a case study of water resource development . . . emphasis is given to the strategies which people followed in seeking to solve a common problem through public actions which could not be solved by individual private actions. The focus is upon the multiple strategies followed rather than the operation of any particular agencies or set of agencies. A study in public entrepreneurship provides an opportunity to develop a natural history of the evolution of a program in public administration where all of the different components can be viewed as being fit together as essential elements in a total program.[12]

That definition begs an important question: Whose idea of "public benefit" will be pursued? Over the following decades, Ostrom studied institutional arrangements for the collective management of natural resource systems worldwide—a multitude of fisheries, forests, and watersheds. Her decades of work led to the powerful conclusion that earned her Nobel Prize: Communities left to their own devices know the most about their goals, desires, and the resources around them and often can manage natural resource systems themselves. In an idea that still frequently dominates our thinking, the seventeenth-century political philosopher Thomas Hobbes described the need for *Leviathan*, the authority handed over to an all-powerful government imposing rules from above to save us from our selfish shortcomings.[13] Ostrom's empirical work found something both different and hopeful. Given the opportunity to communicate and collaborate, people often eschew Leviathan in favor of a governance system they collectively manage for themselves.[14] However, Albuquerque repeatedly confronted a tension. It needed federal funding—Leviathan's money—to pay for the work to be done.

Going to a single place and looking deeply at the evolution of its institutions can be a powerful academic methodology, Ostrom wrote years later as she looked back on her career.[15] That is our goal here. Albuquerque's history shows that the community's first large-scale attempts at collective action to manage the Rio Grande failed to incorporate two of Ostrom's most important advisory precepts—the importance of giving voice to the people using the resource in the development and adaptation of the institutions for its management, and the "proportionality in benefits and costs."[16]

Ostrom identified these as part of what she called *design principles*, often shared by successful collective resource management institutions. We single them out because they are crucial for the story of Albuquerque and New Mexico's Middle Rio Grande: Who will have a say in what must be done and how, and who must pay for the work?[17]

The communities already living on the valley floor knew two crucial things the newcomers ignored. First, the Pueblo communities built their villages on high ground near the Rio Grande but above its high spring and summer flows. The newcomers set out to build a city on the valley floor.[18] Second, where early farming supported modest populations with a grazing economy combined with largely subsistence crop farming, the newcomers tried to brush away the past and engineer a new commercial powerhouse of irrigated crops on the valley floor, ignoring those who understood how unrealistic that goal was.

In our analysis we take seriously the issue of political power. The disenfranchisement of the small farmers on the valley floor created an unstable governance system, wobbling for three-quarters of a century as the city builders tried to sort out its failings. The wobbling is rooted in the political power of those creating the institutions over the objections of many of those being governed.

The tension over these two crucial elements of Ostrom's design principles—Who has a say? Who has to pay?—are at the heart of this book and are central to understanding the evolution of Albuquerque's relationship with the Rio Grande. When Max Gutierrez later split from the collective enthusiasm shown in that 1919 Commercial Club meeting, it was over the newly developing system's failure to give the farmers living on the valley floor a chance to vote on the new institutional arrangement being created. When Pablo Abeita bargained for his community's sovereignty, he was pushing back, asserting his community's power through the act of resistance, demanding a say in what was to come.

Ostrom's broader set of design principles also includes a question vital to Albuquerque's future as the community and the river evolve: How will we adapt the rules to a changing future?[19] As climate change shrinks the Rio Grande while Albuquerque's population continues to grow and community values continue to evolve, the role of democracy in a hotter, drier world becomes central.

Interludes

If the book provides what Ostrom called "a natural history" of the public administration of the river, unraveling how we got to where we are in our relationship with the Rio Grande, then it also is important to give the reader a touchstone to the river today. To help with this, the book includes a set of interludes, placed between the chapters. They provide snippets, month by month, showing how the Rio Grande's institutions managed the river over the course of a single annual cycle—the year 2023, during which much of the book was written. Our institutional choices—how much water to hold in upstream dams, how much to release, how much to divert into the valley's irrigation ditches—produces a *hydrograph*. At their simplest, hydrographs show how a river's water level changes over the yearly cycle. But hydrographs for modern rivers are anything but simple or natural. Like so many rivers, the reach of the Rio Grande known as the Middle Rio Grande Valley is highly managed. The annual movement of water through the Middle Rio Grande Valley follows what might called an institutional hydrograph,[20] heavily influenced by the rules through which we manage the Rio Grande. These interludes are our attempt to pull back the curtains a bit on the Rio Grande's institutional hydrograph—the contemporary link to how evolving institutional arrangements altered the hydrology.

We hope the answers that follow will help our community understand where we came from and how we can mindfully adapt our relationship with the Rio Grande to a changing world.

Figure 3. Downtown Albuquerque and its river, the Rio Grande. Photograph by John Fleck.

INTRODUCTION

> In the ancient legends there was a white, burning desert through which the sacred river ran . . .
>
> —Rudolfo Anaya, *Heart of Aztlan*

> United we drain, divided we drown.
>
> —Aldo Leopold

On the edge of a riverside park in the high desert community of Albuquerque, New Mexico, city workers hastily cleared picnic areas and fishing ponds late on the afternoon of Friday, September 13, 2013. Firefighters positioned themselves on Central Avenue's Rio Grande bridge, watching the river rise.

A flood, once a dominant feature of life on the Rio Grande Valley floor, had become such a rarity that the city's twenty-first-century residents had no idea what to do. The first warning high water was on the way had come in mid-afternoon when staff at the US Bureau of Reclamation's Albuquerque headquarters saw a spike in the Rio Grande's flows at a gauge thirty miles upstream from Albuquerque, the highest flows on that stretch of the river in half a century.[1] Heavy rain, falling on soil saturated by a week of storms, had created a pulse of water headed toward the city. The Rio Grande seemed bent on reminding Albuquerque that it was, after all, a river. The community scrambled to respond.

Nestled against the Rio Grande's riverside woods—called the *bosque* in a nod to the city's Spanish roots—the park known today as Tingley Beach is intimately linked to the history of modern Albuquerque. It was built on forty-three acres of land reclaimed from the river's clutches in the early

1930s.[2] Today, a levee stands tall between the park and the river to fend off the Rio Grande's historical propensity to flood. On the city side of the river runs a parallel ditch that drains away groundwater, turning what was once a swamp into land that's now home to tidy green neighborhoods and a lush, manicured golf course.

Engineered by a newly formed government agency called the Middle Rio Grande Conservancy District, the levees and ditches in the early 1930s remade a river in the blink of an eye. The work included ninety-four miles of levees thrown up in the first year alone to constrain the river's natural tendency to wander a valley floor where residents were trying to build a city. For the valley's Indigenous communities, that was just a river doing what rivers do. For colonial immigrants trying to build a city on the valley floor, that natural wandering had become a flood menace.

The Conservancy District was a project of urban modernity, as community leaders imagined Albuquerque's future as a metropolis surrounded by a garden of rich, productive farmland. This required collective action to provide the extensive engineering works needed, a gardening of the valley at a scale not possible with the old, decentralized institutions of valley communities. The project was born in tension and conflict as those communities—Indigenous Pueblo, deeply rooted Hispanic, and recent immigrant Anglo—clashed over means to the end. From that conflict a community emerged that differed from the imagined future in those heady days of the early 1930s. Still, it made good on the promise of building a modern metropolis on a desert river valley floor. Through its midst still ran, in the twenty-first century, the river that had defined the structure of the community. But it was a river changed.

The commercial agriculture the city builders envisioned stretching up and down the valley beyond the urban core never materialized. But that should not be seen as a failure. Rather, an alternative urban-rural structure arose in its place. Nearly six thousand landowners irrigated their property from valley ditches in 2021, typically parcels fewer than two acres. That is far too little land to make much money but plenty for a lovely green place to make one's home.[3] Some commercial agriculture emerged in the metropolitan area's distant reaches. But New Mexico's Middle Rio Grande Valley became something else. Small irrigators up and down the valley, with their flood control, drainage, and irrigation systems subsidized by the valley's urban core, have created a lovely community of green, a linear core paralleling the river through the heart of a modern American city.

By the twenty-first century, the Rio Grande's natural tendencies to flood and change course had largely been forgotten. The levees' primary civic role was recreation. Paved trails top the levee through the entire length of the city, alive on summer weekends with walkers, joggers, and cyclists.

Inland from Tingley Beach, a former slough on the river's edge had become the Albuquerque Country Club, a lush golf course spun out of a 1930s urban land development scheme that had become one of the greenest patches in the desert city. With its swamp drained and the land safe from flooding, water that had fed a marsh was redirected to a heavily irrigated, tree-shaded, manicured greenspace for affluent recreation.[4]

Between the levee and the river stands a magnificent gallery forest of cottonwoods. It's one of the community's most beloved natural places. Trails twist through the forest, with side paths slipping through the woods to river viewpoints. Yet, in a different way, the long, thin forest of bosque could be seen as every bit as unnatural as the golf course. The same flood-control efforts that made city building possible created ideal conditions for cottonwoods to take up permanent residence in places on the edge of a flood plain where they once would have been swept away.

The gauge that sounded the first warning of the 2013 flood is called San Felipe, the name Spanish colonizers gave to an Indigenous community when the first wave of settlers arrived in the late 1500s. In Keres, the native language of the community of 3,500 people, it is called *Katishtya*. From time immemorial its residents have farmed the edges of the Rio Grande.[5] Katishtya residents and the valley's other earliest residents built their villages on the valley's best high spots—close to the river, to enjoy the river's benefits, but safe from the Rio Grande's annual rise and fall. Katishtya's central plaza is on a bench of land less than five hundred feet from the Rio Grande but nearly ten feet higher than the river. That put it safely above the highest river elevations ever recorded, a sanctuary from flows that once devastated settlers trying to build their communities on the valley floor.[6]

As the river rose that September afternoon, the Pueblo community was in no danger. The same could not be said for Albuquerque in its earliest years. Since the late 1800s, the city had spread across the valley floor, wrestling with the twin threats of back swamps and increasingly common floods.

Just down the road from Tingley Beach in September 2013, at a hastily called news conference on the front walkway of the Middle Rio Grande Conservancy District, water-management officials led by the flood-control team from the US Army Corps of Engineers addressed reporters. The September 2013 news conference was a hurried affair. Federal flood managers briefly explained that they believed the valley's levees, built by the Conservancy District in the 1930s and reinforced over the years, should contain the flood.[7] Five hundred yards to the west, the Rio Grande kept rising.

Van Dyke

It would have been hard to see then, but the Atchison, Topeka, and Santa Fe Railway (AT&SF) was already beginning to change the place when it dropped its travelers into the Rio Grande Valley thirty miles upstream from Albuquerque in the 1890s. Here since 1880, rammed through in haste on its twisting route west, the AT&SF gave little consideration to the place itself.[8] This was a river valley then, not a railroad valley.

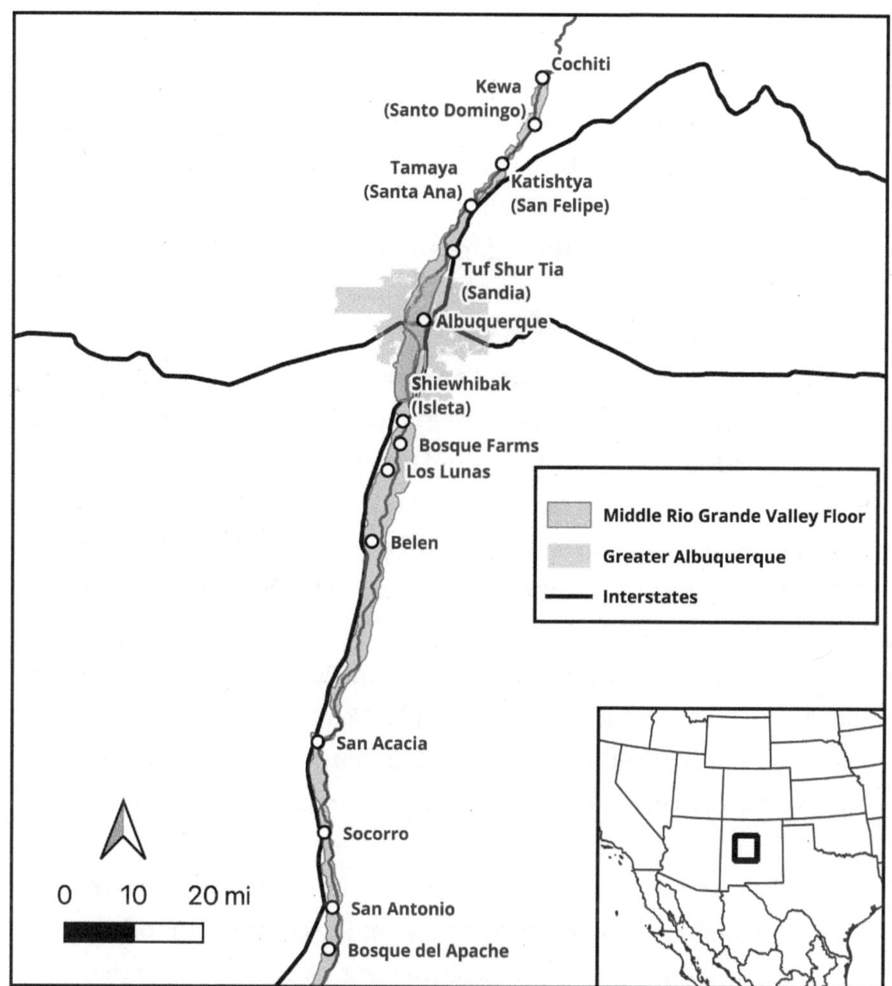

Map 2. A river of green. Map by John Fleck.

After crossing Glorieta Pass, one of the better paths through the mountains available to the railroad engineers at the southern end of the Rocky Mountains, the tracks turned south down the high margin of the river valley—dry mesas to the travelers' left, cottonwoods and patches of farmland to their right. Entering what today we might call the Albuquerque reach of the valley, the tracks carried travelers from the east, a wetter place, down the edge of an old river channel, a "yazoo," past swampy land and salt grass marshes where the river would frequently reclaim its old channel when in flood stage.

For days, those early rail travelers had been crossing the plains of North America's great midsection, a landscape gradually changing from wet to dry. Across the 100th meridian, they would have seen a landscape increasingly unable to support the agriculture exploding across the nation's broad, flat midsection, with rain alone. Everywhere the rails went, they brought dramatic change as they knitted together once-localized communities into a national economy.[9]

It is reasonable to believe this stretch of the Rio Grande Valley is where the eclectic librarian and literary critic John Van Dyke, riding on one of the passenger rail cars of the day, first came in touch with arid southwestern North America's defining geography: the valley of a desert river:

> The desert terraces on either side . . . come down to meet those "bottom" lands, and the line where one leaves off and the other begins is drawn as with the sharp edge of a knife. Seen from the distant mountain tops, the river moves between two long ribbons of green, and the borders are gray and gold mesas of the desert.[10]

Van Dyke's book, *The Desert*, introduced a nation to the idea that the desert was a place of worth, not a wasteland. But he was skating across the surface of this pond, and in places, the ice beneath him was thin. Today, the ribbons of green remain, and they have become more important than ever. But when he arrived in the 1890s, they had long had something Van Dyke largely failed to acknowledge: people.

The Pueblo and Spanish peoples of the valley were farming, diverting water from the river with rock and brush dams into village acequias, spreading across gardens and farm plots along and within the bosque, sustaining community life. These historic irrigation systems were their own piece of localized democracies, developed from their Native American, Spanish, and Moorish roots. In the 1890s, when Van Dyke arrived, they had long had complex governance structures managing communities' relationship with their river.[11] Even then, the ribbons of green down the Rio Grande Valley floor were a garden, a creation of the interplay between people and water. Even then, the farming these people were doing was neither robust nor plentiful. And they were struggling. Life with a wandering river that did not understand the boundaries placed on it by those tasked with turning a floodplain into a city was a central challenge. The existing river management institutions were inadequate for the challenges of living with the river as the growing city approached modernity.

Follett

Less poetic than John Van Dyke, but more in tune with the place of humans in the ribbons of green was W. W. Follett, who surveyed the valley in 1896 for the US and Mexican governments.

The Rio Grande had been dwindling as it reached the communities of El Paso, Texas, and Juarez, Mexico, and the International Boundary Commission was trying to figure out what to do. The Commission dispatched Follett, a hydraulic engineer,[12] to determine how much water was being diverted for irrigation. This was a classic problem of collective rights and responsibilities as communities share a river, reflecting the ever-present tension between upstream users and their downstream neighbors.

Before the 1880s, when the railroad connected the Rio Grande Valley to other markets, crops were grown primarily to feed the people living there. The main agricultural exports were sheep and cattle, and the transportation methods used for exports was the animals' hooves. Herders drove their flocks of "woolies" overland to the mines in Mexico or California.

The railroad changed that. In the river's upper reaches, near its headwaters in the San Luis Valley of Colorado, Follett found growing agricultural communities exploiting the markets opened by the railroads. Vast areas of arable land and the ready availability of irrigation water, combined with their new rail access to markets, fueled a booming agricultural economy. However, the two things that had provided such benefits in the San Luis Valley—plentiful water and the connection to the railroads—had the opposite effect on the lands around Albuquerque.

"The soil is very fertile," Follett wrote, "but the land lies low and nearly level, and has very poor drainage." Follett found some 115,000 acres of arable land in the valleys upstream and downstream of Albuquerque, but only 16,000 acres were being farmed. "Much formerly watered (land) has been abandoned and is now marshland, white with alkali."[13] As farming upstream reduced the Rio Grande's flow, a slower river dumped more sediment in the Albuquerque valley, raising the river's bed. The Rio Grande was steadily turning the valley lands around Albuquerque into a swamp.

Follett also found a second phenomenon central to Albuquerque's evolving relationship with the river. In the two decades since the railroad had arrived in New Mexico's Middle Rio Grande, the valley south of Albuquerque had seen a reduction in irrigated acreage as farmers left the land for jobs building the railroad. Imports made growing local food less necessary, and from the moment of the railroad's arrival, the wage economy was more attractive than farming to those trying to make a living. It was one of the first steps in the demographics of Albuquerque's urban transformation.

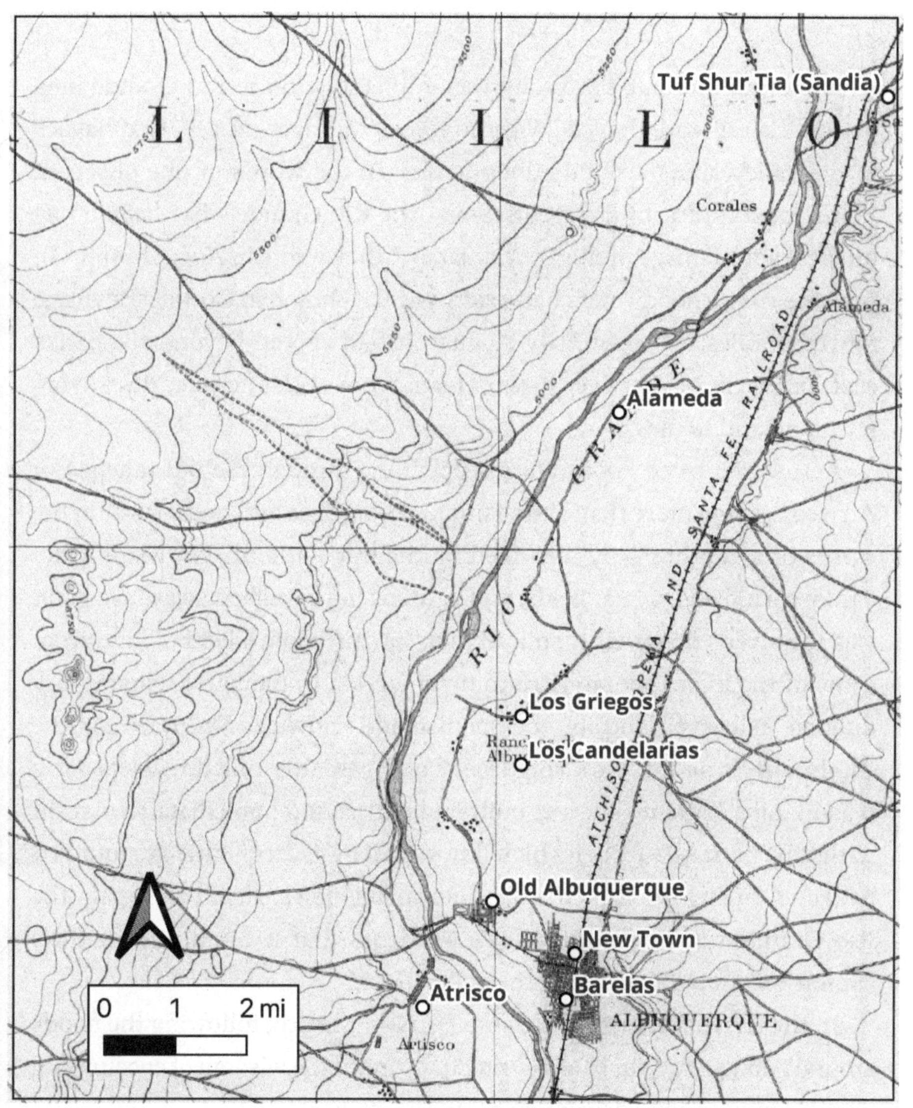

Map 3. Albuquerque as W. W. Follett would have found it in the 1890s. Map adapted by John Fleck.

"That Most Erratic of Erratic Streams"

Albuquerque's broad, flat valley was vulnerable to the Rio Grande long before the railroad arrived. With no levees the river caused "sad havoc" in the valley lands around Albuquerque, in the words of one observer. "That most erratic of erratic streams—the Rio Grande—has been doing unspeakable damage in this county lately," they wrote in August 1868.[14] In July, the river's floodwaters had destroyed the church in Corrales, a village fourteen miles upstream.[15] By August, it had spread beyond the banks east and west of the river downstream from Albuquerque, destroying farmland and homes.

Across the river, floodwaters seeped out through the old ranchos of Atrisco, leaving more than sixty families "homeless and houseless," in the words of an author only identified by the initials H. R. W. "Many vineyards, corn fields, wheat fields, and gardens have washed away." So great was the river's flow that it split in two, leaving a low island of land from some of the high spots in Atrisco downstream to the native community dubbed "Isleta" (island) by the Spanish and known as *Shiewhibak* in the community's native Tiwa language. The Spaniards called it Isleta for a reason. Like Katishtya, it was built on high ground immediately adjacent to the river but safe from its high flows. Isleta was frequently surrounded by water during the Rio Grande's late spring flows. Again and again the Rio Grande reminded the valley's residents that it cared not for their aspirations to build a city on the valley floor.

In the territorial capital of Santa Fe, New Mexico, following the floods around Albuquerque in 1874, a writer questioned the wisdom of encouraging significant economic development in Albuquerque.

> Albuquerque's situation is too exposed to inundation. . . . This town should be removed to a securer site either on or at the foot of the bluffs, where there would be more confidence as to its security. Those who have invested significant amounts

> in improvements will, no doubt, scout such an idea, yet we cannot see much ridiculous about it, because as long as we are exposed to similar disasters as the present one, real estate will always be held at depreciated value and persons desirous of settling and building will always be deterred from doing so at the mere mention of such a probability.[16]

Albuquerque didn't listen. In 1885 the community built a piecemeal dike at Alameda to prevent the river from jumping into the old yazoo during high spring flows. It didn't solve the problem. "The Rio Grande is again changing its course from the west to the east side," an observer wrote in April 1889 as spring snowmelt swelled the river. "If something is not done to preserve the banks that are now rapidly washing away, the road down the valley will soon be a thing of the past."[17] The Rio Grande was doing what it always had done, but now there was a growing city in its path.

Between 1850 and 1930 the Rio Grande caused damaging floods at least forty-four times in this stretch of the river valley, and the Middle Rio Grande Conservancy District was formed to protect it.[18] More modest floods would rejuvenate the valley's soils, but depending on scale and location, larger floods inundated historic Spanish colonial villas, took out bridges, ruined crops, and destroyed homes. Much of the valley floor was never a particularly good place to farm—or build a city.

To an Albuquerque resident in the twenty-first century, that "most erratic of streams" was a lost memory. In September 2013 this was evident in Barelas, along the stretch of early Albuquerque devastated by the 1868 floods. As the floodwaters rose that day, heavy pumps ran at the City of Albuquerque's Barelas Pump Station #32, heaving water out of a low-lying neighborhood and into the river.

Standing on the railroad's namesake Santa Fe Street, just up the ditch-bank road from the Barelas pumps, one can look up at cars driving a levee road that was known as Riverside Drive when the Conservancy District built it in the 1930s. Barelas's far southwest corner has always been a low spot. Here, the Rio Grande is a couple of feet higher than the modest homes dotting the old working-class community, where residents could walk to their jobs at the rail yards. But on September 13, 2013, the Rio Grande kept rising. Absent levees and pumps, this neighborhood would have been underwater.

Gardens and Institutions

Throughout history, the English word "garden" has done yeoman's work, traveling with us as we constructed a modern world. At its simplest it is a noun describing a place behind the house where we grow flowers, vegetables, and perhaps a few fruit trees. At its most expansive, it is "a region of great fertility." Kent was "the Garden of England," "known for its abundance of fruit and crops." The province of Touraine was "the Garden of France." But it is the noun's interplay with garden's verb form that does the word's linguistic heavy lifting—"to bring a landscape into a particular state"—to mindfully and intentionally change the land on which we live.[19]

To understand any community, you can start with its water. Collective action to solve shared problems defines community. Our relationship with our water often poses the first collective action problem a community must solve as it comes into being.[20] Communities grow up around water—bays around which to fish, harbors for our boats, rivers from which to drink, bathe, and irrigate our crops.[21] For cities like Albuquerque that sit astride rivers, the story of collective action around water is a river story. How do we share the costs and benefits of diverting water to irrigate lands? How do we stop the floods? How do we ensure that the drainage from our irrigation doesn't leave our neighbors downstream living in a pestilent swamp? How do we get from one side of the river to the other? The answers to those questions provide the foundation for understanding community.

In Voltaire's classic satirical eighteenth-century novel *Candide*, the title character and his fellow travelers settle into a simple division of duties after a chaotic life. They act collectively on a small plot of land, producing "plentiful crops" and pursuing a common goal.

Candide's final wisdom is famously and most often translated from the original French as follows: "Let us cultivate our garden." But modern translations of Voltaire's "Il faut cultiver notre jardin" suggest a broader interpretation, with the garden not as the plot of land behind the house but as a more expansive landscape: We must work our land. Translating *jardin* as fields or land points toward not just one's personal space but also the larger community.[22]

We think of hoes, shovels, and rakes as the implements of our gardens, as our tools. But the expansive form of the noun—*Candide*'s fields, the Rio Grande Valley as our Kent, the grand Garden of New Mexico—calls for something more, a reliance on collective action. It is impractical for me to build a levee around my house to protect it from flooding or my own bridge to cross the river, and without the cooperation of my neighbors, I am powerless to drain a swamp encroaching on my back garden.

In the deserts of the southwestern United States, in places like Tucson, Phoenix, Los Angeles, and Albuquerque, it was a process, one historian argued, in which communities "blend[ed] competing forces into a new natural harmony in which the desert would yield to domestication and ultimately become a garden."[23] But this was (and remains) a process with no end point, no ultimate equilibrium, ever becoming. Human communities shape rivers, and rivers continue to shape us.

It is easy to turn conceptually to the government agencies we have created to do the work and think of them as our gardening tools. But scholars trying to understand how communities succeed or fail at solving this collective action problem ask us to reach further. Beneath the agencies, they argue, are rules. We establish rules and only then create the government agencies to carry them out. Before there was a Reclamation Service to build the dams that changed the West, the United States Congress wrote a Reclamation Act.[24] In New Mexico the state legislature wrote a Conservancy Act, which enabled the creation of a Middle Rio Grande Conservancy District with the legal authority and physical ability to build Albuquerque's levees, consolidate its irrigation, and drain its swamps.[25]

"The term *institutions* refers to the rules that humans use when interacting within a wide variety of repetitive and structured situations at multiple levels of analysis," Elinor Ostrom wrote.[26] Such rules can be laws, but they can also be informal norms.[27] Notably, the economist Daniel Bromley argues that institutions don't emerge spontaneously. They emerge as the purposeful result of the efforts of elected officials, city leaders, influential civic organizations, and government agents—a coalition of leaders Bromley calls "authoritative agents"—who write rules to induce behaviors and outcomes. These are Ostrom's "public entrepreneurs."[28] They build rules with hoped-for outcomes, providing the rationale and justification for the institutional arrangements they create.[29]

The role of institutions is critical in understanding Albuquerque's relationship with the Rio Grande. Cities and their connected communities establish formal and informal rules around collective water resource management and water resource institutions. These institutions, in turn, shape cities and their rivers. These rules both liberate and constrain how water is allocated and distributed—how to get it when and where we want it and keep it at bay when we don't.

Before there was a Middle Rio Grande Conservancy District to build the levees, drain the swampland, and consolidate the valley's irrigation systems—enabling Albuquerque's rush into twentieth-century modernity—there was a rich and complex public debate, full of multi-party power dynamics. Building this institutional foundation played out intensely over more than a decade as the community struggled to establish the rules. But the work was never done, extending and revising the rules as the river and the community changed. In the Middle Rio Grande Valley, an ever-evolving community response to a persistent set of questions has been required.

- Where should the boundaries around our area of collective action be drawn? In other words, who should be included in the collective?
- What is the purpose of our collective action? Drainage? Flood control? Irrigation? Game refuges? Urban green space? What of flows in the river channel itself?
- How should the district be governed—by an appointed board of experts or through elections? If appointed, who would do the appointing? If elected, who would get to vote?
- Who should pay for the work? In what proportions?

As the Middle Rio Grande Valley's institutions evolved, not everyone had equal access to seats at the table. While its influence was weakening, New Mexico's centuries-old Hispanic community still held substantial political power through its dominance of the Republican Party, controlling state government as legislators made crucial decisions in the late 1920s about the rules Albuquerque would use to manage its relationship with the river.[30] The valley's Native American communities, while not powerless thanks to political skills honed by centuries of struggle for sovereignty and cultural survival in the face of colonization, lacked the right to vote.[31]

The answers on which the community settled shaped the Rio Grande, which in turn shaped the community Albuquerque was to become. Their relationship with the river was both cause and consequence. The institutions, the community, and the river coevolved in the century that followed. But the institutions remain the foundation, and to understand what we have become, we must start there.

Figure 4. "Somos Atrisco"—Modern wheat-pasted signs in Albuquerque's Atrisco neighborhood celebrate the valley's heritage and lay a historical claim to pre-dating Albuquerque proper. Photograph by John Fleck.

A Brief History

The date most often attached to Albuquerque's founding is 1706, which marks the beginning of the Spanish village now tellingly labeled Old Town. But Old Town is not by a long stretch the oldest settlement in what is now considered greater Albuquerque.

Older Spanish villages exist within the boundaries of the modern Albuquerque metropolitan area. However, their age is dwarfed by Native American communities upstream and downstream. These communities have lived along or astride the river since time immemorial and have endured a sometimes-uneasy relationship with the newcomers.

The dawn of "modern Albuquerque" can be traced to the arrival of the railroad in Albuquerque's swampy New Town in 1880,[32] as the idea of Albuquerque as a modern city took root in the minds of its builders and boosters. But to develop their vision of a growing city connected to broader markets, livelihoods, and transportation systems, they first had to solve a bundle of river problems: flood control, drainage, and irrigation. Ultimately, they also needed the buy-in and support of New Mexico's broader political community—an agreement that the growing urban metropolis of Albuquerque would become the economic heart of modern New Mexico. By the late 1920s, that agreement would manifest as a nearly unanimous legislative agreement on the rules for managing the Rio Grande.

From the beginning of human habitation in the valley, communities have faced collective action challenges. For the Indigenous communities that lived in the Rio Grande Valley when Spanish colonizers made their way north in the late 1500s—communities both closely related and diverse, speaking multiple languages, lumped together as Pueblos by the Spanish—the collective action challenges were central to a resilient way of life, questions the communities had to answer for themselves: Who waters and tends the crops? Who shares the religious and cultural responsibility needed for life here to endure?

We have collective analogs for those communities' modern successors: Who performs the legal and scientific rituals to which we shifted in the twentieth century to ensure that ever-larger communities could thrive here? Who measures the depth of the winter snow in the mountains to the north and the river's flow? Who decides how much water a dam can or must release? Who shares the cost of levees to protect from flooding or bridges needed to cross? How do we dispose of our waste without fouling the water on which we, or our downstream neighbors, depend? What rules do we make, and how do we adapt those rules to a changing community and river?

Our modern institutions are rooted in actions taken in the first decades of the twentieth century, as the idea of Albuquerque as a modern city took root in the minds of its builders and boosters. Over a decade or more of maneuvering, dealmaking, planning, and implementing beginning roughly with the end of World War I, they reorganized the hydrologic system of the Middle Rio Grande Valley and the social-ecological system that went with it.

In the answers they found, the builders and boosters not only built a complex system of physical infrastructure, but they also implemented a suite of Progressive Era institutional changes[33] in water resources governance that, in many ways, still carry Albuquerque's history forward today.

We call the resulting metropolitan area Albuquerque, though we must be careful in defining the area we are describing. Municipal boundaries around the modern "City of Albuquerque" fall short of explaining the complex web of interconnections in what might be better called the greater Albuquerque metropolitan area. The US Census counted some 565,000 people living within the Albuquerque city limits in 2020, but nearly 890,000 people in what the census defines as the Albuquerque Metropolitan Statistical Area, a single geographic bundle of employment, commerce, and access to amenities like the river corridor as well as the nearby Sandia Mountains.

The neighboring city of Rio Rancho, or the villages of Los Lunas, Corrales, and Los Ranchos, have separate municipal boundaries and governance but are home to people commuting to work every day at jobs in Albuquerque. They are part of what we mean by "Albuquerque." The Pueblos astride the Rio Grande immediately upstream and downstream of Albuquerque's heart remain independent communities, proudly identifying as sovereign tribal nations, yet are integrally linked, with residents commuting to jobs in the city, sending their children to Albuquerque's colleges, selling their bales of alfalfa to suburban horse owners.

These communities are connected by a transportation network that spills from one municipality to the next—cities, Pueblos, villages, and unincorporated areas. The first stops on New Mexico's commuter rail outside the city's core are at Sandia Pueblo upstream and Isleta Pueblo downstream. These communities share an urban economy and a sense of identity and are connected by the Rio Grande. Their residents fly in and out of Albuquerque's airport. This is what we mean when we talk about modern Albuquerque.

The Middle Rio Grande Conservancy District, a public corporation under the laws of the state of New Mexico that emerged from Albuquerque's water management fog of the 1920s, remains the largest water distributor in the four counties of New Mexico's Middle Rio Grande Valley. Today, it is a multipurpose agency with broad tax and finance powers that operates under an elected board. It charges irrigators a modest flat rate for water per acre, receiving most of its financing from a property tax collected from non-irrigators, primarily those in Bernalillo County, greater Albuquerque's populous urban heart.[34]

Nestled within a broader web of governance—municipal, county, state, and federal—the Conservancy District navigates coordination with many federal and state agencies, local governments, and six sovereign Pueblos. The Conservancy District participates in a multistate water allocation compact, federal water distribution systems, federal flood-control operations, and federal endangered species protection efforts.

The twenty-first-century Conservancy District also has legal responsibility for considering the provision of various ecosystem goods and services, such as open spaces and the corridors of green threaded across the valley floor. That was not always the case. When it was created, its job was to separate Albuquerque from its river, which it did dramatically. Its network of levees and drains, built quickly in the early 1930s, disconnected the community from the river in a geologic instant. Gone were the twin menaces of flooding and swamps. Only a half century later, evolving environmental values led to a halting, difficult task of reconnecting Albuquerque with the Rio Grande.

Our Modern Ribbons of Green

Follett's 1896 survey of the Rio Grande Valley provides one of the keys to understanding the modern nature of Albuquerque's ribbons of green: his observation that the valley's agricultural land was not an attractive place to farm. But there remain enduring myths about commercial agriculture in the Middle Rio Grande Valley and the role of our institutions in perpetuating it. Agricultural data for the four Middle Rio Grande Conservancy District counties tell a consistent story. Year after year federal surveys show that, far from making money, the typical farmer in the valley consistently spends more money in farming than they make from selling crops produced on valley land. Net cash farm income is negligible and has often been negative in recent decades, especially for Bernalillo County and the adjacent counties of Sandoval upstream and Valencia downstream.[35] For most of its farms it has ever been thus. "The traditional agricultural pattern of the valley," wrote historian Ira Clark, "strengthened by the growth of Albuquerque, was one of small farms which returned minimal profits, with family members seeking employment elsewhere to supplement their meager incomes."[36]

Yet a myth persists of a lost garden that can be reclaimed if only we twiddle the right institutional knobs. Across history, we see enthusiasm for the next commercial, exportable cash crop that will turn things around—pinto beans, tomatoes, a vegetable cannery, commercial-scale wheat farming, sugar beets, and even a remarkable 1920s effort to turn

Albuquerque into a tobacco-exporting powerhouse. Again and again the next big thing fails.

It was a belief in that myth, at a time when farming was still central to the nation's economy, that led the Middle Rio Grande Conservancy District's founders to concoct a financing scheme dependent on cutting down bosque forests and rehabilitating every acre of the floodplain's marginal soils to turn the valley floor into a rich agricultural garden. The scheme would provide jobs to support a growing city, they believed, with revenue from booming crop sales to pay for the levees and drainage the community desperately needed. Ultimately, those founders were proven profoundly naïve. The agricultural dreams foundered, and the Conservancy District could not pay its bills.

Only a few crops have overcome the valley's agricultural shortcomings. Alfalfa, which covers over 80 percent of the Middle Rio Grande Conservancy District's irrigated lands today, is its modern low-risk staple. Alfalfa's labor costs are low, its resilience to drought makes it ideal in a place with a variable water supply, and local horse owners provide a ready market. New Mexico's iconic green chiles play a small role, too, and expanding orchards of pecans, creeping north, are enabled by the warmth of climate change.[37] Some lands, generally those farthest from the city, produce positive cash flow for their farmers. But closer to Albuquerque, mortgages became the only reliable cash crop in the growing urban area. Yet the greater Albuquerque metropolitan area, through its democratic institutions and all-important urban and suburban property tax subsidy, continues to support an expensive agricultural irrigation system threaded through the metro area's heart.

To understand the benefits, travel south of Albuquerque to a community known today as Bosque Farms. In the floods of 1868, the land then known as El Bosque de los Pinos was underwater.[38] By 1932, with the levees in place and the lowlands drained, the lands' new owner, the sheep-ranching scion Eduardo M. Otero, was marketing home sites just a short commute from the city—a middle-class suburb for people working in the city who wanted to farm tomatoes on the side.[39] "They are generally agreed by all competent authorities," the ads read, "to be the finest farm lands available in the Middle Rio Grande Valley." Otero and his family even developed a short-lived tomato cannery to support the part-time farmers he hoped to attract to his land.[40]

History shows emphatically that they were not "the finest farm lands." The alkaline soil, left behind by the river's swamps, proved largely unfarmable. Otero, one of the largest landowners and wealthiest people in the state, strongly backed creating the Conservancy District, understanding the importance of drainage and flood control to developing his land. He died in 1932 before it was clear his Bosque Farms development was a failure.[41] His estate sold the land to the federal government, which tried using Bosque Farms as a New Deal–era Resettlement Administration colony for forty-two farm families displaced by the Dust Bowl. The federal government invested more than eleven times the land's purchase price in improving farmers' chances of making a go of it.[42] But the federal project failed as a commercial crop enterprise even with that massive subsidy. It served briefly as a dairy center before its commercial agricultural base died off completely.[43]

Yet Otero was on to something that helps explain why irrigation remains robust in the Middle Rio Grande in the twenty-first century, even if commercial farming is not. With a levee confining the Rio Grande to a narrow channel and a network of ditches to drain the land and deliver irrigation water, Bosque Farms is today home to a community of four thousand people, a patch of garden a short drive from the city. Bosque Farms is one of several such treasured communities stretching out from Albuquerque along the Rio Grande's ribbons of green. Most of the valley green belt communities are affluent, but not all. Otero was right about the desirability of the land for people working jobs in the city, and he was ultimately right to think it might be farmed, but not for the reason he thought. Judging by the Department of Agriculture's data, most of the people irrigating there are spending more on their green space than they are making in dollar

Figure 5. A cottonwood over a building awaiting the development of Bosque Farms. Photograph by Dorothea Lange, 1935. Courtesy of the Library of Congress.

Figure 6. Figure developed by Brennan Davis using InVEST model from the Stanford Natural Capital Project. Darker area represents cooling benefits.

terms. But Bosque Farms is turning that water into something equally valuable—a garden, threads in the valley's ribbons of green.

With nearly a million people in 2022, Albuquerque is the sixty-first largest of the nation's 384 metropolitan statistical areas (MSAs). Extending beyond mere city limits, MSAs are federal demographers' attempts to formalize geographic boundaries around groups of people with shared housing, labor markets, and transportation systems that extend beyond mere municipal borders.

Greater Albuquerque is modest as United States metropolitan areas go. But Albuquerque dominates New Mexico with nearly half the state's population and economy. If you placed a circle over Albuquerque's central core, there isn't an MSA even one-fifth of its size within a radius of over 250 miles in any direction. Albuquerque is the financial and commercial center of New Mexico.

Albuquerque, as a modern city, has a defining feature rooted in the history of its institutional relationship with the Rio Grande: the metropolitan area's core, flanking the Rio Grande, is one of the least dense among large urban areas in the US, threaded with old irrigation ditches—Albuquerque's "ribbons of green."[44] In debates about what we want our modern cities to look like in a climate-altered world, Albuquerque represents one side across that spectrum. An argument can be made that more than 95 percent of large urban areas in the US have insufficient open space.[45] It is hard to conceptualize the cost of retrofitting a metropolitan area with a broad green strip several miles wide of irrigation ditches and associated biking and walking trails running lengthwise through its core.

Like many modern metropolitan areas, Albuquerque grapples with questions of urban density.[46] Urban density conveys many benefits: efficiencies in public transportation, municipal water provision, economic network effects, economies of agglomeration, productivity gains, and energy efficiencies.[47] However, it also conveys cons, the so-called demons of density: rising land prices and gentrification, pollution concentrations, urban heat islands, and congestion. Collectively, we navigate these pros and cons with our institutions.[48]

From the perspective of one hundred years ago, creating the Conservancy District as a multipurpose institutional arrangement is one of the primary mechanisms for making the heart of modern Albuquerque less dense, more rural, greener, and cooler. As a social-ecological system, the Rio Grande runs through it—both the river and the ditches and drains spread across the valley floor where the river once spread of its own volition. It does this because of the rules the community wrote a century ago to guide its future. This is an example of an "institution carrying history forward."[49] History matters. Things are the way they are because of a long, complicated history that can't be ignored. In a world where many of our traditional political institutions for solving collective problems are frayed, the Conservancy District represents a relatively small but regionally important piece of working democracy. Climate change is writ large in water problems, and these working pieces of democracy represent critical components of adapting to a climate-altered world.

2013: The Flood That Wasn't

The sum of all of this, of a century of institutional and hydrologic change, played out across the Middle Rio Grande Valley floor during that flood of September 2013. "That most erratic of streams" was anything but erratic. Upstream, flood-control dams contained the runoff, and through the city's heart, levees safely kept a docile river within its narrow main channel. Far from fearing their river, residents flocked to overlooks to watch the Rio Grande flow. When the flood peak reached Albuquerque's Route 66 Bridge shortly before midnight, the only things vulnerable to its flooding were the low spots on the community's bicycling and walking trails. The levees held, protecting the community beyond.

Downstream at dawn the next day, the muddy torrent seemed well-behaved as it passed through the Middle Rio Grande Conservancy District's Isleta Diversion Dam gates. The community of Isleta itself, always safe from flooding because it was built on a high spot, was untouched.

Since its origin the Conservancy District has been more about protecting people and places, culture and community, and the distribution of green than just commercial crop production. Even in lower spots downstream, the levees protected places like Bosque Farms, which would have been swamped by such a flow at a different time before the institutions we created to guard it.

The Middle Rio Grande Conservancy District may not have given us the garden its founders intended, but it is a garden, nevertheless. To understand how we got here, we must next travel to Santa Fe, New Mexico, in early 1927 to one of the most consequential legislative debates in young Albuquerque's history.

Interlude: Winter

Albuquerque's riverside woods wore their muted winter colors and frost-ringed sandbar islands on cold mornings as the low-flowing Rio Grande meandered through Albuquerque during the winter of 2022–2023. Two big pulses of water pushed the river up during December and January, briefly submerging the islands, not because of nature, but because of a dam and the rules used to manage it. River managers were moving water that had piled up behind Abiquiu Dam on the Rio Chama downstream to comply with the Rio Grande Compact, a 1938 agreement over river management rules between Colorado, New Mexico, Texas, and the federal government. It's an example of what Elinor Ostrom called a cross-scale linkage, the connecting relationships upstream and downstream for any selected reach of river governance—in this case, the Middle Rio Grande

Figure 7. Frost rings sandbar islands as the Rio Grande creeps through Albuquerque, January 2023. Photograph by John Fleck.

Valley. The Compact imposes the terms for those relationships, but within those terms, there is still much that must be sorted as each year proceeds.

With the Compact accounting completed, the Rio Grande had dropped back to its winter base flow when Middle Rio Grande Conservancy District Water Operations Division Manager Anne Marken delivered her first water management report to the District's board of directors on January 9.

The nondescript office building that houses the headquarters of the Middle Rio Grande Conservancy District seems to fold in on itself. With few windows, it has the feel of the fortress-like buildings erected in the 1960s at the height of Cold War fears over nuclear Armageddon. As you enter its main door, a glass-boothed receptionist waits to admit visitors to the main building entrance to the left—to pay their irrigation assessments, look at old maps, or discuss the water rights attached to their property. To the right, on the second Monday afternoon of each month, an open door beckons to a small meeting room where the democracy of Rio Grande management plays out.

The small room lacks the architectural signaling of grandeur many government agencies build into their governing spaces. A few dozen slightly uncomfortable movable chairs for the public and staff are crammed into a space that feels too small for their presence. The district's seven board members sit on a semi-circular raised dais, but they also mingle freely through the crowded room before and after the meetings. If they have to take a break to use the bathroom or take a call, they have to slip through the audience.

But what is most singular about the meetings, to those who have spent their lives watching government in action, is the intimacy of the conversation: how the community thinks about the relationship between this river, its flood control, drainage, and irrigation systems, and the communities that live on the valley floor.

Step into that room in the winter of 2023 to begin to make sense of Albuquerque's complex relationship with the Rio Grande. Each month, Marken explained the *institutional hydrograph* to the board—how much snow was in the mountains, and what the rules said about how it would be moved down the river.

The early snowpack, the reservoir of frozen water accumulating in the mountains to the north, was a little low, but it was still early in the year. "There's a lot of winter left," Marken explained. Summer rains in 2022 had left mountain watershed soils moist, which was expected to help the 2023 runoff, but the institutional piece of the hydrograph remained the most important influence on how much water would pass down the Rio Grande in 2023 and when. New Mexico was behind on its water deliveries to Texas under the Rio Grande Compact. Under the rules, users in the Middle Rio Grande Valley owed water to their downstream neighbors in Southern New Mexico and Texas, Marken explained. That would mean more water in the river's narrow main channel and less in the network of ditches spreading water across the valley floor.

CHAPTER 1

WHO HAS A SAY, AND WHO HAS TO PAY?

Frank Alaric Hubbell[1] was long past the height of his political power when he rose to address a committee of New Mexico legislators in February 1927 to complain about the unfairness of what was being done to the small farmers of greater Albuquerque's Rio Grande Valley floor.

Nearly a decade had passed since the Commercial Club's 1919 meeting, which brought together Pablo Abeita, Max Gutierrez, Aldo Leopold, and the valley's other public entrepreneurs to begin creating the institutional arrangements—writing the rules—that would allow the project of flood control, drainage, and irrigation to remake New Mexico's Middle Rio Grande Valley. Planning was well underway, but no earth had yet been turned, and as the project emerged more clearly, the rules were increasingly being contested.

The first critical step was the approval of the original Conservancy Act by the New Mexico legislature in 1923. The community's public entrepreneurs had rushed to create the government agency needed to carry out their will: the Middle Rio Grande Conservancy District.

The effort to transform the valley's communities from a collection of villages into a metropolis was bold. But Gutierrez, Leopold, Abeita, and the many others engaged in the effort grappled with a fundamental question: How would the benefits and burdens of progress be shared? It was an easy question to pose in the abstract in 1919 when the community

Figure 8. Octaviano Larrazolo, former New Mexico governor, who as a legislator chaired the 1927 hearing over the future of the Conservancy Act and later became the nation's first Hispanic US Senator. Courtesy of the Library of Congress.

leaders were in hot pursuit of federal funding. But by 1927 it was proving stubbornly difficult to sort out in practice. The pursuit of federal funding had failed, and the realization had set in that the law's authors had made it easy for a small group to trigger the formation of a conservancy district with the power to aggressively tax the residents of the traditional communities who had long made their homes on the river valley floor and to force them to change their way of life. But those residents were given no direct democratic say in the process. Many were angered at their lack of voice.

The struggle came to a head in a dramatic clash in 1927 before the body entrusted with the job of writing, and possibly rewriting, the rules: the New Mexico legislature. The question before the heavily attended meeting of a special committee of state legislators that day was one of governance. Should the valley's residents be entrusted with the vote to choose the leadership of the Middle Rio Grande Conservancy District, the new government agency being created to bring irrigation, flood control, and drainage—to reshape the river to enable a growing city? Or should a board of appointed experts be left in charge? From the answer to this question flowed the next: Who would pay what portion of the cost of the work? The implications of Elinor Ostrom's design principles for collective governance of natural resource systems[2] were emerging in two simple questions, which would linger over much of the following century: Who has a say, and who has to pay?

The drama played out in public hearings before the state legislature's Special Committee on Conservancy Act, chaired by Republican Octaviano Larrazolo. Larrazolo had proposed a bill to revise the law to require elected boards for conservancy districts, to give those being taxed a say. The special committee's majority was both Hispanic and Republican, much like the Hispanic-dominated Republican Party, which at the time controlled both houses of the state legislature and the governor's office.[3] The Republicans appeared sympathetic to the call for a shift to democratic elections for the Conservancy District board.[4] Democrats, at the time dominated by New Mexico's Anglos, opposed the change. But they were in the minority.[5] The stage appeared set for a shift to democratic governance.

Frank A. Hubbell

Frank A. Hubbell was an entrepreneur in both senses of the word—as a businessman, and as a civic leader. He was one of the sons of the Gutierrez-Hubbell did not object to the Conservancy District's primary goal; he agreed that flood control, drainage, and improvements to the valley's irrigation system were needed. It was how they were to be financed—by placing a significant new tax on the valley's small farmers, calculated on the assumption that their previously unproductive land would instantly gain value as arable property, and forcing them to pay taxes at this inflated rate immediately.

Hubbell claimed that Albuquerque's First National Bank was only charged $1 in taxes for the flood control and drainage to be provided by the Conservancy District. At the same time, the South Valley's Melquiades Turrieta, farming to feed a family whose primary income came from jobs in town, and whose farm was only valued at $1,600, would be charged $14.50. The bank's assets were valued at $427,000. Why, Hubbell asked, must Turrieta pay more than a banker whose property was worth nearly three hundred times as much?

The community's civic leadership, dominated by a mix of boosters and downtown merchants, had an answer rooted in their hopes and dreams for what Albuquerque was to become. They believed a belt of commercial agriculture surrounding the growing city would provide jobs and an economic base. It would provide food that didn't need to be shipped in by rail and some that could be exported. They would turn the small farmers of the valley from

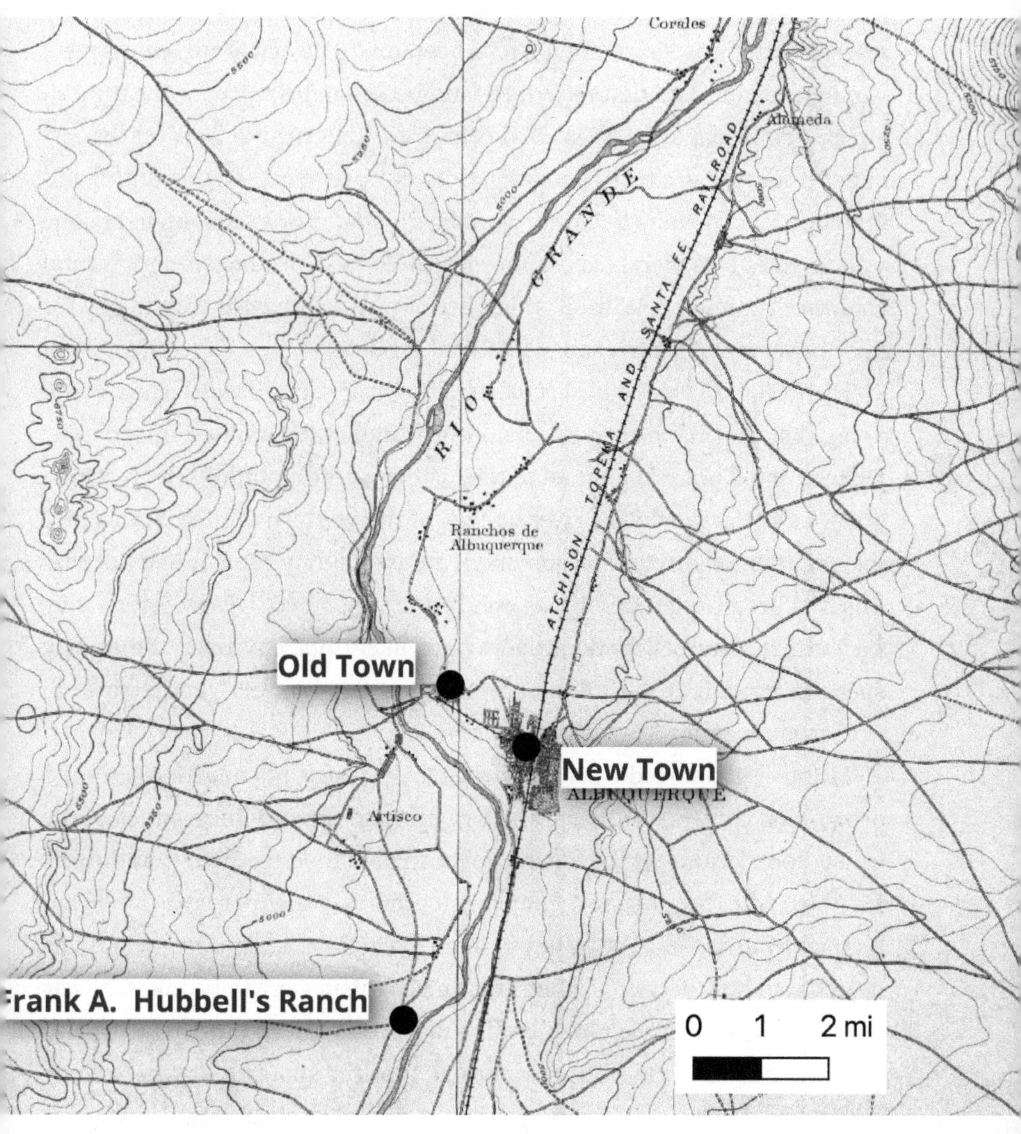

Map 4. Frank A. Hubbell's Albuquerque. Map adapted by John Fleck.

a subsistence lifeway, growing food to feed their families and for small local markets, into prosperous commercial operators. The newly affluent farmers would be taxed from that reclaimed land benefit to help pay for the project. For city-building purposes, such a tax base was the only way to cover the cost of flood control, drainage, and irrigation improvements. Flood control and drainage, the boosters believed, would turn land now locked up in bosque woods, salt-grass marsh, and dunes into a rich and productive agricultural engine of commerce. Without this, there would be no clear way to pay for the Conservancy District absent federal funding.

Hubbell understood desert valley agriculture and life with the river in a way that the financial engineers of the Middle Rio Grande Conservancy District could not. He pointed to the history of the ambitions of "reclamation," bringing the desert river valleys of the western United States into the twentieth-century commercial-farming economy. He pointed out that this had been tried many times and repeatedly failed. Desert river valley agriculture, Hubbell understood, could likely not pay back the money spent to provide it with flood control, drainage, and irrigation water in new crop revenues.[8]

Hubbell supported the idea of the conservancy, of collective action to bring flood control, drainage, and irrigation to the 160 linear miles of the valley floor, as long as the federal government stood ready to foot the bill. He objected to the shift to a financing mechanism that placed a significant financial burden on the valley's small farmers and, more crucially, he objected to how decisions about that mechanism were to be made. It was only fair, Hubbell argued in one of the most consequential political debates in the history of modern Albuquerque, that the small landowners being asked to pay so much of the project's cost should be given a democratic say.

There is a risk of a simplistic moral tale here: Frank. A. Hubbell, a noble leader acting on behalf of the little guy versus the rapacious urban power brokers—bankers and railroads, standing to benefit while paying little of the costs of the flood control and drainage they so needed for their investments to prosper.

Or an alternative moral tale: Frank. A. Hubbell, wealthy scion of a sheep empire, former longtime political boss/patron of Bernalillo County—with all the baggage that entailed,[9] clinging to the economic and political power of his family's and communities' past, blocking the road to progress pursued by the well-intentioned civic leadership in pursuit of prosperity for all.

The Making of a Modern American City

By the late 1920s in America, the charge of modernity was leading a population shift from farm country to the city. The US Census in 1920, for the first time, found more people living in urban areas than in the nation's rural countryside.[10]

The transition from an agricultural past to an increasingly globalized and centralized economy had whipsawed farming long before the lash of the Great Depression struck in 1929. Crop and land prices had boomed during and following World War I with the collapse of European agriculture, but Europe's quick recovery devastated US farming.[11]

The municipality we today label Albuquerque was, in the early twentieth century, a small chunk of modern urbanity wedged between sandhills and the Rio Grande, still struggling to build the water, sewer, and road systems it needed, but also the cultural markers of a modern city. The villages scattered up and down the river, places with old names drawn from old cultures—Sandia, Alameda, Los Griegos, Los Candelarias, Atrisco, Pajarito, Los Padillas, Isleta—maintained separate identities. "Old Albuquerque," the village that had loaned or lost its name to the growing metropolis built around the railroad depot, would not be formally annexed into Albuquerque's municipal boundaries until 1949.[12]

The jobs and connections to the broader economy created by the railroad's arrival represented an inexorable force that had already been reshaping the valley's human geography for nearly half a century. It brought jobs in the city, the decline of the prominence of the old sheep economy, and new waves of immigration to the valley.[13] Imports and exports—of commodities, but also people and ideas—were linking the Middle Rio Grande Valley with the rest of the nation in a way that had once been impossible.

Collective action at a new, larger scale, beyond villages and the more personal relationships of rural life, seemed inevitable. But the struggle to manage the newly forming urban area's relationship with the Rio Grande brought tensions between old and new, rural and urban, to a head.

On one side were the civic boosters—merchants, bankers, real estate developers, and other elites (often but not always part of the newest generation of immigrants) who wanted to reengineer the city and needed to reengineer the Rio Grande to do so. This public entrepreneurship was steeped in a Progressive Era faith in scientific expertise and central planning,[14] seeking to solve the problems of flood control, drainage, and irrigation to maximize the Middle Rio Grande Valley's economic potential.

For a time there appeared to be shared values around the goal. As we have seen, people like Frank A. Hubbell, who had emerged from the old village cultures of the valley floor, had long agreed that those villages would also benefit from creating institutional arrangements to manage the river through large-scale collective action. But when those ideas moved from worthy abstractions to the concrete institutional changes needed to turn them into real levees and ditches, a countermovement emerged that by 1927 was on full-throated display.[15]

Decisions on river control necessarily led to broader questions about making a modern American city, including questions around urban development, agricultural transitions, economic growth, political power, and community identity. As Frank. A. Hubbell stood before the legislators in 1927, river management had become a proxy for deeper currents of change.[16]

Hubbell's Strategy

Melquiades Turrieta, his family, and the land they called home for perhaps three centuries is a story of how the landscape of modern Albuquerque came to be. Hubbell was playing a clever game when he used Turrieta as his example in the Santa Fe legislative debate in which Albuquerque's future hung in the balance.

Among the well-known names of the city's surge into modernity—the Atchison, Topeka, and Santa Fe Railway, and the First National Bank—Hubbell slipped in the little guy. Melquiades Turrieta is the sort of person whose name is often lost to historical retelling, but people like him are the foundations of a community. Turrieta was part of Hubbell's community roots in Pajarito in Albuquerque's South Valley, and he grew up several minutes' horse ride from Hubbell. Like his father, Melquiades Turrieta (1879–1950) spent his life farming on the family land. He is buried in the Pajarito Cemetery, built like most of the communities' cemeteries on high ground at the base of the sand hills, a heritage carefully preserved above the flooding of the valley floor.[17]

Neither were Hubbell's other choices of the First National Bank, with Alonzo B. McMillen as a longtime bank officer, and the AT&SF, with William C. Reid as their attorney and chief lobbyist in New Mexico, simply random or impersonal. McMillen and Reid were wealthy lawyers and landholders and had served on the Governor-appointed state Rio Grande Commission of 1921–1925. Like Hubbell, they were among the public entrepreneurs who had pushed toward the Conservancy District's creation in the first half of the 1920s, but by 1927 their aims had diverged.

Hubbell was no antagonist to progress. Prominent in the Albuquerque Commercial Club, he supported city building as much as the other boosters of the day. His wealth by the 1920s came partly from the great transition then underway, as the land he had assembled in support of his sheep empire was increasingly connected to the suburban fringe. After moving from his rural estate in Pajarito to a home in the city, he now lived a short stroll along high-end city blocks from McMillen and Reid.

"If for no other reason," the *Albuquerque Journal* wrote about him in 1892, "Frank A. Hubbell is a true friend of Albuquerque because as the town grows, his large suburban interests will make him a rich man."[18] By the early decades of the twentieth century, Hubbell's many land holdings included large areas—several thousand acres—of the valley floor southwest of the city center, land that would grow in value as flood control and drainage promised to turn it from swamp and floodplain into a growing metropolis.

But in his impassioned plea to the legislators, Hubbell singled out Melquiades Turrieta. He asked that the little guys, who owned land spread across the valley floor—five or ten acres here, maybe as many as fifty acres there—not be left behind and disproportionately taxed out of their land in the community's effort to finance progress.

Turrietta Lane

In the third decade of the twenty-first century, Turrietta Lane—its single trailing "t" at some point doubled, the spelling having wandered over the years—was a private road, more dirt driveway than street. It cut east off the old Camino Real toward the Rio Grande, past increasingly affluent homes, ending in a secluded 5.94-acre parcel of farmland being advertised in 2022 for sale for $1 million: "Build your dream home or MANSION on this secluded lot with a culvert for irrigation."[19]

A century earlier, the land told a different story: a microcosm of a landscape in which the river shaped human geography and human institutions, and their engineering shaped the river in return. Some ten miles south and west of downtown Albuquerque, the neighborhoods known as Pajarito and nearby Los Padillas were still rural in the 2020s, the traces of its rural past still evident despite its formal Census Bureau designation as part of greater Albuquerque's "urban" area.[20] By the first decades of the twenty-first century, large horse estates, often irrigated for pasture, were mixed with older middle-class homes.

Settlement of the valley floor, dating back to the valley's first Indigenous inhabitants, has followed a familiar pattern. It is a floodplain built by a river that, most years, rose out of its banks in spring, swelled by the melting snows of winter, and spread across the valley floor, leaving sediments in its wake. We think of rivers carving through a landscape, cutting down through the surface of the earth, but this is the opposite, a river bringing sediment and building up the land along its banks. In doing so, the Rio Grande slowly, inexorably, built up the land flanking its main channel, ever so slightly higher than the surrounding floodplain. Since the beginning, the valley's residents have built their homes, trails, roads, and irrigation systems on that higher ground. Low spots beyond were swamps until the river finally detached from the high ground it had built and claimed a new channel, turning swamps into river channels on the valley's opposite side and starting the process over again.

Today, the river is pinned between levees, with upstream flood-control dams to limit the flow. Without a spreading river acting as a level to mark the valley's high spots above the water line and low spots below, it is easy to ignore the subtle ups and downs of the valley floor. But in a time before levees, as the Rio Grande rose from its channel in the high spring flows to spread across the relatively flat valley floor, these spots, even a few feet above the surrounding terrain, made apparent the places humanity could claim.

In this stretch of the Rio Grande Valley, this can most clearly be seen at Isleta Pueblo. Built on the highest piece of the valley floor, it is home to the Indigenous Pueblo community named "Isleta" by the Spanish because of how the river in high flows would split and surround the community. The later Spanish villages of Los Padillas and Pajarito, a mile and a half to the north, where Hubbell grew up surrounded by orchards and a stop on the Camino Real, were also built on such spots.[21]

The area in the twenty-first century bears the imprint of humanity's response: a web of irrigation canals and drains that draw on the last four hundred years of engineering to replace the Rio Grande's natural function across the valley floor. People have been slowly but steadily gardening this landscape for a long time.

Along the back of the million-dollar Turrietta Lane parcel is a drain that was dug in the 1930s by the Middle Rio Grande Conservancy District to drain the swampy lands in this reach of the valley, and that is still present today. Along the property's front side is the Los Padillas Acequia, an irrigation canal snaking along the contour of the riverside land that dates to the 1700s, continuously irrigating this land ever since.[22]

And curving down one edge of the property is something even more intriguing: the ghostly outline of what was once called the "Isleta Indian Ditch," carrying irrigation water to the rich farmland of Isleta Pueblo to the south. Its age is uncertain. In the first formal inventory of the age of the valley's irrigation infrastructure it was recorded as simply "Pueblo—old," the surveyor's equivalent of "time immemorial." Arguably, it represents one of the oldest irrigation ditches in North America.

Turrieta Family Roots

The Turrieta family's roots reach back to the first wave of Spanish to arrive in New Mexico's central Rio Grande Valley when Don Juan de Oñate and his party of colonizers arrived in the late 1500s. Much of the record of that time is lost. Still, there are indications that the Turrieta brothers could trace ancestry to Don Fernando Jose Gomez Duran y Chavez, who may have been one of the earliest Spanish settlers in this stretch of the valley, on the northern edge of the lands of the Native American community of Isleta.[23] While the bulk of Oñate's party settled to the north, in the Española

Valley, a few modest outposts were established along the route of what would become the Camino Real. Los Padillas was likely one such outpost.

In the 1700s, Los Padillas and its neighboring villages of Pajarito and Atrisco, the villages strung along the Camino, were by far the largest communities in what we now call the greater Albuquerque area.[24] Before Albuquerque became the dominant population center, the entire valley was known as the Valle de Atrisco, from the Aztec word "Atlixtco," or "on the surface of the water."[25] This valley has long been identified with the river and its swamps.

In the 1920s, the Turrieta brothers owned some 250 to 300 acres of land on the valley floor between the sand hills on the west and the Rio Grande on the east. Melquiades Turrieta grew equal parts corn and alfalfa, with his brothers growing other crops, including grapes in small vineyards, chiles, and beans. Importantly for our story, though, is the land they owned that wasn't being farmed. Large chunks are marked in the early Conservancy District maps as weeds, desert, sand and gravel, salt grass, dunes, and bosque.[26] This was the kind of land the Conservancy District was meant to rescue, to bring into a modern, engineered, commercially productive landscape. And to do that, the district would seek to tax the Turrietas—a lot. The worse the condition of the land parcel for current production, the more significant the hoped-for *change* in agricultural production and the higher the relative tax burden.

Taxation Structure

This tax structure was crucial. As established under state law, the newly formed Conservancy District had the power to levy taxes to pay for the work to come—the construction of drains and levees, the consolidation of irrigation works, and the construction of an irrigation supply dam to capture high snowmelt flows in the spring and early summer for use on crops in the late summer and early fall dry seasons. The plan assumed farmers like Turrieta would turn their weeds, desert, sand and gravel, salt grass, dunes, and bosque into commercially productive farmland. The tax structure devised by the Progressive Era central planners, focused on taxing the value of incremental benefits to reclaimed land, demanded it.

The Turrieta brothers and the other small farmers like them did not have the capital and, therefore, could not convert the land, even if they had wanted to. But the question of whether they wanted to transform their land and lives into commercial farming was central. The valley's traditional communities were being told that they must change. And in this, they were given no say. The creation of the Conservancy District had been initiated by a petition of largely urban, predominantly Anglo, Albuquerque businessmen and civic boosters. Just 116 landowners signed the original petition, meeting the requisite minimum of 100 under state law in 1923.[27] If the Turrietas and the other small farmers like them objected, that process left them limited political or legal recourse. They did object, in the thousands. But the Conservancy District was governed by a judicially appointed board, with no direct role for voters or democracy. The rules created to reshape the valley left nowhere for the objections to go.[28]

Progressive Era expertise of the early twentieth century was telling the valley's farmers that it knew what was best for them, leaving them to adapt to new rules and a new hydrological system. The previously decentralized web of more than seventy separate acequias spread up and down the Middle Valley—each led by an elected *Mayordomo*—would be replaced by the centralized management of a newly created entity—part public corporation, part government agency, with the powers of taxation and eminent domain. Mayordomos from each acequia-based village were replaced by Conservancy District employees known as ditchriders.[29] In creating the Conservancy District the public entrepreneurs were turning the tools for managing the Rio Grande into a tool for reshaping the community. Some in that community were increasingly vocal in pushing back. The story of how the consensus so clearly in evidence at that 1919

Commercial Club meeting fell apart shows that, in the messy real world of collective action problem solving, who has a say and who has to pay matters. This allowed the tiny minority of initial petitioners and their hand-picked board to impose a crippling financial burden on all those who lived on the valley floor.

Interlude: March

By early March of 2023, there was reason to be optimistic about the coming year on New Mexico's Middle Rio Grande. Coming off a miserable, chaotic 2022 that saw the Rio Grande dry through Albuquerque for the first time in four decades, the early snowpack looked good. Flow down the river's main channel was modest, though higher than the dismal 2022, a steady base flow created by shallow aquifers slowly discharging through the winter. The ditches that for centuries spread water across the valley floor through Albuquerque neighborhoods remained dry.

But in a hydrologic system as human-altered as New Mexico's Middle Rio Grande, it takes more than melting snow to get water to the places where humans want it. It takes physical infrastructure—dams, siphons, and canals, many of them aging. It also takes institutional infrastructure—the rules that govern the system. As 2023's water season dawned, neither were working in the Middle Valley's favor.

Upstream, on the Rio Chama, El Vado Dam was out of commission, with long-needed repairs underway on the eighty-eight-year-old structure. Built in the wake of the green light the New Mexico legislature had given the Conservancy District in 1927, the dam had fundamentally changed the Middle Valley's relationship with the river, reducing spring flows to store water for late summer irrigation, smoothing out the natural hydrograph to shift water to the time when water users needed it most.

This year, there would be no such water. "After spring runoff," the Conservancy District's Anne Marken told her board of directors at their

March meeting, “MRGCD will be operating with a run of the river supply, and without summer rains, supply could get tight.” Even without the problems at El Vado, the problem would have been the same—not because of infrastructure and hydrology, but because of rules. The rules meant paying off the Middle Valley’s water debt to its downstream neighbors were forcing Marken’s hand. She had no choice but to reduce flows in the ditches to pay down the debt. The only hope was rain. The rules would allow irrigators to use the rainwater that fell on the valley.

“Let’s all pray for a spring that’s not too windy. And summer rains,” Marken said.

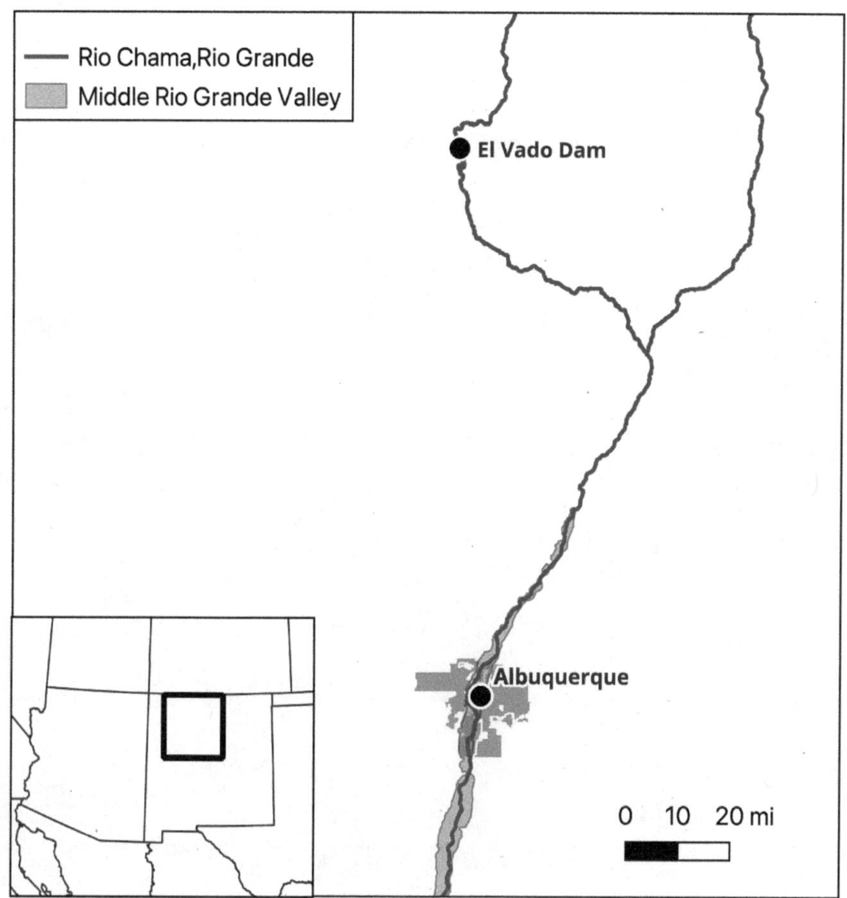

Map 5. El Vado Dam. Map by John Fleck.

Figure 9. The Albuquerque Main Canal awaits its first water of spring, March 2023. Photograph by John Fleck.

CHAPTER 2

A FLOUNDERING TURN TOWARD MODERNITY

To understand the roots of that 1927 legislative battle so crucial to the shape of modern Albuquerque, we must go back to the early 1920s. Efforts to turn greater Albuquerque into a modern metropolis were floundering, mired in Albuquerque's inability to overcome the challenges posed by the Rio Grande. The 1920s saw an enthusiastic pursuit of federal money to pay for the work of flood control, drainage, and irrigation. But when the possibility of federal funds largely evaporated, Albuquerque's boosters were left with a question that would take decades to solve—how to pay for the river management needed to turn their cluster of villages into a modern metropolis. Embedded in that question was a second: Who would have a say?

The arrival of the Atchison, Topeka, and Santa Fe Railway in 1880 offered a historical turning point. The AT&SF did not much care about commerce in New Mexico itself. There were too few paying passengers and too little paying freight for New Mexico to contribute one way or another to the ATS&F's economic fortunes. Albuquerque merely sat astride a convenient route to California, where the real money was. Local leaders saw it differently, heralding the railroad's arrival as a ticket to prosperity.[1]

Their challenge was managing the Rio Grande. The AT&SF was built along the high road at the base of the valley's eastern sand hills, and the Albuquerque station was built at the edge of a swamp, low-lying lands in an old Rio Grande side channel that wasn't good for much else but the railroad, and its local real estate development partners could acquire it cheaply.

Figure 10. The railroad in 1925 dominated Albuquerque's urban structure. But the challenge of managing the Rio Grande stood in the boosters' way. Courtesy of the Albuquerque Museum, PA1982.181.098.

With AT&SF representatives seeking a Middle Valley site for a rail depot, repair shops, and administrative offices, the wealthy Perea family famously demanded $425 an acre for land in Bernalillo, the nearest village upstream from Albuquerque. AT&SF representatives instead quickly accepted an offer of $1 for deeded land from a group of Albuquerque land speculators for "marshy farmland east of the villa." Those prominent citizens (Franz Huning, William Hazeldine, and Elias Stover) then acted as agents for The New Town Company (a subsidiary of AT&SF), partnering in selling connected town lots from the extra land.[2]

Consider the Rio Grande's "poised stream" and its flanking natural levees. Beyond these lay a floodplain, lowlands awaiting the river's eventual course change. In the late 1800s, the boosters hoping to bring Albuquerque into modernity chose that old swampy lowland to build their growing city's new, modern downtown. By the early 1920s, the tools to keep the river at bay and manage its waters were not up to the task.

A patchwork of community-built levees was insufficient to fend off the Rio Grande's frequent flooding. Attempts to respond by building and maintaining dikes regularly drained county coffers. During the Rio floods of 1904, it was Frank A. Hubbell who organized the labor that cut through a North Valley irrigation ditch levee that was damming flood waters and water logging lands. An equally disconnected patchwork of irrigation ditches, each managed by the local community that used its water, was also breaking down. Acequia governance structures had been sufficient to manage irrigation at the scale of small communities. Most importantly, the valley floor on which a city might be built was plagued by rising water tables, shallow marshes, and alkaline soil.

Solving this bundle of related problems—drainage, flooding, and irrigation—required broad collective action, which the valley's scattered communities had been unable to muster. The situation was ripe for public entrepreneurs to take up the challenge of creating a new institutional arrangement. In response, they turned to Progressive Era scientific resource management to remake the river and build a city. The traditionalist Hispanic farmers and their powerful but fading political leaders fought against the boosters' imposition of unrealistic costs on their homes, land, and way of life.[3] The resulting clash shaped the contentious birth of the government agency created to realize the dream of building a modern city on the valley floor—the Middle Rio Grande Conservancy District. The Conservancy District's turbulent origins marked a pivotal point, as Albuquerque leaned toward a future for the city and the river that was only dimly envisioned.

Phoenix Provides a Model

Like Albuquerque, Phoenix was a former Spanish colony facing similar challenges managing its river, the Salt, and transitioning to modernity. Although Albuquerque was larger in 1900, by the 1920s, Phoenix had surged ahead in economic and population growth, offering insights into the path of urban development.

The key to Phoenix's progress lay in a large federal program designed to funnel resources to small western communities to help them on the path to economic growth. In 1902 Congress created the United States Reclamation Service to "reclaim" arid Western lands using federal money. In response, the public entrepreneurs of the communities of Maricopa County, Arizona, in greater Phoenix, banded together to create a new institutional arrangement capable of doing things beyond the scale and reach of existing governmental structures. They formed the Salt River Valley Water Users Association, pledging more than 200,000 acres of farm and ranch land as collateral to serve as the financial foundation for the nation's first multipurpose reclamation project. At the community scale, they created the institutional framework needed to coordinate with the federal government on the project and, in the process, obtain other people's money to do the work required.

Within two years the United States Reclamation Service (Reclamation) began building Roosevelt Dam and a broad set of additional facilities to store and distribute irrigation water, protect the valley from the Salt River project's tempestuous floods, and ultimately drain waterlogged farmlands.[4]

It was the spark Phoenix needed. Between 1900 and 1920 Maricopa County's population quadrupled. Meanwhile, Bernalillo County—greater Albuquerque—was stalled.[5] The model was clear. "The Salt River project . . . made Phoenix a city," the *Albuquerque Morning Journal* argued in a December 1921 editorial.[6] "In 1910, Albuquerque, N.M., and Phoenix, Ariz., had about the same number of inhabitants. Now Phoenix has about twice as many population (sic) as has Albuquerque. Why? Because Phoenix has developed her valley and put it into production and Albuquerque has not done so," wrote Conservancy District advocate Jay Turley.[7]

By the 1920s, Congress was considering a new and larger infusion of federal funding for more reclamation projects. To get the money, Albuquerque had to be ready. Albuquerque's boosters realized they needed their own version of Phoenix's Salt River Valley Water Users Association.

The Public Entrepreneurs

To the list that includes Aldo Leopold, Pablo Abeita, and Max Gutierrez, we must add the names of three attorneys and civic leaders who, sometimes publicly and sometimes quietly behind the scenes, did critical work to establish the institution of the Conservancy District.

Pearce C. Rodey did much of the heaviest lifting in the boosters' push for flood control, drainage, and irrigation. After graduating from Harvard Law School in 1915, Rodey led the 1920s political fight for the Conservancy District as a community leader, project spokesman, and Conservancy District attorney. William C. Reid, another key figure, was counsel to the AT&SF during the Conservancy District's development in the 1920s. Reid served as New Mexico's Territorial Attorney when the state's Territorial Water Code was adopted in 1907, and he also served on the Rio Grande Commission, developing early plans for what would become the Conservancy District.

Behind them stood Rodey's father-in-law, Alonzo B. McMillen (1861–1927), an Albuquerque attorney who did prominent work on land grant cases. He also was a land developer and businessman. As often was the case, McMillen was both a public and private entrepreneur. He started a prominent insurance company and owned stakes in a newspaper, an electric trolley company, and the water supply company—ironically, given the political battles to come, as a partner in the private municipal water business with Frank A. Hubbell.

McMillen was the son of a pioneer Ohio farmer. He came to Albuquerque in 1893 and went to work as the attorney for the First National Bank of Albuquerque, where he would remain involved for many decades. He was an early advocate in Bernalillo County for the national goods roads movement and, with it, the necessary drainage—two of the crucial areas where public entrepreneurship played a role in filling a gap where existing institutions were incapable of solving the problems at the scale needed in growing Albuquerque. A man of his time, as of early 1912 McMillen owned an electric car when they were briefly popular.[8] Like Frank A. Hubbell, McMillen was active in the Commercial Club and involved in the push to statehood.[9] Through multiple corporate entities, McMillen had extensive land holdings on the valley floor and the connecting mesa lands to the west in what is now present-day Rio Rancho, New Mexico. Like Frank A. Hubbell, McMillen's extended family was heavily involved in the sheep industry into the 1960s.[10]

In a Progressive Era push toward good governance, McMillen helped write the new city charter, successfully moving Albuquerque to a city commission form of government in 1917. McMillen's vision statement for the city included a heavy focus on drainage, home building, industrial development including farming and agriculture, home markets for food production, conventions, a clean city, and the endorsement of Aldo Leopold's idea for a new riverside park.[11]

Armed with extensive, state-commissioned drainage survey maps of the Middle Valley produced in 1917–1918,[12] McMillen looked for a fix. One of his first moves was to hire Aldo Leopold as secretary of the Chamber of Commerce. Like Reid, McMillen served on the three-person state-sponsored Rio Grande Commission from 1921 to 1925.

"It's the Well-Drained Land That Earns the Money"

"The man who said, 'Too many cooks spoil the broth' overlooked the fact that if you can get all the cooks to work together, the more cooks the better." So wrote Aldo Leopold in Albuquerque's *Evening Herald* in May of 1918.[13]

Leopold, one of the great voices of twentieth-century American environmentalism, was a young family man living in a small house on the edge of a valley swamp near downtown Albuquerque when he wrote those words. With a World War I victory garden out back, his home was built several feet above the surrounding land, as its land sat at the edge of a swampy, alkaline Rio Grande floodway.[14] Today, it is a short walk up and over the levee to visit the city park he helped create.[15]

In essential ways Leopold's civic activism in Albuquerque laid a foundation for the environmental leader he would become. During his time here, you can see his early environmental thinking taking shape, including protecting public parks and wilderness. Perhaps more importantly for Albuquerque's story, it was here that his skills as an organizer and a communicator first appeared on the public stage, a crucial piece of the public entrepreneurship needed to bring the Rio Grande to heel.

In a detour from a life in forestry, land, and game management, Leopold had resigned from the US Forest Service to take a job in January 1918 as secretary of the newly formed Albuquerque Chamber of Commerce.

The same 1918 day McMillen's Chamber announced it had hired Leopold, its board approved a resolution throwing its civic and political muscle, and Leopold's singular talents, behind the effort to reshape the valley floor.[16]

Two salient features of the Chamber's resolution were crucial to the story of what followed. The first, as Leopold's civic zeal and communications genius quickly showed, was the need for community organizing to create the collective action tools to support the development of the institutions needed to solve the valley's drainage problems. "United we drain, divided we drown," a line penned by Leopold, became the movement's slogan, posted on special stationery donated by the Chamber.[17] By May 1918 civic leaders had banded together to form the Rio Grande Drainage Association.[18] "We pledge our support to the initiation and completion of the general Rio Grande drainage and irrigation project by local, state, and federal help," read the group's founding resolution.[19] The second salient feature was the financing mechanism to carry out the work. At that January 1918 meeting, the Chamber of Commerce endorsed the pursuit of federal funding—other people's money—to get the job done.

Science and the Gospel of Efficiency

The United States' Progressive Era of the late nineteenth and early twentieth centuries is most often identified with the clash between the corruptions of monopolist capitalism and social reforms, a response to Gilded Age excess. But for the western United States, it had as one of its most important components a rethinking of our relationship with the land.

At the heart of this manifestation of progressivism was science—hydrologists, foresters, agronomists, geologists, anthropologists, and engineers bringing their tools to bear on the West's challenges. "Its essence," the historian Samuel Hays wrote, "was rational planning to promote efficient development and use of all natural resources." The environment was a "resource" to be turned to human use, and science was the tool.[20]

Aldo Leopold exemplified the movement. In the years to come he rose to become one of the great American environmental thinkers and writers, authoring *A Sand County Almanac*.[21] His early professional training and work were rooted in science-based, "progressive" land and resource management. A graduate of the Yale School of Forestry, the movement's philosophical and technical launching pad, Leopold moved to New Mexico in 1909 to bring scientific management tools to the southwest's forests. With a new job as an information officer for the US Forest Service in Albuquerque, he quickly began to engage in local civic affairs and state issues around game management. In the latter, he pushed hard to appoint a professional state game commissioner and, somewhat ironically, politically argued vociferously for avoiding political appointments. As a community leader in Albuquerque, he was active in civic groups, especially the Chamber of Commerce, from its formation in 1918 until 1923, shortly before he left New Mexico in 1924. His eighteen months as the secretary of the Chamber in 1918 and 1919 represent a whirlwind of activity.

While Leopold's thinking evolved over his life, there is no evidence he ever discarded his support for draining the Middle Valley. In the near term, after his time as secretary for the Chamber of Commerce, he remained on their board for several years, later served on the Rotarians' drainage committee, and continued to give public statements pushing collective efforts for drainage throughout his time in Albuquerque.[22] During that crucial period in both Albuquerque's and Leopold's history, he placed the ideas and values of the progressive tradition front and center in the effort to tame the Rio Grande and bring order to the valley floor.

The vanguard of scientific resource management had first appeared in the Middle Rio Grande in 1896 in the person of W. W. Follett, the hydraulic engineer dispatched in service of the International Boundary Commission to figure out where all the water that used to reach El Paso and Juarez via the Rio Grande had gone.

Follett's report did not judge the many decentralized irrigation systems he found. But those who came after did not shy from a normative application of their principles. "Since each ditch was constructed to serve its own little community or area," Joseph Burkholder would write in the late 1920s as he helped engineer what the Pearce C. Rodeys and Alonzo B. McMillens and W. C. Reids of the world hoped would soon be built, "there was no attempt to construct a comprehensive irrigation system for the valley as a whole. It was inevitable that a great duplication should result with a consequent waste of effort, excessive cost of maintenance, and loss of water. This condition continues at the present time."

It was, in a word, "inefficient."[23]

As we shall see, there was an arrogant naivete in the scientific understanding the hydraulic engineers, mainly from the East, brought to remaking desert agriculture. But they were backed by political power, creating an inevitable momentum to shape the Middle Rio Grande Valley.[24]

Other People's Money

The lure of other people's money is an enduring thread in the history of the reclamation of the West.[25] Boosters knew they needed engineering help to manage their uneasy relationship with water—there was sometimes too much, sometimes too little. They needed levees to manage floods, drainage to turn swampy valley floors into farms and cities, and dams to store water to use when their rivers would otherwise drop away into useless trickles, as the Rio Grande of the nineteenth and early twentieth centuries did through central New Mexico most years in the late summer and fall. This cost more than tiny frontier communities like the proto-Albuquerque, whatever the boosters' city-building ambitions, could afford. That was the context as the Albuquerque Chamber of Commerce enthusiastically welcomed the head of the United States Reclamation Service to Albuquerque in December 1921. The federal government was "seriously considering a reclamation project for the middle Rio Grande valley from White Rock Canyon to Socorro," the federal leader told the Chamber's members at a December 19, 1921, meeting.[26]

Arid land could be brought into commercial production and added "to the agricultural assets of the state," he told the Chamber. And while irrigation was at the core of the Reclamation Service's work, the need for drainage would be a key to the effort. "With the irrigation will, of necessity, come drainage," he said, "because the two go hand in hand."[27] The response was enthusiastic. The Chamber thanked him for his visit and offered the Reclamation Service "the closest co-operating in working out the proposed project." They endorsed a piece of federal legislation known as the Smith-McNary bill, which they saw as providing the vital missing piece—other people's money to fund the work.[28]

Albuquerque's city-makers knew they needed engineering to make it possible to build a city on the valley floor. But it was expensive. Initial proposals by Alonzo B. McMillen and other developers and politicians, carried to Washington DC, to fund drainage efforts out of the proceeds from selling off federal public lands in New Mexico had fallen flat.[29] However, with a proposed $250 million federal revolving fund and generous project terms, Smith-McNary seemed to offer an answer.

First proposed in 1921 by Rep. Addison Smith of Idaho and Sen. Charles McNary of Oregon, the bill would have expanded what began with the Reclamation Act of 1902—more money for more projects. It also expanded the notion of "reclamation" beyond bringing irrigation water to arid lands. For the first time, the federal government would also encourage (and fund) the drainage of swamp lands.[30]

New Mexicans were enthusiastic.[31] Senator McNary personally reached out to Albuquerque organizers, supporting their efforts to develop a drainage and reclamation project and encouraging them to get the state legislation in place to square with the rules and requirements of the Smith-McNary proposed funding mechanism.[32] Existing New Mexico laws on single-purpose drainage or irrigation districts couldn't meet the multipurpose needs of incorporating flood and river control. New Mexico's public entrepreneurs would need to create something new. But they were excited about the task. "Response to the bill in New Mexico was enthusiastic, and even community leaders concerned with the welfare of subsistence Hispano farmers saw promise in the McNary measure," concluded historian Kenneth Orona.[33]

In December 1921 New Mexico Governor Merritt C. Mechem returned from a meeting of his Western colleagues to report that "proper reclamation and drainage of the middle Rio Grande valley is more of a possibility than ever before."[34] The following months marked a pivotal point in Albuquerque's history, as city leaders scrambled to prepare for a bounty of federal money, which would allow them to follow Phoenix in their quest to build a city on the valley floor.

Pursuit of Smith-McNary

Enthusiasm over the promise of Smith-McNary led to a frenzy of glowing rhetoric and institutional preparation. Now that the reclamation of swamp lands would explicitly be part of the reclamation bargain, Albuquerque boosters dreamed of 200,000 acres reclaimed and irrigated, with the increased agricultural production more than enough to repay the heavily subsidized Smith-McNary money to the federal government "and produce a good profit," and that "the Middle Rio Grande valley"—the "M" having grown to a capital letter—"will become a garden spot of the west."[35]

And there at the founding, shoulder to shoulder with the other boosters, was Frank A. Hubbell himself. "The federal government is the only institution which can successfully put over such a project in such a way that it will prove a benefit instead of a detriment to the land owners," Hubbell said.[36] In June 1922 several years before he led the opposition, Hubbell helped form the Middle Rio Grande Association, which was created to lay the institutional foundation needed for Albuquerque to get Smith-McNary money. A local government agency to oversee the work, conduct surveys, and estimate costs had to be created by the time Congress, as was widely expected at the time, approved the Smith-McNary bill.[37]

In the discussions during the summer of 1922, financing emerged as a key to the project's success. While the federal money would pay for the upfront work, the communities to benefit would have to pay the US Treasury a portion of the money back.[38] Gov. Merritt C. Mechem assured community leaders that the burden would be shared evenly. "The burden of taxation will spread over every bit of property which gains benefits from the project," he said. "This will shift part of the burden of the repayment of the Federal appropriations from the land owner to the city property owners and the railroads—every bit of property which derives benefit from the scheme in increased values."[39]

Hubbell's support was enthusiastic but qualified in a way that foreshadowed conflict to come. He "declared himself in favor of drainage emphatically," one local paper reported, but with a caveat: "He only wished to see the project brought about based on economic costs and not to have any confiscatory tax levies made on land owners and farmers."[40]

Conservancy Legislation

By March 1923 the New Mexico legislature, eager to leverage Smith-McNary money, cleared the way by rushing through legislation enabling the creation of "conservancy districts," government agencies to oversee the building of the things Albuquerque knew it needed to make its peace with the Rio Grande and follow in Phoenix's footsteps.[41] As historian Kenneth Orona notes, the Act had the support of both Anglo and Hispano legislators.[42]

Under the new law, creating a new district was made easy. Deliver the signatures of one hundred landowners to the District Court, and a community could have its new agency as a ready vessel for the federal money to come. Albuquerque's boosters wasted no time forging ahead, pursuing sweeping authority to remake the Middle Valley landscape under the broad powers of the new Act.[43] When it was done, the local agency to be created was granted authority to remake the landscape: "To regulate the stream channels of the Rio Grande and Rio Chama and to regulate the flow of said streams . . . and thereby to reclaim, drain, or fill the wet and overflowed lands and to protect public, municipal and private property from inundation and injury; and to reclaim and irrigate the arid and unproductive lands adjacent to said rivers as herein described."[44]

Death of Warren Harding and Smith-McNary

Just as the forces to transform the Middle Rio Grande Valley floor from swampland to a garden spot of the West seemed aligned—federal money combined with the local institutional tools to spend it—an accident of history upended everything. On August 2, 1923, President Warren Harding died suddenly, likely of a heart attack, in a San Francisco Hotel. The effort had lost a champion.[45] McNary appeared to distance himself from his own bill,[46] and a revision left the sentiment but dropped the requested funding.[47] In the months that followed Smith-McNary died. Absent federal money, the project struggled. But the zeal for reclamation and the creation of a Conservancy District to carry it out was in motion. The community's leaders had to find other ways to come up with the upfront cash.

A critical dimension of that was embracing support for the lands of the sovereign Native American Pueblos, which comprised one-fifth of the river valley land and had drainage needs. This was not an obvious path in 1922–1924, as Pueblo land rights were under attack. But project leaders generally eschewed efforts to encroach further and strip Puebloans of their lands. Instead, they endorsed the position that the federal government would cover this Indigenous portion of project funding, and they intended to get this part started sooner rather than later.

The other funding path lay in the lure of the private bond-buying houses of the day in places like Chicago and the big East Coast cities. Unlike the decentralized acequia system, a Conservancy District would have tax and finance powers. It could issue bonds that the Conservancy would commit to paying off with collected tax revenues.[48]

The prominent consulting engineer Arthur E. Morgan had helped introduce the Ohio Conservancy Act of 1914 in response to devastating floods in Dayton, Ohio, in 1913. The law enabled the creation of the successful Miami Conservancy District, which became the model Albuquerque and other communities followed. The Miami Conservancy District was a public corporation crafted before World War I, when municipal powers were too narrow, and federal involvement in flood control was far less than it would later become.[49] This provided the example on which New Mexico's original Conservancy Act had been modeled. Morgan was also the consulting engineer for the Pueblo Conservancy District, formed under new Colorado legislation in 1922. The steel-producing town of Pueblo, Colorado, formed its Conservancy District to control the Arkansas River as it recovered from the devasting floods of 1921. For a city built in a floodplain, the Pueblo flooding offered attention-grabbing stories and pictures in the Albuquerque papers.[50] Several years later, tracked down by Pearce C. Rodey, Morgan would come to Albuquerque to help the boosters engineer an institution to pursue similar goals here.

It is hard to know whether the financing and institutional problems that persistently beset the effort would have manifested themselves regardless of whether the community had access to federal money. Even with the federal financing, residents of the valley would have been taxed to pay the Treasury back. Without it, the question of where to get that upfront money needed sustained attention for much of the next decade. But the 1923 Conservancy Act legislation had shortcomings that quickly became clear. While it was easy to form a district—supporters needed to submit just 100 signatures—it was hard for everyone else to object. And when it became clear by year's end that there was no significant federal money to fill the vessel and that local funds would be needed to pay the bulk of its staggering costs, conservancy district opponents did object, in large numbers.

Without Federal Money, Trouble

Smith-McNary's demise threw efforts to create a conservancy district in the Middle Rio Grande Valley into disarray, sparking an intense conflict over the project's leadership and direction forward. Without the lure of significant federal funding to pay for the work of flood control, drainage, and irrigation system improvements, the discussion over creating the Middle Rio Grande Conservancy District in 1924 and 1925 changed dramatically.

The idea that one hundred landowners could force the district's creation, giving this special government agency—a public corporation—the power to tax all the valley's landowners without their democratic permission, struck Frank A. Hubbell as "confiscatory."[51] One critic called the Conservancy Act "a mustang without a bridle."[52] Octaviano Larrazolo—attorney, legislator, former governor, and political ally of Frank A. Hubbell and the Hispanic farmers on the Middle Rio Grande Valley floor—filed a legal objection signed by 3,125 protesting parties, mostly farmers concerned that the financing mechanism would force them off their land, concerned that the means of making the decisions—a board appointed by the court—left them with no say on the question.[53] Far from the egalitarian vision laid out by Gov. Mechem in 1922, who had said that "The burden of taxation will spread over every bit of property which gains benefits from the project," the financing structure that emerged placed a heavy burden on the valley's small farmers that they seemed unable to pay. This would happen under the governance of a board of directors of Progressive Era experts appointed by a single judge, leaving the farmers no say in the matter. Progressivism was crashing headlong into populism.

By 1925 the New Mexico state legislature seemed to agree, passing legislation that significantly raised the bar for creating a district (requiring signatures of at least 60 percent of the land owners and 60 percent of the land area) and would have handed management of the district over to a democratically elected board.[54] Given the clear need for drainage and flood control, there is no certainty about what might have happened had the legislation taken effect, but to the Middle Rio Grande Conservancy District's supporters, it appeared to be a death knell. But in a surprising political twist, Democratic Gov. Arthur T. Hannett "pocket vetoed" the bill, allowing it to die without either signing it or explicitly rejecting it with a formal veto.[55] The Conservancy District continued to live, but barely, as it was enveloped in a fierce political debate.

There remained a shared belief that the underlying tasks—flood control, drainage, and consolidation and improvement of the valley's irrigation systems—were needed. But the battle now centered on two related questions: Who has a say in the district's governance, and who will pay the costs of the work? The broad agreement among the valley's public entrepreneurs had fallen apart.

In settling those questions, the struggle highlighted a deep underlying cultural division between the descendants of Albuquerque's traditional Hispanic village and acequia culture and the wave of Anglo immigrants who followed the railroad's arrival. Meanwhile, the valley's Native American Pueblo communities stood patiently but insistently to one side, rarely mentioned but destined to play a crucial role.

With their opponents' legislative path at least temporarily blocked, the Conservancy District's backers were ready to proceed. On August 26, 1925, New Mexico's Second Judicial District Court formally created the Middle Rio Grande Conservancy District.[56] But the fighting did not stop. Another round of litigation to effectively block the Conservancy District's formation also failed in late 1925, as the boosters plowed forward, and others extolled the virtues of conservancy districts as needed public corporations.[57] "Reclamation Assured," the *Albuquerque Journal* announced on December 13, 1925.[58]

The Myth of 125,000 Irrigated Acres and a Lost Eden

The writer Anna V. Huey did not use the word "Eden" in early 1927 when she laid out the case for the embattled Middle Rio Grande Conservancy District, but its shadow was there. "85,000 Acres of Farms Lost in Middle Rio Grande Valley Since Year 1850: Vast Garden Gone Back to Alkali and Swamp," read the headline atop her January 31, 1927, stemwinder of a pitch for conservancy in the *Santa Fe New Mexican*.[59] The story of a mid-nineteenth-century 125,000-acre Middle Rio Grande Valley irrigated paradise—at a time (1850–1880) before the widespread use of steel plows, or the advent of tractors to plow, or trucks and trains to ship and home to only a sparse population—met a need and became a narrative that remained widely believed in the twenty-first century.[60]

This narrative is false.

The first months of 1927 were a time of peril for the project of flood control, drainage, and irrigation in the Middle Rio Grande Valley. Without federal funding to pay for the work, the goodwill and shared purpose of Aldo Leopold's 1918 "United We Drain, Divided We Drown" crusade had evaporated.[61] In their pursuit of the project, the Conservancy's backers settled on a persuasive narrative: the Middle Rio Grande Valley had once been home to a vast garden—an idyllic paradise of 125,000 richly productive irrigated acres, lost to an assault by the ill-behaved Rio Grande. "Out of this enormous and non-productive waste the Middle Rio Grande Conservancy District Board purposes [sic] to reclaim and irrigate over a hundred thousand acres," Huey wrote. Opponents were not standing in the way of progress. They were standing in the way of a return to an Eden lost.

The inflated irrigated acreage claim appears to have made its first public appearance in the Conservancy debates in a July 1925 talk to the Albuquerque Rotary Club by Conservancy District attorney Pearce C. Rodey.[62] It occurred in the weeks just before the legal creation of the Conservancy District. As legal and political efforts to reverse this continued, the acreage claim was often repeated, commonly during talks with civic organizations. At the Albuquerque Kiwanis Club in September 1926, Rodey claimed that "In 1880 the area in the valley under irrigation was 120,000 acres, but that rising water level had reduced the acreage to 40,000 acres."[63]

The claim first appeared in a 1925 report by C. R. Hedke for the Rio Grande Valley Survey Commission, which conflated land *capable* of irrigation in the 1800s because of "suitable soil and surface topography" with land *actually being irrigated*.[64] To the modern eye, Hedke's sleight of hand is clumsy, converting land previously identified as having the potential to be irrigated to "the definite conclusion that the entire valley was under cultivation" as early as 1850. If it *could be irrigated*, Hedke argued, we should assume it *was being irrigated*. His source for the claim is "those who are conversant with the history of the development of the region." They are never named.[65]

Despite its flimsiness, the claim took on a durable life because it served three purposes.

First, it was a key piece of New Mexico's legal claims against its upstream neighbors in Colorado. The US Supreme Court had ruled in 1922 that, absent an agreement between the states, the doctrine of prior appropriation applied to interstate rivers.[66] If New Mexico had once irrigated all of that land and then lost that opportunity because of Colorado's use in the headwaters valley of San Luis, it would strengthen New Mexico's claims in interstate struggles.[67] There was thus pressure for New Mexico to act decisively and establish a conservancy district with a strong water rights claim—the larger and earlier the dating, the better. Within New Mexico, with the Conservancy Act of 1923, there were immediate—if ultimately unsuccessful—efforts to establish a competitive conservancy district in the Santa Fe tributary basin to the north and a massive proposal in the San Juan basin.[68] To put a fright in New Mexico political leadership, there was even a scheme for a Los Angeles syndicate to buy New Mexico water rights claims from the San Juan River basin in northwest New Mexico.[69] From Albuquerque, influential early New Mexico irrigation engineer and lawyer Jay Turley was at the center of all this while simultaneously pushing the Middle Valley to act.[70]

Second, without federal money, the Conservancy District's backers had settled on expanding commercial agriculture to create a stream of new tax revenue to pay for the drainage and flood control needed to build a city on the valley floor.

Third, and related to the other two, was crafting a powerful narrative to support the community-building goals embodied in the first two.

Huey's language—a "vast garden" lost—is telling, in keeping with the idea of "reclamation," of nature tamed and perfected by human hands.

But it took the argument a step further. The boosters of drainage had been outlining an imagined future. Huey was turning that to argue for a reclaimed past. The Middle Rio Grande Valley was not just any land; it was a garden lost, and those who opposed Conservancy District opposed its redemption.

Despite its dubiousness, the number has persisted. Why? Because it met, even into the twenty-first century, a need. Whether they realized it or not, what Huey, Rodey, Chief Engineer Burkholder,[71] and the others were doing when they conjured an idyllic historic garden along the valley floor was turning away from an accurate tale of the past and turning it into a cartoon in service of political rhetoric. "[U]sing the past to make an argument about the future," the historian Jill Lepore has written, "is far from exceptional; it is instead a feature of political rhetoric, always and everywhere. Politics involves elections and votes and money and power, but the heart of politics is describing how things came to be the way they are in such a way as to convince people that you know how to make things the way they ought to be."[72]

1927 Legislative Debate

Rarely in US history, an impassioned Octaviano Larrazolo thundered, "has such an infamous law ever been enacted."[73] Thwarted by Governor Hannett's pocket veto of the 1925 legislation that would have forced democratic governance on the Conservancy District, in 1927 Larrazolo and his allies had once again returned to the New Mexico legislature. The "infamous law" to which Larrazolo was referring was New Mexico's 1923 Conservancy Act, the law under which the then-nascent Middle Rio Grande Conservancy District had been formed. The debate that day in 1927, a raucous six-hour "barrage of speeches" before the New Mexico state legislature,[74] focused on the two central questions at the heart of the struggle to shape the future of the floor. Embedded in an argument over structures of governance and goals for reengineering a river, it was a battle over what Albuquerque was to become and how.

Larrazolo—Mexican immigrant, former New Mexico Republican governor (1919–1921), soon to be elected the first Hispanic US Senator, a fierce defender of the Spanish-speaking people of the state—saw the 1923 Conservancy Act, in its answer to those questions, as a betrayal of democratic principles.[75] The law allowed the tiny minority of initial petitioners and their hand-picked board to impose a crushing financial burden on all those who lived on the valley floor; Larrazolo said the law "couldn't be more un-American if it had been enacted in Soviet Russia or by the Emperor of Japan."[76]

Four years after the Conservancy Act's original passage, Larrazolo, a lion in New Mexico political history—if not always on the winning side—was back before New Mexico's legislature, trying to change the law and defending the little guy.

"On to Santa Fe!"

On the other side of one of the most consequential political debates in shaping modern Albuquerque were those enamored of the progressive ideal of expertise in solving the Rio Grande Valley's dilemmas. "Big Men, Big Problems," the *Albuquerque Journal* said of those who preferred appointed experts to more direct democracy.[77] "Duke Citians Storm City for Conservancy Bill Hearing," the *Santa Fe New Mexican* blared on February 10, 1927. A caravan organized by the Albuquerque Chamber of Commerce drove north to the capital city. Arriving perhaps five hundred strong, they wore yellow tags bearing the slogan "Let Conservancy Alone."[78]

Representing Albuquerque's merchant class ("100 business men . . . promised to leave their establishments in the interest of the conservancy") the caravan embodied Albuquerque's push toward modernity.[79] Pearce C. Rodey, a lawyer for the Conservancy District as it then existed and one of the leading opponents of elections for the District's board, said he was "for democratic measures" but noted (as paraphrased by the *Journal*) that "not long ago there was a world war and he did not have a chance to vote on it. He said no one complained." If a decision as monumental as war could be entrusted to experts, surely something as simple as a Conservancy District could as well.[80]

Rodey spoke for a dominant view in 1920s America—keeping natural resource management out of the dirty, messy hands of democratic politics, entrusting it to the white gloves of scientific expertise. A young Aldo Leopold would have approved, as this replicated the political arguments he had made in 1918–1919 over the New Mexico Game Commissioner position—that an appointed expert should hold the job rather than filling it through a political process.[81] The Conservancy District debate was the latest example from New Mexico of a thread that repeats through United States history: the tension between governance by elites versus the will of the masses.[82]

Rodey "said he believed large engineering problems should be decided by men who had time to study them. He quoted leading engineers who had said there should be no change in the present conservancy law. Any proposed change in the law would cripple the financing of the district, he contended." Rodey represented the vanguard of that Progressive Era thinking in 1920s New Mexico—wise men calling on the tools of science and engineering to bring order to the disorder of the Rio Grande Valley floor. As key expert witnesses before the special legislative committee hearings, the consulting engineer, Arthur E. Morgan, and the Denver bond house representative agreed with him.[83]

Never mind that the questions at issue were questions of community values, representation, and agricultural economics, not engineering. Democracy, Rodey insisted, was a dirty business not to be trusted over the views of Big Men (in 1927 they all were men) on these Big Problems. It was a familiar refrain. Less than a decade before, Aldo Leopold had made efforts to include Puebloan, farmer, and community interests in his early Albuquerque conferences of 1918 and 1919, rallying support for drainage actions. But at a September 1919 meeting organized by Leopold, the consensus was to set democracy aside, issue bonds to pay for the work, "and let the people fall in line."[84] Speaking before the 1927 New Mexico legislative hearing, Pearce C. Rodey argued for democracy's limitations. "Speaking of the dangers of elections," said Mr. Rodey, "there was a fight at the Atrisco acequia election and I understand there was a mobbing affray."[85]

His choice of example should not be overlooked. Atrisco was part of the South Valley home turf of Frank A. Hubbell's political machine.

The District Stands

For weeks after the February 1927 hearing, wrangling over the state's Conservancy law continued. But by March, it was clear that Octaviano Larrazolo had lost his fight to have New Mexico conservancy district boards selected by democratic vote. Beaten on the central question of democratic representation, Larrazolo and Hubbell agreed to a compromise that expanded the judicial appointment process for the Conservancy District's board so that a judge representing rural communities around Albuquerque would play a role. The deal also critically provided some near-term financial protection for small farmers, deferring tax payments for five years for those owning fewer than twenty acres (more than 75 percent of landowners, but not a majority of acreage). But after that, taxes would be based on the expected benefits to farmland.[86]

The final governing structure for the Conservancy District then adjourned to a back room. A "meeting of Albuquerque business men" gathered on a Saturday evening in March 1927 to settle on the names of a new Conservancy District board. Upon receiving the names, the judge overseeing the process responded: "The passage of a good conservancy act is promised and it appears that the sentiment of this community favors the acceptance of the plan as the means of saving the conservancy project."[87]

The following Monday, the legislature passed a bill revising the Conservancy Act, allowing the Middle Rio Grande Conservancy District to stand, with only a single vote opposing in the Senate and unanimous support in the House—both with Republican majorities. It was signed into law by a Republican governor, absent any requirement for an elected board, and contrary to the party's legislative platform. The Progressive Era vision of turning to expertise rather than democracy to manage Albuquerque's relationship with the Rio Grande had won. Albuquerque's civic boosters and the Conservancy District's agents had created a persuasive case for a well-drained, well-irrigated, flood-protected city, with a District run by a judicially appointed board. The cards appeared stacked against the Conservancy District's survival, but the legislative events in early 1927 represented a marker in the political recognition of Albuquerque's growing economic ascendency in the state.

Octaviano Larrazolo was not there for the vote and resigned his seat in the New Mexico legislature two days later, citing his health. "His condition was believed due largely to his labors on the Conservancy act," wrote one observer.[88]

Epilogue: Power and Wealth Still Hold Sway

An odd epilogue to 1927's political battle and the underlying argument played out the following year. Frank A. Hubbell and Octaviano Larrazolo, fighting on behalf of small Hispanic farmers on the valley floor, were not the only ones to argue the financial structure made no sense. Downstream, near the bottom end of the Conservancy District's proposed project lands, sat the newly forming district's largest landowner, prominent Dallas businessman and banker J. Fred Schoellkopf. If any piece of land was situated to make a successful turn to commercial agriculture and generate the cash flow needed to finance conservancy, it was Schoellkopf's holdings on the old Bosque del Apache land grant.

The land ownership was large enough to support the economies of scale of commercial agricultural crop production relative to the valley's many small Hispanic, primarily subsistence farmers with their traditional "long lots." Large parts of the area had already gone through significant clearing and leveling, and a new thirteen-mile irrigation ditch had already been dug to improve crop production. This occurred through several rounds of early twentieth-century corporate colonization efforts surrounding the former settlement of Elmendorf, marketing farm sites to Anglo immigrants in Albuquerque and elsewhere. It had a train stop at Elmendorf.

Schoellkopf, with deep pockets, was much better positioned to put the lands into commercial agricultural production. But he wasn't interested in such a conversion. Some of the lands were being grazed, but the owner was also pursuing oil and gas development. Schoellkopf made the same argument Hubbell and Larrazolo had made—that the costs being placed on farmland were unreasonable. "The protest gives as the main objection that the expenditure incurred by the owner will far exceed the benefits."[89]

Where identical arguments made by Hubbell and Larrazolo on behalf of the small Hispanic farmers were rejected, the boosters, faced with a challenge from a wealthy owner of a large tract of land, quickly changed course in response. In the early weeks of July 1928, as the Rio Grande was running dry from Barelas to Elephant Butte reservoir, the District, through its chief engineer Joseph Burkholder and lead attorney Pearce C. Rodey, submitted a modified plan, trimming Schoellkopf's 8,300 acres of Bosque del Apache bottom lands from the project. At the same time, the boosters dropped the community of San Marcial to the south.[90]

The Dallas businessman's projection of the negative net farm income of commercial crop production for his large-scale lands was prophetic for the coming decade, especially for small-scale farmers in the Middle Valley with limited capital and who had no access to federal farm loans in the period. By the mid-1930s, the Bosque del Apache lands were sold to the federal government upon recommendation of a New Deal–era national wildlife committee that included Aldo Leopold, who had left Albuquerque

Figure 11. (*above*) The trees of Corrales still wear their winter colors as the first water of spring makes its way through the village ditches, April 2023. Photograph by John Fleck.

and emerged as a leading national conservation advocate. In 1939 they were designated the Bosque del Apache National Wildlife Refuge.[91] Drains through the property are still in use today and connect to the Middle Rio Grande Conservancy District's broader ditch and drainage system. Today, annual expenditures from birdwatchers visiting the internationally recognized site are on the same order of magnitude as the market value of sales for all crop production in Socorro County.[92]

Interlude: April

As the Middle Rio Grande Conservancy District board of directors met in April 2023 for their monthly conversation about managing the Rio Grande, problems were brewing. Anne Marken's prayer call had been answered. Like a great frozen reservoir, a growing snowpack awaited the spring warming to bring green to the valleys below. But the rules controlling the institutional hydrograph were making it hard to get that water out of the river's main channel and into the valley's irrigation ditches.

As runoff gained momentum, the Army Corps of Engineers dam managers began allowing more water down the main channel, into the Middle Rio Grande Valley. The Rio Grande through Albuquerque had been swelling since mid-March. But Marken cautioned against undue optimism. Water was starting to flow in the ditches, but slowly. Irrigators were grumbling about all the water flowing past them down the main channel, while they waited to get theirs. The reason, Marken reiterated, was the rules. More water that moved downstream to pay off the debt to the Middle Valley's downstream neighbors in Southern New Mexico and Texas meant less water in the irrigation ditches. The Middle Valley outside the river's main channel was already greening up, but less than it would have absent the Rio Grande Compact problem.

"It's important that we are all conservative with water use and balance irrigation needs with river obligations," she said.

Figure 12. (*below*) A once-failed Middle Rio Grande Valley tobacco farm, preserved as community open space, grows alfalfa for the local horse market. Photograph by John Fleck, 2020.

CHAPTER 3

TOBACCO COMES TO ALBUQUERQUE

The 1928 *Albuquerque Journal* advertisement seems profoundly out of place:

> GROW TOBACCO: Farmers of the Rio Grande Valley Near Albuquerque, the Consumers Tobacco Company is offering you the opportunity of growing tobacco. We believe that this crop promises a cash return well worth your efforts. A few acres of tobacco added to your farm may mean many extra dollars in your pocket next fall.[1]

The signatories, founders of the Consumers Tobacco Company, were an odd assortment for an agricultural enterprise: an insurance agent, a lawyer, housing developers, a warehousing and shipping firm, the Albuquerque Gas and Electric Co., and the First National Bank.[2] Why were non-farmers so enamored of a crop that seemed so out of place in the Rio Grande Valley? Tobacco thrives in humid climates like the southeastern United States, not a near-desert river valley like Albuquerque.[3]

The story of Albuquerque's failed experiment in tobacco farming illustrates one key to understanding the trajectory of Albuquerque's relationship with the Rio Grande and the collective action challenges of managing life on the flood plain. While the pursuit of commercial tobacco farming demonstrated the naivete of the boosters trying to build their city on the valley floor, what followed in its wake demonstrated the remarkable success of the alternative.

The 1928 newspaper advertisement enthusiastically explained the economics behind the boosters' motivation. "Any crop that can increase the per-acre yield of the acreage we have under cultivation will react to the benefit of the farmer and the community alike."[4] Despite not being farmers, the 1920s civic boosters viewed the growth of commercial agriculture as key to Albuquerque's future.

Victory in the 1927 legislative fight seemed to have ensured the Middle Rio Grande Conservancy District's future. With the institutional tool needed to transform Albuquerque's relationship with the Rio Grande now in place on paper, work to convert those ideas into changes on the ground was by 1928 well underway. The civic boosters behind the Consumers Tobacco Company understood that managing the city's relationship with the Rio Grande was central to their community's future. Albuquerque needed flood control and drainage to grow on the valley floor and create jobs to support its boom. By draining the swamps and protecting the valley from the river's rampages, and consolidating the valley's irrigation systems, the creation of the Middle Rio Grande Conservancy District could provide both. They were turning the city's relationship with the river from obstacle to opportunity. Tobacco, they hoped, would provide the key, and they were willing to invest their own money to help make it happen.

"If I were a farmer in this valley I would jump at the chance to grow tobacco this year," wrote Clinton P. Anderson, a former newspaperman turned insurance entrepreneur. Anderson's political rise to Congress, the US Senate, and eventually a cabinet seat as Harry Truman's Secretary of Agriculture began here. "It's a real opportunity," he said about tobacco farming, "one you've never had before."[5]

The tobacco business failed. Anderson and the others lost money, then lost some more. A century later, the Isleta Boulevard site of the processing plant was a combination Taco Bell / Kentucky Fried Chicken. Across the street, a Long John Silver's fast-food joint on Tobacco Road in 2023 advertised $6 shrimp baskets. Nearby is a small park named for Anderson, flanked by suburban homes built on the failed tobacco farm. One of the last two remaining pieces of farmland from the project was for sale awaiting a housing development. The other was held in public ownership, preserving open space and using Rio Grande water to grow alfalfa for local horse owners.

Farther from the city center a few commercially viable farms existed in the Middle Rio Grande Valley a century after the Conservancy District's formation, perhaps three or four dozen based on land ownership, with some unknown additional number of farmers who lease land from others. Most of the irrigated acreage in the valley was, in the third decade of the twenty-first century, devoted to noncommercial irrigation.[6] But while the agricultural dreams of those 1920s boosters failed repeatedly and spectacularly, their underlying goal—to build a modern city on the valley floor—was a dramatic success. The city's *peri-urban* fringe—the broad transitional zone between urban and rural—was filled not with the Jeffersonian yeoman farmers[7] Clinton P. Anderson and the other tobacco farming boosters had imagined. Pastures and small alfalfa fields are still irrigated, just not for the money. The valley is still cool and green in the summer, and the ribbons of green remain.

Shaped by a River

Albuquerque's modern South Valley has been fundamentally shaped by the area's relationship with the Rio Grande. By the late 1800s, farming in the Middle Valley was already fading. Its decline was partly the result of physical challenges: flooding, a rising water table, and alkaline soils. But the change was socioeconomic as well. The railroad's arrival created far more attractive economic opportunities than the sheepherding and subsistence farming life.

If measured against the goal of Clinton P. Anderson and the other boosters—of creating a thriving agricultural industry—the river management institutions created in the 1920s must be judged in this part of the Rio Grande Valley as a failure. The only productive farms by the twenty-first century were in public ownership, land purchased by local governments and leased to alfalfa farmers to preserve open space and the valley's "agricultural heritage." Yet the institution created to provide flood control, drainage, and irrigation has not only endured; it has thrived.

In 1896 when W. W. Follett surveyed what is today known as Albuquerque's South Valley, a ten-mile stretch of Rio Grande Valley floor south of Albuquerque, he found agriculture already in decline. Valley residents irrigated just a quarter of Rio Grande bottomlands from five ditches.[8] Follett's survey, conducted on behalf of the US and Mexican governments, was to determine why the Rio Grande's flows to the south were shrinking. In the river's upper reaches, near its headwaters in Colorado two hundred miles to Albuquerque's north, Follett found the primary explanation: booming agricultural communities. Vast areas of arable land and the ready availability of irrigation water, combined with access to markets provided by the extension of railroads into the San Luis Valley in Colorado, 175 miles upstream of Albuquerque, had fueled a booming agricultural economy.

The same could not be said for the river's Albuquerque reach. The two things that had provided such benefits in the San Luis Valley—plentiful water and the connection to the railroads—had the opposite effect on the lands around Albuquerque. "While there is fully 75,000 acres of arable land in the district," Follett wrote of his survey of the lands south of Albuquerque, "less than one-fourth of this amount is cultivated. Much formerly watered has been abandoned and is now marsh land, white with alkali." Increased farming in the San Luis Valley was reducing flow in the Rio Grande, in a way that was paradoxically turning the Rio Grande Valley lands around Albuquerque into a swamp as a smaller, slower river dumped its sediment load in the Middle Valley.[9]

Follett also found a second phenomenon that would bedevil efforts to develop commercial agriculture in Albuquerque in the coming century. In the two decades since the railroad arrived in New Mexico's Middle Rio Grande, acreage farmed in the valley south of Albuquerque dropped 10 percent as farmers left for jobs building the railroad. The wage economy was displacing subsistence farming from the start.

A Long History of Marginal Agriculture

True or not, narratives that serve a useful purpose are sticky. Thus, insurance man Clinton P. Anderson and his colleagues believed that commercial agriculture could succeed in the Middle Valley and that they were reclaiming the idyllic past of a garden paradise of large-scale irrigated agriculture up and down the valley floor. That belief persisted into the twenty-first century. The historical record suggests it was more myth than reality. Farming had long been there. Since the arrival of the Puebloans, irrigation was critical to feeding New Mexico's earliest communities. It is one of North America's oldest continuously irrigated human geographies. But throughout that long history, irrigation was little practiced at any significant scale.

"This has never been done otherwise than in the simplest and most inexpensive modes," the *Santa Fe New Mexican* explained in 1868, before the railroad's arrival.[10] What might have seemed primitive and backward to the newly arrived Anglos was meeting the needs of the communities strung up and down the Rio Grande Valley. But without mechanization, irrigation from hand-dug ditches was laborious, limited to small communities growing the food they needed to feed their families. And the number of people in New Mexico at the time was small. Without a modern dam to store spring runoff, farmers' late-season irrigation was limited to whatever meager flow the Rio Grande could provide during the late summer and early fall harvest seasons.

Records from the time are scarce, with the earliest estimates focused on "cultivated land" rather than land under irrigation. This is because irrigation beyond that sufficient to meet subsistence needs was not done in the mid-1800s in what would become the United States. In the first survey, US Army Major George McCall found 72,000 acres under cultivation, some irrigated and some not, in the entire Rio Grande Valley between Cochiti and the US-Mexico border.[11]

The first tally of what would come to be called the Middle Rio Grande Valley was done in 1860, but it is little help in doing anything other than constraining the upper bound of what might have been farmed in the Middle Valley. With county boundaries extending east of the Rio Grande across what is now Arizona to the Colorado River, it tallied a total of 46,646 cultivated acres (some irrigated, some not) in an area that included not only the Middle Rio Grande Valley but portions of the Rio Pecos, the Gila River, and the Colorado.[12]

Given the population of the time, the small number of cultivated acres is unsurprising. It stood out to visitors, who repeatedly pointed to the potential the valley might offer, "land which heretofore counted no more than barren waste" once irrigation systems were built, as the *Daily New Mexican* put it in 1875.[13] Thus it remained in 1880, as the Atchison, Topeka, and Santa Fe Railway line arrived. "One thing is prominently noticeable to the traveler to this valley; there is but a very small portion of the tillable lands under cultivation," a chronicle by one of the first passengers explained.[14]

Von Thünen Rings

The Middle Rio Grande Valley's place in the nation's transition from an agricultural to an urbanizing economy is crucial to understanding the thinking of Clinton P. Anderson and the other investors in the tobacco farming enterprise. These civic boosters were committed to greater Albuquerque's growth and economic development. But it was hard for them to imagine moving beyond agriculture as society's economic underpinning. They believed commercial farming would serve as modern Albuquerque's foundation. They believed this so strongly that that they were willing to invest their own money to help make it happen.

Urbanization in the nineteenth century had followed a familiar pattern. Driven by the need to feed urban populations and the costs of land and transportation, agricultural land clustered around cities, a model famously laid out by the early nineteenth-century German economist

Johann Heinrich von Thünen. Von Thünen argued that the development of cities would follow a natural pattern, with concentric rings of farmland surrounding a city center, providing food and economic underpinnings for the growing urban centers.[15] In the idealized version of his work, what has become known as the "von Thünen ring" would emerge to meet cities' needs. The rings were an abstraction. Natural landscapes and the availability of soil, water, and transportation routes shaped the actual growth of urban areas and their peri-urban fringe. However, the model laid out a spatial pattern crucial to transitioning from an agricultural world to an industrializing urban one.

You can see this in Albuquerque. Shortly after the railroad arrived in 1880, immigrants like the Herman Blueher and John Mann families set up truck gardens on some of the most productive and well-watered land, a short wagon's haul from the rapidly expanding New Town.[16] Dairies filled swampier lands unsuitable for irrigated agriculture but close enough to get milk to the growing city. "Wanted—Everybody to try; Albers' ice cream; made of pure cream only. At Ruppe's fountain, or at Albers' dairy, end of street car tracks," read one 1899 newspaper advertisement for a dairy built on swamp land downstream from Old Town.[17] Farther downstream, on the east side of the river, stockyards and slaughterhouses settled in to meet Albuquerque's needs.

Beyond these patterns driven by a growing city's need to eat was agriculture's role in the US economy. In von Thünen's nineteenth-century Europe, a substantial fraction of the population produced food. The same can be said for the United States. In 1900 about one-third of all workers in the US population farmed.[18] While the proportion dropped as Anderson and his friends advocated for their desired future for a growing Albuquerque in the 1920s, it was still hard to imagine a city without agriculture as a foundation.

But it also was a deliberate act to change the community's character. The villages around what was becoming modern Albuquerque had always been agricultural. But the farming had been largely subsistence, with families growing food to feed themselves. This clashed with the boosters' ambitions. Rather than abandoning agriculture, they aimed to change the agricultural landscape to suit their city-building goals. But by the time Anderson and the others were advertising for local small farmers to take up their tobacco farming cause, the relevance of von Thünen's ideas was already colliding with the changing reality of America.

Expanding urban centers attracted workers with the promise of steady wages. Follett had already identified this three decades before as South Valley residents abandoned irrigated land for jobs in the city. Mechanization transformed agriculture, increasing productivity while reducing the need for labor. Agriculture's share of employment was shrinking, and a massive demographic shift was underway from rural areas to cities.

Railroads also reshaped the human geography von Thünen described in the nineteenth century. Rail shipping, especially advancements in refrigeration, made it possible to import foods over long distances. A successful vegetable farm no longer needed to be next to the city it served. Thus, even as Anderson and the others were pushing for an expansion of commercial agriculture in a belt around Albuquerque, the most successful existing operations, the truck gardens west of town, were losing their economic competition with food imported by rail. Except for dairies, which clustered around cities until the 1970s,[19] von Thünen rings were no longer essential for a city's existence.

In this context, the Albuquerque boosters' plan for commercial farming around the city can be seen as an attempt to straddle these two worlds—to keep a foothold in the agricultural past while embracing the urban-industrial future. Anderson and the other boosters could not imagine a Middle Rio Grande Valley without agriculture at its core. But their interest was also self-serving. They believed they could only pay for flood control and drainage by drawing on the revenue created by commercial agriculture. By promoting tobacco farming, with a centerpiece farm, a processing plant, and cooperative arrangements with smaller farmers, they aimed to make agriculture more profitable, hoping to retain and attract residents in an era of rapid urban migration. They saw the opportunity to create a unique urban-agrarian blend, allowing the city to benefit from the industrial urban revolution while preserving its agricultural heritage.

But the trend had passed them by. Follett had already seen this in the 1890s. South Valley residents abandoned agriculture for work with the railroad, which connected Albuquerque with import and export markets, and built a sizable locomotive maintenance shop and administrative offices in Barelas.[20] Wool processing and a sawmill offered jobs. Tourism was also emerging, luring travelers first by train, then in early automobiles.[21] With the wage economy's opportunities, old patterns of subsistence farming and community life in the villages around Albuquerque were breaking down.[22]

The Legacy of Tobacco

Like much of the development of early twentieth-century Albuquerque, the tobacco farming enterprise is entangled in politics. Clinton P. Anderson and the other Albuquerque boosters who invested in the project believed they could profit from it—that commercial agricultural success was possible. But their purchase of the land also was an attempt to solve a political problem.

By the mid-1920s, Frank A. Hubbell's opposition had become the most significant obstacle to their efforts to bring flood control, drainage, and a modernized irrigation system to the valley through the institutional mechanism of a conservancy district. Hubbell did not object to the goal. Born in Pajarito in the South Valley to mixed Hispanic-Anglo parents, head of a *rico* sheep empire, and Bernalillo County's Republican political boss at the onset of the 1900s, Hubbell had begun amassing South Valley lands. As one of the valley's largest landowners, he stood to benefit handsomely from reclamation. But he objected to financing it based on unrealistic expectations for commercial agriculture.

Hubbell's political machine was aging, but it had already been central in defeating an earlier effort at setting up a drainage district in the South Valley. The vision was clear, but the devil was in the details for Hubbell, and he still had the political wherewithal to organize opposition. Reasoning that Hubbell's interests were purely economic and disagreeing with him about the potential of agriculture, the boosters put their money on the line. Led by banker George Kaseman (another immigrant drawn to Albuquerque in the 1880s by a railroad job), the group created the Valley Development Company, composed of pro-conservancy stockholders. In one of the most consequential real estate transactions in this crucial period in Albuquerque's emergence as a twentieth-century city, they bought 1,700 acres of Hubbell's lands in the South Valley. "A group of public spirited Albuquerque citizens purchased 1700 acres from Frank A. Hubbell for $100,000 to turn that large acreage from an opponent of conservancy to a proponent of conservancy," Anderson explained years later.[23]

With much of the land yet to be drained, the Valley Development Company quickly leased out 400 acres of their new purchase to Louisville tobacco grower R. G. Mewborne, president of Consumers Tobacco Company. Mewborne would set up shop on the land to launch a tobacco-growing experiment. They couldn't lose. Or so they thought.

"Syndicate buys F.A. Hubbell Farm as First Move in Development of Tobacco Industry in River Valley," the *Albuquerque Journal* told its readers on December 6, 1925. The story laid out an ambitious plan. The syndicate, led by a group of local investors "and capitalists from Los Angeles" would lease land to Mewborne, setting up a tobacco processing plant and "educating the farmers of the valley . . . so that a large amount of acreage will be planted to the weed in 1927."[24] In November 1926 Mewborne claimed success in the first years' tests. "We have demonstrated that tobacco can be raised profitably here and our first year's crop has been a decided success," he told the Lions.[25]

Agricultural records suggest a different story. Maps drawn up for Conservancy District planning show some effort to plant tobacco in the farms in 1927, most of it on the land the boosters had bought from Hubbell.[26] However, according to federal agricultural census records, in 1929 only fifteen acres on three farms were commercially productive. By the next census in 1934, total tobacco acreage in New Mexico had dwindled to just five acres.[27]

The failure was about more than the questionable suitability of the Middle Valley climate, soil, and water for tobacco farming. Tobacco failed for the same two fundamental reasons every other attempt at commercial

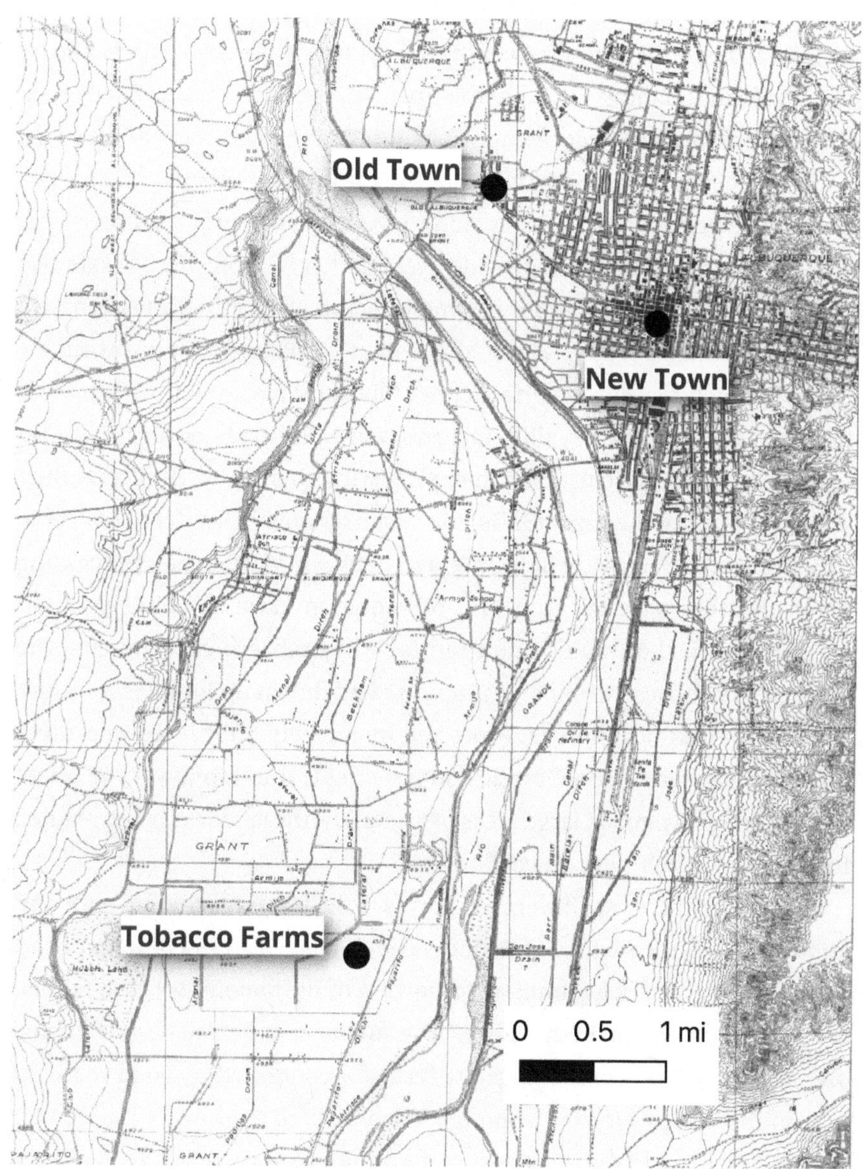

Map 6. Tobacco farms. Map adapted by John Fleck.

agriculture failed in the Middle Rio Grande Valley. First, successful commercial agriculture would have required operating at scales impossible on the small landholdings left from the Spanish, Mexican, and early US eras. Second, and probably more importantly, farming as an occupation could not compete with the attractions of jobs in the growing urban economy, nor could it compete with the value of land converted to peri-urban subdivisions.

Even as tobacco's failure provided yet another in a long list of examples of the valley's unsuitability for commercial crop production, an alternative framework was already taking shape that explains tobacco farming's failure, which would come to define Albuquerque's relationship with the Rio Grande. While valley farmers were uninterested in taking up tobacco's call to agricultural arms, preferring to stick to the crops they already knew, by the early 1930s, early Conservancy District maps show a different "crop" already being planted between Mewborne's processing plant and the river: the neat grid of "Tobacco Farm Subdivision." On land that even then was being used for early tobacco experiments, the Consumers Tobacco Company syndicate had drawn up lot lines for more than a hundred new homes. Protected by a newly built levee to protect it from a wandering Rio Grande and a riverside drain to lower the water table that had swamped large areas of the valley, the land was being readied for Albuquerque's next phase.[28]

"Sale of Property at Clover Leaf Farms is the fastest ever known for any subdivision in the history of Albuquerque," gushed a 1934 newspaper ad for a housing tract being built on "a portion of the famous Tobacco Farms, some of the finest land in the valley." The subdivision, served by good roads, was advertised as "small bungalow farms"—connected by good roads to jobs in the nearby city, with enough irrigated land to grow a bit of food.[29]

While the shift from commercial farming to subdivisions looks like a haphazard adaptation to the failure of commercial agriculture in the case of Tobacco Farms, the same pattern quickly appeared in more intentional ways. Eduardo M. Otero, who, like Hubbell, was the head of one of the old sheep ricos, added to his landholdings in 1927 by buying the lands of an old Spanish land grant in Valencia County, south of Albuquerque. The purchase, notably, came after the Conservancy District's formation. Again, drainage and flood control would add value to this land.[30] Until he died in 1932, Otero—the half-brother-in-law of Aldo Leopold—was a staunch supporter of the Conservancy District.[31] In a model similar to the failed tobacco enterprise, Otero set up a vegetable cannery to buy crops grown on the land he hoped to develop. But from the beginning, Otero's model grasped that a country home on the city's edge, with good roads so its residents could commute to a job in the city, was crucial to the valley's evolving economy.

Otero's 1932 pitch for Bosque Farms was aimed directly at "the man who works 8 hours a day," offering tracts of 2.5 to 8 acres with a comfortable home and a chance to put spare time to use growing food for the new cannery. The levees and drains of the newly formed Conservancy District were the key. "These farms are effectively drained and protected from floods by the canals and dikes of the Conservancy District," Otero's ad explained.[32]

As commercial agriculture, Bosque Farms failed in the same way as tobacco farming. Several years after Otero died in 1932, the family sold the land to the federal government, where it became part of a Depression-era relocation program for a small group of displaced Dust Bowl farmers.[33] It went through several iterations, including dairy farming, before becoming what it is today: a suburban neighborhood a short commute from the city center, still drained and irrigated by Conservancy District canals. It now supports horse properties with a few small vineyards, much as the modern properties once planned for tomato and vegetable farming.

Dairyland followed a similar trajectory. With expected drainage to be provided by the coming of the Middle Rio Grande Conservancy, the Albers dairy and hog farm in a swampy and flood-prone area along the Rio Grande near Old Town was sold in 1927 to become a country club and golf course and residential real estate development. Clinton P. Anderson became the vice president of the Albuquerque Country Club in January 1927, and the Club had an option on the land next to the river by October 1927.[34]

Commercial Farming in the Twenty-First Century

This is not to say that there is no commercial farming in the twenty-first century in the lands of New Mexico's Middle Rio Grande Valley. Farther from greater Albuquerque's urban center, the landscape becomes more rural. Irrigated fields are larger, enabling agriculture's economies of scale. Consider the lands of the late Corky Herkenhoff, the descendent of a multigenerational farming family in San Acacia, once a railroad stop village along the Rio Grande sixty miles downstream from Albuquerque. From the 1960s until he died in 2024, Herkenhoff farmed in part on land that had been in his family for more than a century and in part on land he acquired after he started. His great-grandfather, mining engineer Philip Zimmer, first started buying up land at San Acacia in 1882, shortly after Atchison, Topeka, and Santa Fe Railway construction crews re-routed the Rio Grande through his little patch of the valley to make it more convenient for their bridge construction.[35] By the second decade of the twenty-first century, Herkenhoff had grown his commercial alfalfa operation to some seven hundred acres.

Like many commercially successful valley farmers, the capital to support Zimmer's agricultural enterprise came from elsewhere—in his case, mining. But in the years since his great-grandson Corky took over the farm in the 1960s, the acreage was expanded, turning it into one of the most extensive alfalfa operations in the valley. Unlike many smaller-scale operations that cater to the local horse market, Herkenhoff grew forage for the dairy industry, shipping off flatbed hay trucks for milk cows 250 miles away. But in the beginning, Zimmer's efforts to farm at San Acacia were plagued by the same struggles found elsewhere in the valley. In the 1920s, when Zimmer ranched the land, the maps tell a familiar story: "cattails-swamp," "marsh grass," "salt grass," "swamp," "mud flat," "old abandoned dike." One old map shows a feeble drain running along the southern edge of Zimmer's land—where his great-grandson farmed into 2024. But the labels make clear the drain was losing its battle with the swamps.[36]

But while swamps and flooding suggest the challenges of coping with too much water, Zimmer's modest early farming efforts also show struggles with the opposite: too little water. In 1903, Zimmer was one of the early valley residents who experimented with pumping groundwater to supplement the river's meager summer flows.[37] Two decades later, Zimmer supported the emerging idea of the Conservancy District, which would provide drainage and flood protection for his farm. On stationery from his *Indian Hill Orchards and Poultry Yards*, Zimmer wrote on May 18, 1922, to the Albuquerque-centric drainage booster group: "I am preaching Drainage" and "enroll my name on the books of the association and advise me to whom the dues $10.00 have to be sent."[38]

By the 1930s, the Conservancy District was aiding these farmlands, but by the third decade of the twenty-first century, the chronic water shortages of a climate change–altered Rio Grande were taking their toll. The southernmost field on Corky Herkenhoff's San Acacia farm had long been ideal for wintering cattle. They could browse on alfalfa stubble, and when they were thirsty, all they had to do was drop down an embankment to drink from the San Acacia drain. Drains—gently sloping ditches dug a dozen feet below the valley's pan-flat land surface—are the same ubiquitous feature here as they are in the rest of New Mexico's Middle Rio Grande Valley. Without them, the valley's high water table, an extension of the surface manifestation of the Rio Grande, made difficult what humans wanted to do on the valley floor. But in the winter of 2021–2022, for the first time in Herkenhoff's deep memory, they had to truck in water for the cows. The drain had gone dry as aridification drained the nearby Rio Grande, and the water table dropped away from his Indian Hill Farms.[39]

Making a living in commercial farming here has always been a struggle. Herkenhoff joked that he was "the fifth generation to go broke on this operation."[40]

Despite his self-deprecating humor, Herkenhoff made a decent living farming at San Acacia. But he was an exception among the roughly quarter million residents living on a valley floor made livable by the collective action needed to provide flood control, drainage, and irrigation. An analysis of 2021 data found just forty-two people farming at least a hundred acres—what Herkenhoff identified as the minimum acreage needed to make a living farming. Only 17 of those farmers were irrigating more than 180 acres.[41]

The numbers do not include the land of the Pueblo nations, where larger parcels remain in more significant numbers than on non-Native land. And they do not include the hardscrabble farming life of leasing land one irrigated field at a time. But they reflect why the Census of Agriculture shows that "net cash farm income"—the revenue from farming, minus its cost—is consistently marginal in New Mexico's Middle Rio Grande Valley.[42]

In a final twist, at his death, Herkenhoff was finalizing a deal to sell his entire farm to a company developing a massive power line through New Mexico to serve the growing renewable energy market in the West. The plan was for the farm to become an environmental restoration site, offsetting land developed elsewhere. Thus, the farm would be returned to the river from whence it came.

A Few Acres to Grow Things and a Job in Town

It is tempting to view the story of Tobacco Farms as a moment of transition in the history of Albuquerque, and in one sense, it is. The formation of the Conservancy District, intended to enable commercial agriculture, had instead enabled something else. In the twenty-first century, the resulting properties, irrigated green and lovely with a bit of pasture for a horse or a few acres of orchard trees and garden, are often called "hobby farms." People are not farming to make a living. They are farming for other reasons—a connection to the land, the rural lifestyle, and the value of living amid a patch of green.

But to suggest that a break had occurred, a fundamental change, misses the vital way in which the development of Clover Leaf Farm, Bosque Farms, and Tobacco Farm Subdivision represents a move along a continuum that dates to at least the 1800s and perhaps beyond in the Middle Rio Grande Valley.

Before the railroad's arrival, sheep, not crops, dominated commercial agriculture astride the Rio Grande. There was a modest agricultural exchange with New Spain and Mexico to the south, and the Comanche empire to the east,[43] but exporting crops for money at scale was only possible once train tracks arrived. Sheep, and to a lesser extent cattle, were the exceptions, an agricultural commodity that could walk to market. Farming on the valley floor before the railroad's arrival was largely subsistence in nature—families growing their food on family plots while participating in the sheep economy as laborers. Sheep grazed on open range beyond the valley floor.

The arrival of the train brought the opportunity to export. However, the industry never conducted significant feeding on the valley bottomlands. Instead, the ricos shipped sheep to Kansas, Colorado, and Nebraska, where they were fattened and then shipped to larger markets.[44] In the early 1900s, there were some attempts to increase the fattening of sheep in the valley. Most notably, this was led by Frank A. Hubbell.[45] That is why Hubbell amassed the valley land that he eventually sold to the tobacco farmers. But the experiment was short-lived.

Meanwhile, commercial crop farming never took hold. Instead, rail commerce worked in both directions. The railroad allowed not just exports but also the import of cheap and plentiful food. Valley residents no longer needed a plot of land to feed their families, and a job in the growing urban wage economy proved more attractive than commercial farming. That importation doomed the truck gardens of the Mann brothers and Herman Blueher. The trains had changed the mathematical logic of von Thünen's rings. But the need or desire for that patch of irrigated land did not go away.

This shift away from von Thünen's postulated need for a belt of agriculture to feed a city, and from the boosters' belief in commercial agriculture as the community's economic engine, would take decades to play out. Tobacco is a pointed example, but it was not the first, nor the last, effort to find a profitable commercial export crop for the Middle Rio Grande Valley: sugar beets (more than once), tomatoes, pinto beans, a vegetable cannery, commercial-scale wheat farming for export. For decades after the failure of tobacco farming, alfalfa (a forage crop for animal feed) persisted with some commercial success. Into the twenty-first century, it remained the dominant crop grown with Rio Grande irrigation water.

Today, if you are looking for something that looks more like a conventional farm in the Rio Grande Valley downstream from Albuquerque, head away from the river a few blocks from Tobacco Road, down Clinton Boulevard (named after Clinton P. Anderson), through a subdivision called Adobe Acres built on Anderson's old Tobacco Farms land, and to a patch of land that bears a familiar name—Tobacco Farms LLC.

Shimmering green in the summer sun after its once-every-two-week shot of Rio Grande irrigation water, it is one of the last large farms in the urban part of this stretch of the Middle Rio Grande Valley. The farm is approximately 230 acres of alfalfa, a mile and a half long and a half mile wide at its widest. The land was broken in two in the twenty-first century, split by a Walmart, a development site awaiting multi-family housing (and farmed in the meantime), and a dangerously busy highway, uncrossable by the same neighborhood equestrians who can so easily negotiate the valley's dirt ditch banks. The ad valorem property tax that funds the majority of Conservancy District revenues each year is much more heavily supported per acre by the high-valued Walmart lands than the patchwork of nearby alfalfa and hay fields that commonly receive a greenbelt agricultural tax break introduced in the 1960s.[46] Sitting on twenty acres of land, Walmart pays 250 times as much in property taxes to support the Conservancy District as the eighty acres of Tobacco Farms land remaining in private ownership and still growing alfalfa.[47]

But as farming goes, this stretch of agriculture is an odd thing. Local governments own the larger plots of land, the product of further late twentieth-century and early twenty-first-century efforts to preserve Albuquerque's connection to its past. "Farmland connects us with our agricultural heritage," the City of Albuquerque explains.[48] Visit this land on a Saturday afternoon, and across the shimmering green, you'll see a stream of pickups as valley horse owners stream in to get bales of alfalfa hay. The connection here with "our agricultural heritage" is tenuous. Before the Conservancy District's drainage canals arrived, this land was swampy. The shallow lake on its western edge served private duck-hunting clubs for early Albuquerque's elites (including Aldo Leopold). The lakes are gone, but some wetlands and waterfowl spots have been preserved along the Rio Grande south of Albuquerque.[49]

Even as the Conservancy District was barely getting off the ground, one of its primary purposes—creating a commercial agricultural foundation for Albuquerque's economy—was being rendered irrelevant. But a new evolution was already underway, a shift toward a hybrid urban form—suburban, peri-urban, slightly rural but comfortably close to the city—reshaping the landscape and Albuquerque's relationship with the Rio Grande.

Developing Tobacco Farms

Despite all of this, the old Tobacco Farms property remained in alfalfa production in 2025. But its days were numbered. In the summer of 2023, the owners began advertising it for sale. The real estate advertisement was decorated with pictures of farming, but the intent, and the price, were pointed in another direction:

> DEVELOPMENT OPPORTUNITY! Develop, Farm, or Land bank! The Old Tobacco Farm is in a Bernalillo County approved Sector Plan allowing for 450 single family housing units. Utilities & access available and planned. The property has a long and storied history in the Valley Farms area of Albuquerque and is an ongoing hay farming operation today. It is one of the last large private acreage land holdings in an area of new commercial and residential development. Located only a block off Coors Blvd, just south of Rio Bravo, the location is in a rapidly developing area of town. 23 acres of the property are designated as an open space donation to the County to facilitate the quality of the development. There are also another 147 acres of county-owned open space adjacent to property.[50]

The price: $10.99 million. The selling points were the agricultural heritage and green open space, but the goal was a subdivision.

Figure 13. A swelling Rio Grande begins rising out of the narrow channel built for it in the 1950s, spilling into the bosque. Photograph by John Fleck.

Interlude: May

By May 2023 the big snowpack was beginning to show itself in rising Rio Grande flows. As Anne Marken gave her monthly water supply report to the district board in early May, the river at Central Avenue in the heart of Albuquerque was the highest it had been at that point in the year since 1992.

But the complexity of managing a river for multiple goals—irrigation for farms (and yes, some yards and lawns), water through the valley's neighborhood ditches, environmental benefits, and delivery to downstream users—was rearing its head. From an environmental perspective, the view of the river's main channel was glorious. Since April, the river had been high enough to spill up and out of the channel and into the riverside woods, refreshing an ecosystem and beloved community open space that rarely saw flowing water. Complaints about mosquitoes were common, but they were only complaints because members of the community were so excited about going down to see the water.

While that overbanking was but a tiny echo of the vast floodplain the Rio Grande once wandered, it was what the engineers had been trying to avoid. In the eyes of twentieth-century engineering, water spreading out into the woods rather than speeding downstream to human users, whether farmers in the Middle Valley or irrigation districts and communities in southern New Mexico, was water wasted.

The entire legal structure of the river's management under the 1938 Rio Grande Compact was predicated on swiftly getting water down the river's main channel. That goal was at the heart of the Bureau of Reclamation's "river rectification" efforts of the 1950s. Overbanking might have been more in tune with the community's contemporary environmental values, but the rules written in the Compact still applied. With New Mexico still in debt to its downstream neighbors, the rules prohibited storage of water for late-season irrigation. Without good summer rains, the river was again at risk of going dry by autumn.

Subject to the Action of the Bernalillo County Republican Convention, I Hereby Announce Myself as a

Candidate for the Office of

SHERIFF

I am a native born citizen of Bernalillo County and I received my education in St. Michael's College at Santa Fe. I am a stock-raiser and farmer by profession and I am thoroughly acquainted with conditions in Bernalillo County.

Should I be nominated by the Republican convention, and later elected, I pledge myself to a clean, impartial and energetic administration of the office.

Respectfully,

MAX GUTIERREZ

Figure 14. Max Gutierrez circa 1918, *Albuquerque Tribune*, Oct. 17, 1918.

CHAPTER 4

MAX GUTIERREZ AND THE THREE DITCHES

Max Gutierrez has a jaunty cock to his head in the October 17, 1918, announcement of his candidacy for Bernalillo County sheriff. He wears a suit jacket, a button-down collar, and a tie. An untamed cowlick sneaks out of otherwise carefully combed hair. "I am a stock-raiser and farmer by profession and I am thoroughly acquainted with conditions in Bernalillo County," his announcement explained. "Should I be nominated by the Republican Convention, and later elected, I pledge myself to a clean, impartial and energetic administration of the office."

The story of Maximiano Gutierrez is largely lost to the retellings of Albuquerque's history. When he does enter the narrative, it is as a simplified stereotype: the leader of a farmer's revolt—the practitioners of the old Hispanic ways rebelling against the Middle Rio Grande Conservancy District juggernaut, bent on imposing a different notion of the role of agriculture in community life and the urban economy.[1]

The rebellion had its iconic stand—what came to be known as the 1930 Los Chavez Riot, a *Rashomon*-like event, the truth obscured by conflicting perspectives, much as in Akira Kurosawa's famous film. Did Max incite a riot as he led farmers blocking the construction of the riverside drain through the community of Los Chavez, thirty miles downstream from Albuquerque? Was he a champion of the little guy and an old culture being crushed by the growth of a modern city? Did the farmers hold the Conservancy District dragline operator *at gunpoint*?

But to understand Max Gutierrez and, in so doing, understand Albuquerque's complex, messy history, you must go back a dozen years to the 1918 political campaigns, where Max represented the tensions of Albuquerque's slow slog into modernity.

Gutierrez was a leader rooted in the old Hispanic village culture of sheep grazing, farming, and acequia irrigation. His rise as a leader of the farmers' revolt shows those roots. Yet he and his family were also navigating the changes wrenching the old rural economy. His civic roles pushing for good roads, drainage, and flood control reflected the views of a modernizer, embracing Albuquerque's dreams of urban growth.

In the process, he played a sometimes contradictory role in the tension between Albuquerque's past and future. He was one of the leading public entrepreneurs in developing the collective action institutions needed to manage the growing community of Albuquerque and its relationship with the Rio Grande, playing a crucial role in creating what would become the Middle Rio Grande Conservancy District. But as the details of who would run the Conservancy District and how it would be financed became clear, Max Gutierrez became one of the leaders of a powerful counterforce of resistance.

His switch came in response to the answer being offered to Elinor Ostrom's two central questions: Who has a say, and who has to pay?

Closing of the Range

As we have seen, Albuquerque's economy since before the railroad arrived in 1880 had been based on sheep. It had a centralized economic structure, dominated by large sheep-owning capitalists—first, the old Hispanic sheep dynasties, or ricos, followed by Anglo mercantilists and increased capitalization with New Mexico's annexation into the United States and the arrival of the railroad. The enterprise depended on the labor of sheepherding families living on the valley floor, farming near their homes and using already-old irrigation ditches to feed their families. They grazed sheep, which were predominantly owned by the ricos or merchants in a system known as *partido*, on the open range beyond the river valley.[2] Max

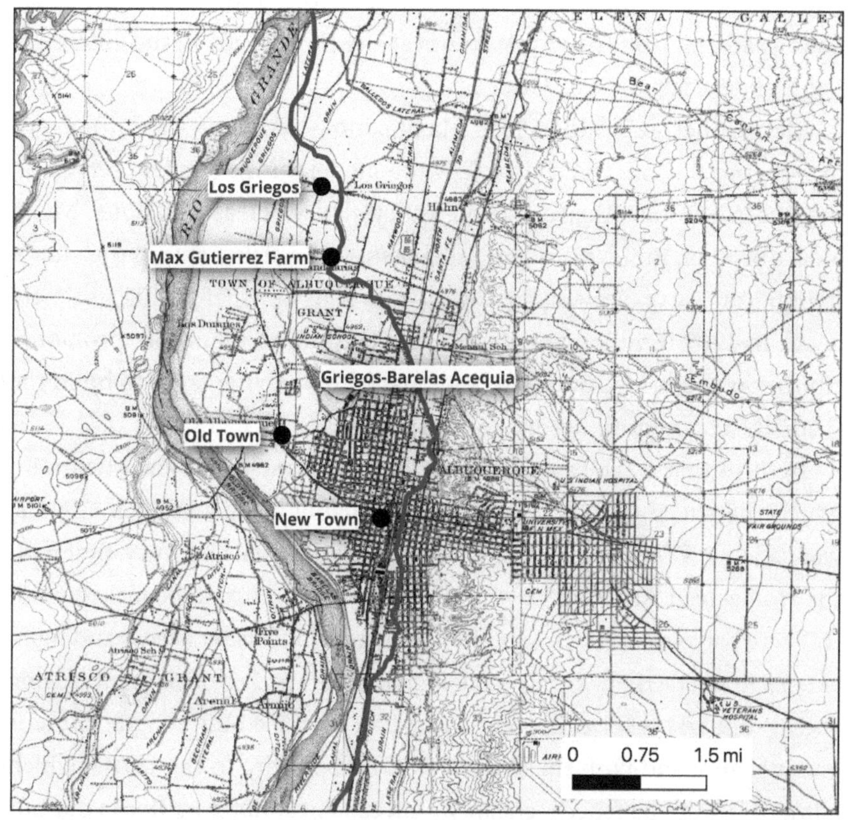

Map 7. Max Gutierrez's Albuquerque. Map by John Fleck.

Gutierrez's family was deeply rooted in these communities, on the valley floor upstream from Albuquerque, near the Rio Grande in the villages of Los Candelarias and Los Griegos.

Max Gutierrez's father, Jose Maximiano—Max Sr.—was prominent in wool processing. His civic role was a model for his son. He served on the Sheep Sanitary Board and the valley's livestock associations. Max's oldest brother, Emiliano, also a stockman, was a rising star in the state's Republican Party, serving as a territorial legislator before his untimely death in 1901. Emiliano served on the acequia commission, promoted education and bridge building, and pushed for levying taxes to build the roads the community needed to prosper.[3]

By 1918 that world was changing. The open range in New Mexico on which the sheep economy depended, arguably at unsustainable levels, was closing.[4] The changes were gradual, reaching back a century, first with the Homestead Act of 1862, which allowed open range to be locked up in 160-acre parcels and often exploited for controlling water access and more extensive tracts; then with the expansion of railroads, which in increasing access to markets for cattle and sheep had increased the competition for grazing land; and with the invention of barbed wire in the 1870s, which allowed land to be fenced, cheaply. Fences kept wandering flocks out but also controlled stocks within, allowed pasture rotation, allowed cattle and sheep to be raised next to each other, and reduced labor costs—and thus the need for sheepherders.[5] Within its first decade of statehood, New Mexico law began to allow the closing of open range.[6] Change also came with late nineteenth- and early twentieth-century Progressive Era federal land management policies on public lands. In combination, all this rescaled and altered the nature of the grazing industry, including closing the open range that had spread out west and east of Albuquerque.

Max Gutierrez was part of this. In 1922 the public order allowing trespassing grazing animals to be seized for damages in the Pajarito area in Bernalillo County, from the Rio Grande westward, was signed by Max Gutierrez as acting chair of the Board of County Commissioners.[7]

As a result, land ownership patterns on the valley floor were changing. Occasionally, sheepherders deeply in debt to the sheep capitalists lost their land titles or sold parts of their valley lands.[8] Much more extensively, parts of the connecting communal grazing lands from Spanish and Mexican land grants around Albuquerque and elsewhere in the valley were gobbled up in tax deed sales and dispossession,[9] to be further later broken up and resold. Historical patterns of economic geography when sheep was king were being dissolved by the forces of modernity. This pattern of change was underway long before the Middle Rio Grande Conservancy District was formed.

As the sheepherding life declined, a new urban economy was rising to take its place. The growing community increasingly saw a need for the urban amenities of a modern city—paved roads, schools, and a municipal water system. Max Gutierrez and his family were navigating that change, sometimes leading, sometimes swept along by events. In 1918, at age thirty-two, Max Gutierrez was already a veteran of Bernalillo County's rough-and-tumble politics. Eleven years earlier, Gutierrez was charged along with his brothers Natividad and Justo and two of his future in-laws with inciting a riot at the Los Griegos election house, with an added charge of trying to break into the home where the election booth was stored.[10] Four years later, party leaders chose him as a delegate for the state Republican Convention. The *Albuquerque Journal* derisively labeled him a "puppet" of political leader Frank A. Hubbell, head of the Pajarito Gutierrez-Hubbell sheep dynasty.[11]

By 1917 Max supplemented his income as a stock-raiser and farmer by working as a Bernalillo County Deputy Sheriff. It was in that role that Max and his brothers Justo and Natividad engaged in a running gun battle in March 1918 after stalking rustlers who had been using an abandoned adobe two miles west of the Barelas Bridge as a slaughterhouse for stolen cattle.[12] But it was on the civic side of politics, rather than the pursuit of cattle rustlers, that Max Gutierrez's political life began to take shape. While chasing cattle rustlers as a deputy sheriff, Gutierrez had also joined with the Chamber of Commerce to establish "defense councils," part of the US World War I effort to help coordinate home front efforts.[13]

At the October 1918 Republican Party Convention, Gutierrez failed to win the nomination to sheriff he had sought. Instead, he was the party's choice to represent the Second District on the Bernalillo County Commission. His opponent on the Democratic side? His brother, Ofimiano Gutierrez.

Thick History, Thick Places, and Three Ditches

Max, Ofimiano, and eight other brothers and sisters grew up in the decades surrounding the coming of the railroad to Albuquerque; their family lived in Los Griegos, an old Spanish village on the valley floor three miles (an hour's walk) north of the old village of Albuquerque.

We tend to focus on prominent characters and big events when telling history. Main characters and big events matter—they are central to the narrative. But in that focus, there is a risk of missing the way significant characters and big events ride deep waves of social, economic, and political factors that shape communities as they interact with the physical world in which they are embedded. Place changes people, and people change place, what historians and anthropologists describe as "thick history" and "thick places."[14]

Just up the acequia from the neighborhood where Max grew up is one such thick place, where three old ditches come together, layers of Albuquerque history stacked one on top of another. The Griegos Lateral dates to the 1700s, intersecting with the 1800s-era Barelas Ditch, the water of both shunted in a culvert over the 1930s-era Griegos Drain. The tree-lined corridor is popular on warm summer days with the neighborhood walkers, who seem oblivious to the function of the canals, much less their history.[15]

Max Gutierrez arrives at our storytelling doorstep as a significant character in a series of big events—the leader of the late 1920s farmers' lawsuit against the Middle Rio Grande Conservancy District and the hero

Figure 15. The Griegos Lateral, which once irrigated the Gutierrez family's farms, still flows through peri-urban Albuquerque three hundred years after it was built. Photograph by John Fleck.

or villain of the Los Chavez Riot. But his life is better understood as one spent riding the wave of complex social, political, and economic change, shaping what would become modern Albuquerque.

To experience the thickness of place, time, and communities and to understand Max's place in it, ride your bike or walk toward the junction of the three ditches, east from Rio Grande Boulevard down this shady, tree-lined dirt path along what is today called the Griegos Lateral, in the Village of Los Ranchos, New Mexico, toward the past and the history of Max Gutierrez.

Today's waterway, a small, primarily earthen canal, carries irrigation water to sixty acres each spring, summer, and fall.[16] The ditch follows a graceful curve in the landscape, past backyards in a neighborhood that, by the third decade of the twenty-first century, had become one of Albuquerque's greenest and most affluent.[17] A metal gate blocks what, officially and legally, serves as a service road for the Middle Rio Grande Conservancy District's maintenance crews. A wooden horse walk to one side, a structure designed to block vehicles but allow easy passage for horses, walkers, and the occasional bicyclist, makes clear the service road's more practical role—as a community path.

Walking the ditch bank, you tread on three centuries of earth, piled one year at a time by community members as they cleaned the ditch each spring in the annual ritual known as *la limpia*.[18] Layers of history, cultural traditions, and stories help us make sense of the past in a way significant characters and big events cannot. Here, you are surrounded by the layers left by Albuquerque's historic struggles to make peace with the Rio Grande. It is easy to imagine Max and his brothers out in the ditch, joining la limpia in their youth. We do not know if Max himself wielded a shovel. Families could pay others to do their work, and Max's family had modest affluence. Tax assessment rolls for Bernalillo County for 1903, when Max was seventeen years old, list all individuals in Albuquerque with assessed property greater than $1,000 and list all significant sheep owners in a clear sign of the times. The Gutierrez family is not listed under the property assessment but is for sheep ownership: The father, Maximiano Sr., had 1,000 sheep, and a brother, Justiniano, had 300 sheep.[19] Whether Max worked la limpia or not, we know that he grew up in a community with a shared responsibility for this ditch, already nearly two centuries old when he was a boy.

The modern river channel is less than a mile to the west. The street that bears the river's name—Rio Grande Boulevard—follows the old horse and footpath connecting the Hispanic villages of the 1700s, which followed the pathways of the Indigenous Puebloans who have lived on this valley floor since time immemorial. Two hundred yards to the north runs Montaño Road, a thoroughfare built in the 1990s after a tortuous political battle. In the third decade of the twenty-first century, it carried twenty-five thousand cars a day across the Rio Grande. If you look at an old map and then squint and imagine—glance down at the map, then up at the modern landscape—you can conjure beneath Montaño Road the old farm of Melquiades Montaño, whose name the modern roadway bears. By the 1920s, Montaño's farm had become a useless swamp. The existence of that swamp in the 1920s is a case study, one of many examples of the enduring tension between the Rio Grande and the communities on the valley floor.

Los Griegos

The census of 1790 gives us a snapshot of Hispanic village life in Los Griegos before the railroad's arrival. It lists 109 people in 25 households: "Six men were farmers, one was a day laborer and nine processed wool."[20] The village supported two tailors and a shoemaker; one family was affluent enough to afford a servant.

By the mid-1800s, the local economy's core was still rooted in small-scale farming, sheep grazing, and wool. Still, it had become affluent enough to have the only grocery storekeeper in the valley north of Albuquerque and the only schoolmaster. The best date we have for the Los Griegos y Candelaria Acequia, the ditch running down Los Griegos' eastern edge, comes from W. W. Follett, who in his 1896 report on behalf of the US and Mexican governments listed it as "before 1800." Follett estimated the ditch was irrigating 530 acres of land when he came through the valley.[21] The ditch likely dates to the early 1700s; the King of Spain bestowed this patch of land on Juan Griego, a descendant of one of Oñate's soldiers, in 1708. The community was small, with no central plaza, and homes stretched out along what is now Griegos Road between the Rio Grande and the irrigation ditch. Like all the early settlers, Juan Griego and his party took the high ground. While the little satellite church on Griegos Road was responsible for the village's spiritual salvation, the ditches in the early years assured the village's economic deliverance.[22]

When the agents of modernity swept over the valley, such as chief engineer Joseph Burkholder[23] and the Middle Rio Grande Conservancy District's surveyors and hydraulic engineers, they drew straight lines on their maps and dug ditches to match. But in the times before, the exquisite vernacular engineering of the community ditch builders followed the contours of the land. A hundred yards from Rio Grande Boulevard (a street that, like the ditches, carries its old curves), you'll find the tiny Barelas Acequia, sometimes called "Little Ditch" on the old maps, branching off on a journey that once took it across the Albuquerque valley floor, attaching at its downstream end to another piece of Albuquerque history: something you might think of as the city's first suburb. Dug in the 1820s, the Barelas Acequia is a youngster compared to its older Griegos sibling. But in its twisty, tree-lined, slightly chaotic form, the Barelas *looks* the oldest, bearing the unmistakable signs of two centuries of use. In 2021 there were still six properties irrigating from the Barelas—affluent homes with a bit of garden, some pasture, or a hay field around them, not "farms" in the most common sense of the word, but emblematic of the twenty-first-century urban Middle Rio Grande Conservancy District.[24]

Beneath the Griegos and the Barelas runs the real youngster: the Griegos Drain, dug beneath the other two in the 1930s, ruler-straight, the product of twentieth-century engineering.

Lake Montaño and the Floods

Standing on the Griegos ditch bank on a warm spring afternoon, one can, with a bit of imagination, see the problem Max Gutierrez and the communities he represented faced in the early 1900s. Upstream, a lush, small alfalfa field is greening up with the year's first irrigation, and the cars of Montaño Road stream past on the field's far side. But there is a striking difference if you shift your eyes from the pastoral scene to the homes on the downstream side of the Griegos. The farm on the upstream side of the Griegos is three feet lower in elevation than the yards on the downstream side.

Making a bend here perpendicular to the river, the Griegos acequia effectively served as a dike, not only delivering the irrigation water on which the village of Los Griegos depended but also protecting the high ground of the village from the Rio Grande's flood waters. And flood the river did, especially during a handful of high-flow years in the late 1800s and early 1900s.[25] Valley residents struggled to build a flood-control levee five miles upstream, once in 1885, and then rebuilding it in 1891.[26] But the floodwaters found a way around the community's modest protections.

Oldtimers told the story of the flood of 1904, which led to the abandonment of much of the Village of Los Ranchos upstream from the Griegos:

> A man from Mexico—a lawyer—paid the Chávez family five pesos to take the statue of the Virgin out, and just after one of them entered and removed the Virgin, the entire church collapsed. I was just a little boy, but I went with my father all along the ditch to see if the church would fall, and when the man went in to get the Virgin, the water was up to his chest as he carried the Virgin in his arms.[27]

"Almost the entire harvest of corn, wheat, and oats was destroyed and the orchards and vineyards damaged to a large extent," the US Geologic

Survey reported, tallying the Middle Rio Grande flood as one of the nation's most damaging that year. [28] The survey report also noted an odd benefit: the flood had washed away the alkali building up in the valley soils, leaving a layer of fresh soil in its stead. The Rio Grande was doing what rivers do—spreading across its natural floodplain. But to the communities who had chosen to build their villages and farms where the river wanted to flow, it was a problem.

In a theme that repeats in modern Albuquerque's relationship with the Rio Grande, dealing with the river was often more of a governance problem than a problem of physical engineering. "The cooperation problem—the human problem—is greater than the physical problems encountered by the district," said Conservancy District chief engineer Joseph Burkholder. "We are beginning to see solutions to the difficult problems of a rising river bed. But we have yet to work out the solutions to the problem of cooperation."[29]

Beginning in the 1880s in the Territory of New Mexico, each county along the Rio Grande elected river commissioners. Their primary responsibility involved protecting cities, villages, and farms from flooding by constructing dikes. Initially, the commissioners would submit bills for days spent overseeing and managing volunteer crews. The piecemeal but growing system of dikes and levees often failed. Increasingly, counties sought ways to pay for improved efforts, levying taxes in either labor or money.[30]

The communities of New Mexico's Middle Rio Grande were confronting what Elinor Ostrom identified as one of the central challenges of collective resource management—identifying the correct scale needed to solve a problem.[31] Following the flooding of 1903 and 1904, growing Albuquerque confronted Ostrom's question. With Rio Grande floods in the North Valley in both 1903 and 1904, there was tension between the downstream city, Albuquerque, and the regional government of Bernalillo County over who would pay for dike and levee construction and repairs north of Albuquerque, especially in the Alameda area along the Rio Grande. An improved dike at the north end of the valley's Albuquerque reach would protect the city as well as Alameda and the North Valley. But neither government agency was willing to foot the bill to benefit the other. Greater Albuquerque was increasingly becoming a single community connected by shared geographic concerns but separated by county, city, and village boundaries. By 1904 the Bernalillo County government faced bankruptcy in considerable measure because of flood-control costs.[32]

But until flood protection would come, as the water spilled down from the Alameda area, the Griegos acequia often overflowed into the inter-linked Barelas Acequia. It then spilled down into the lowlands in Albuquerque's New Town area, with no drainage.[33] All this would have been tangible to a teenage Max Gutierrez. We have no record of what Max did during the floods of 1903 and 1904 and whether he participated in dike repair crews. But it is hard to imagine an adventurous teenager not getting involved, in some way, in perhaps the most dramatic events of his young life.

What followed—the unceasing flood risk, the rising water table, and the swamping of the valley's communities—was central to the political actor Max Gutierrez would become. Standing on the Griegos ditch bank a few hundred yards north of the home where Max grew up, you can look out across the landscape and imagine how the communities' uneasy relationship with the Rio Grande was playing out.

Max Supports Flood Control and Drainage

The struggle with the Rio Grande dominated the agenda Max Gutierrez and his fellow Bernalillo County commissioners faced at their January 5, 1920, meeting. More importantly, it dominated their budget. Proposed work for the year included bridge repairs and reinforcement of the flimsy earth embankments that had been thrown up along the Rio Grande to protect the rapidly growing communities on the valley floor. The total cost of flood works to the county taxpayers was $7,750, more than a quarter of the county budget of $24,000.[34] That March, Gutierrez and the other county commissioners approved spending $300 for a jetty to protect the intake of the Los Padillas ditch—the ditch that irrigated the land of Melquiades Turrieta and his brothers.[35]

The river drama played out in large and small ways. In June, an Alameda resident appeared before Max Gutierrez and the other Bernalillo County commissioners, asking for a break on his annual tax bill. During the high flows of 1920, the resident explained, "It had been necessary to cut certain ditches and borders adjacent to his lands and crops to save pressure upon the big dam [the Alameda dike], which action agreed to by him ruined his crops totally this year." The commissioners agreed to reduce his annual property taxes on condition that he agree not to sue the city and county.[36]

It is thus no surprise to see the name of Max Gutierrez, county commissioner and community leader, among those leading the effort to solve the valley's collective action problem of flood control and drainage two years after Gutierrez, Aldo Leopold, Pablo Abeita, and the other community members had gathered at the Commercial Club to launch their collective action. "Commissioners Urge Drainage as of First Importance to Central Rio Grande Valley," reads the headline on the front page of *The Evening Herald* of August 11, 1921. Max Gutierrez and a contingent of civic leaders were the main attraction at that week's Rotary luncheon at the Alvarado, the railroad hotel in downtown Albuquerque. "Max Gutierrez explained how drainage would eliminate the dreaded alkali, which is discouraging farmers and eating into their earnings, while the land remains water-soaked."[37] The county's agricultural agent sketched out Albuquerque's dreamy future if they could solve the problems Gutierrez described. More than 30,000 acres of arid and waterlogged land could be brought into production, he explained to the Rotary Club's members.

> "It is only by drainage that we can realize the possibilities of the Rio Grande Valley," said Mr. Reynolds. "When the valley is prepared for agriculture we will save the freight on the tons and tons of grain that must now of necessity be shipped in. Right now there is 10 percent less land under cultivation than

there was 10 years ago, and I predict that five years from now Bernalillo county will have less than 5,000 acres of tillable land, unless a drainage program is put through at once."[38]

Gutierrez v. MRGCD

Things were very different in 1929 than they had been eight years earlier, when Max Gutierrez stood before the Rotary Club, championing the need for a system to provide flood control, drainage, and irrigation for his community. Broad community support in the abstract had collided once again with the reality of the institutional scholar Elinor Ostrom's two crucial questions: Who has a say? And who has to pay?

The answer to the second question flowed from the first. The farmers presumed to be the beneficiaries of the District would bear a substantial share of its costs through tax assessments on the anticipated increase in the value of their land. Those farmers, disenfranchised from the District's formation and governance, and angry at what they saw as the unfairness of the tax burden about to be placed on them, pushed back. They also understood that the dreams of commercial agriculture on which the whole edifice was being erected and imposed on them against their will would never be realized. Their local knowledge of the resource was being ignored. In their search for leadership they turned to Max Gutierrez.

On May 5, 1929, the newly formed Farmers and Water Users Association met in Albuquerque's Old Town and elected Max Gutierrez president.[39] Twelve days later, the District Court ruled against a lawsuit filed by Gutierrez on behalf of the farmers, finding that the Conservancy District formation and the bond sales about to be undertaken to finance the construction of the Conservancy District's dams, levees, and ditches, were legal.[40]

Three days later, two hundred Farmers and Water Users Association members, led by Max Gutierrez, assembled at the Conservancy District board meeting to open bids for the sale of the bonds needed to finance the work. When Max tried to speak, Conservancy board chairman Fred Huning shut him down, explaining that "the session was for the sole purpose of receiving bids."[41]

The back and forth continued in the summer and fall of 1929. The Conservancy District struggled to raise the money needed to start the work, as bond buyers balked at the risk that the Conservancy District's financing scheme—with its financial burden on the small farmers with presently unproductive or uncultivated land, the things Max Gutierrez and the Farmers and Water Users Association were complaining about—would not work. The bond buyers recognized the farmers were right.

The Association rallied under Max's leadership, appealing the District Court's decision to the New Mexico Supreme Court. Considerable public sentiment seemed to be against the Association, as flooding struck the valley in 1929, wiping out the town of San Marcial in August and striking Albuquerque in September. On August 15, 1929, the *Albuquerque Journal* targeted Max personally as an obstacle to progress: "People who have been deluded by Max Gutierrez and his followers who oppose the conservancy district program should put themselves in the place of those whose homes and crops have been swept away in the lower valley."[42]

The legal questions in the decision handed down by the New Mexico Supreme Court on September 9, 1929, in the case of Gutierrez v. Middle Rio Grande Conservancy District, were technical. The core of the argument Max's lawyers made, on behalf of valley farmers, was that the costs of building and financing the works of the Conservancy District would exceed the benefits "and that, as a result thereof, perpetual liens will be placed upon plaintiff's property far above the benefits that can ever be expected to accrue, and that therefore no benefit whatever will result to plaintiff's lands."[43] The court disagreed: "Since the benefits assessed admittedly exceed the approved estimated costs, we have no case of confiscation."[44]

Further, the court rejected arguments disputing the constitutionality of the Conservancy Act of 1927. The court ruled that it fell within the state's powers to allow the creation of conservancy districts to protect public health and safety, such as for mitigating flood risk. The farmers and their lawyers argued that the flooding risk didn't rise to the level seen in Dayton, Ohio—leading to the creation of the Ohio Conservancy Act, or Pueblo, Colorado, that had led to the creation of the Colorado Conservancy Act, on which the New Mexico's law was modeled. The court declared itself "compelled at the present time to take judicial notice of the recent disastrous flood covering a considerable portion of the Middle Rio Grande Conservancy District and the havoc, damage, and destruction of property occasioned thereby" and further congratulated the legislature for exercising "great wisdom" passing the Conservancy Act and affording New Mexicans the opportunity to protect people and property.[45]

In ruling that the Conservancy District could proceed, the court recognized the ability of greater Albuquerque and its civic boosters to collectively organize under state authority, drain an extended area, and protect themselves from flooding while financing a significant share of the *projected* irrigation benefits from commercialized agriculture.[46] We can only imagine his thoughts several September weeks later when Max stood watching the flood waters sweep down North Fourth Street in Albuquerque's North Valley.[47]

Los Chavez

Despite losing in the state's courts, the challenge by Max Gutierrez and the Farmers and Water Users Association exposed the underlying weakness of the Conservancy District scheme in its current form. The capitalists of the bond market seemed to agree with Gutierrez that the farmers would be unable to provide the tax revenue needed to pay off the bonds. A syndicate of banks bought the bonds in only limited amounts—$2 million of the more than $8 million needed—even at a discounted 87.5 percent of par value, meaning the Conservancy District had to agree to repay $100, plus

Figure 16. Middle Rio Grande Conservancy District dragline from the 1930s. Farm Service Administration image LC-USF34-001946-E. Courtesy of the Library of Congress.

interest, for every $87.5 the District received to pay for the work.[48] It was a fire sale, but enough to start construction, if allowed.

In December 1929 the farmers' group issued a series of demands. Two were crucial and prescient, given what followed. The first was the pursuit of ever-elusive federal money to lessen the cost burden on the farmers, something to which the district was willing to agree. The second was to change the governance structure to an elected board rather than the current appointment process. The Conservancy District would not agree, so Max Gutierrez and the farmers' group appealed the state court's denial of their claims to the US Supreme Court.[49] It was a futile gesture. In January 1930 the US Supreme Court declined to take the case.

Later that month, an odd (if temporary) détente emerged as Max Gutierrez and the Farmers and Water Users Association's attorney, W. A. Sutherland, emerged from a mediation session praising a spirit of compromise as work was about to get underway. The agreement would allow New Mexico's Middle Rio Grande Valley to become "a garden spot for the homes of a united, successful, contented people," Sutherland said.[50] But as the "draglines," the Conservancy District's giant excavating machines, began scouring drainage trenches across the valley floor, the détente did not last. And, again, Max Gutierrez found himself in the middle of what had become a fight against the very thing he had once championed.

Draglines are enormous earth-moving machines, cranes with a bucket suspended from the end of a boom. They were invented in the early 1900s to move a river—the Chicago Sanitary and Ship Canal's excavation, which reversed the Chicago River's flow.[51] For the boosters, the draglines' arrival in Albuquerque in the spring of 1930 was a cause for celebration. Businesses closed for the "eventful occasion," and a cheering crowd gathered at the river near Old Town.

> The staccato exhaust of the drag-line shovels that are to shape out the future of the Middle Rio Grande valley, through conservancy, was heard at Albuquerque for the first time Thursday

> afternoon by an enthusiastic outpouring of citizens estimated at 3,000 in number. . . . Prosperity, for Albuquerque and the entire valley, was the keynote sounded in every address, and speakers pointed to a promising destiny as the culmination of years of effort to secure conservancy.[52]

The president of the New Mexico College of Agriculture and Mechanical Arts expressed his hope that the Middle Rio Grande Valley would become "the garden spot of the Southwest."[53] But as the draglines remade the Rio Grande, crawling through the valley to dig drains and pile the dirt into simple levees, not everyone shared the boosters' enthusiasm.

In a fracas that echoed his rough and tumble youth, Max Gutierrez was called on a Saturday in mid-April to the village of Los Chavez, twenty-five miles down the Rio Grande Valley from Albuquerque. A dragline had cut through the Los Chavez Ditch. It was early in the irrigation season, and the Conservancy District juggernaut had suddenly and without warning, the farmers claimed, cut off their water.

Max Gutierrez's statement after the incident brings the tensions in the valley into sharp relief. Max Gutierrez said he asked Joseph Burkholder, the District's chief engineer, if the District was going to honor the agreement with the farmers brokered at the January "détente" meeting. "Mr. Burkholder," Gutierrez related, "answered that they were not going to carry out that agreement, and added, 'I haven't got any use for the Mexican people anyhow.'"[54] On the stand, Burkholder denied uttering the "Mexican people" epithet, and the truth of who said what is beyond our reach. But Burkholder clearly was deeply angered by Gutierrez's fight against the Conservancy District's formation.[55]

The stories offered after were both murky and contradictory.[56] It seems clear that guns were drawn, though it is less clear by whom. "Not a single person among the farmers was armed," Gutierrez said, accusing the Conservancy District leaders who were responding to the fracas of bringing guns. Pearce C. Rodey, the Conservancy District's attorney, offered a different version. "One of them (the farmers) had poked a gun at the foreman and told him either to stop the work or they would stop him," Rodey said.[57] Max Gutierrez was arrested for allegedly threatening Burkholder, an allegation he denied. No charges were ever filed. By Tuesday, Gov. R. C. Dillon had intervened, meeting with farmers and Conservancy District officials and urging Gutierrez "to use his best efforts to preserve order."[58]

Farmers again stopped draglines in a similar confrontation in May in Duranes, a village upriver of old Albuquerque, this time with the farmers—again led by Gutierrez—charging that the Conservancy District's engineers changed the route of the drainage canal through twenty farmers' land without their permission.[59] Fears of violence spread across the valley,[60] and the following June, Max Gutierrez was arrested and charged with "conspiracy to alienate the confidence of Indians of the Pueblos from the government as a result of speeches and talks they are alleged to have had with the Pueblos of Tamaya, Kewa, Cochiti, Isleta, Sandia and San Felipe."[61] Prosecutors seem never to have pursued the charges against Max, but the arrest made clear the depth of the conflict.

The Los Chavez and Duranes clashes were about specific, narrow issues: cutting an irrigation ditch and questions about proper access to private property. But the tensions also reflected something more profound. The draglines and the Progressive Era engineering culture they represented were fundamentally reshaping, in an instant, the relationship between the Rio Grande and the communities and landscape that surrounded it. Ultimately, the draglines and the engineering culture won, but the dreamy rhetoric of harmony and a "garden spot" following the brief détente of January 1930, after what had seemed to be compromise and collaboration, was gone.

The complaints of Max Gutierrez and the farmers he led that the land could never generate the agricultural paradise and therefore could never generate the tax revenue the Conservancy District's institutional and financial engineers had claimed were proven right. The physical engineering worked, especially the drainage. The new ditches dug by the draglines quickly drained the valley's swamps, and the dirt thrown up in spoil bank levees further separated what had once been a floodplain from a narrowed Rio Grande. In many places, those dirt banks still stand today between valley communities and what would otherwise be Rio Grande floodwaters.

But the institutional engineering was a disaster. Beginning almost immediately and continuing for decades were backtracking, federal bailouts, and hunts for alternative ways to pay for the levees, drains, dams, and canals needed to bring flood control, drainage, and irrigation to the Rio Grande Valley floor.

Ultimately, the Max Gutierrez story is a testament to the adaptability of communities confronted with change.[62] Within a few years, rescued by the Depression-era federal Reconstruction Finance Corporation, the flow of bond money into central New Mexico, which Max Gutierrez had so aggressively fought against, made the Middle Rio Grande Conservancy District the economic salvation of unemployed New Mexicans. Max is never mentioned in any joint leadership efforts in the second half of the 1930s protesting Conservancy District assessments and tax delinquencies. In 1938 Max Gutierrez was an employee of the Conservancy District, working on the district's side in a conflict with farmers in Socorro County fighting against the District's takeover of their ditch,[63] but also in distributing federal rehabilitation funds to San Marcial families in the lower valley whose farms had been wiped out by early flooding.[64]

In the following decades, his family played critical roles in the evolution of Albuquerque as a community. One nephew, Robert Gutierrez, worked in real estate and served in the 1970s on the Middle Rio Grande Conservancy District's first elected board of directors. Another nephew, Ofimiano, worked for the federal government on water development projects across the west and was the developer of the Ofimiano J. Gutierrez Lower Terrace Subdivision on land the family had homesteaded in what became the city's Northeast Heights—old grazing land turned into suburbs.[65]

Interlude: June

Runoff from 2023's big snowpack lingered large still in June, as the river continued to spill out of the main channel dug by the US Bureau of Reclamation in the 1950s to try to straighten and narrow the river's flow. Spring 2023 was the coolest in Albuquerque since 2010, Anne Marken told the agency's board of directors in early June, as her monthly report again provided a rich public window into the way the arcane interplay between climate, weather, rules, and infrastructure influence the flow of the Rio Grande through the Middle Valley.

The cool weather combined with the big winter snowpack to stretch out the high flows on the Rio Grande. The cooler the temperatures, the more slowly the mountains upstream released their grip on the snow stored on their slopes. But on the Rio Grande the complex of rules governing the water's management and their interaction with infrastructure continued to play as large a role as the weather in influencing how quickly the melting snow made its way down from the mountains of Colorado to New Mexico's Middle Rio Grande Valley.

There were, as always, conflicting demands on the river. The rules required New Mexico to move as much water as possible downstream, to meet its debt to farms and cities in southern New Mexico, Texas, and Mexico. But farmers in the Middle Rio Grande Valley wanted as much water as they could get for their crops, and residents of valley neighborhoods wanted their ribbons of green.

Meanwhile, downstream from Albuquerque, the river had risen so high by early June that it threatened the old levees built by the Middle Rio Grande Conservancy District in the 1930s. Little more than dirt piles nearly a century old, they were a source of trouble and risk in years like 2023, when the river saw sustained high flows.

The overbanking was a quiet process, a gentle flow wetting the bosque. In places, it reached far enough out of the channel to reach the riverside

Figure 17. A water-submerged swimming dock at Cochiti Reservoir, May 2023. Photograph by John Fleck.

levees, seeping through and creating repeated risks of breaks. Conservancy District heavy equipment crews dropped all their other work and swarmed over the Valencia County levees, backfilling over a mile of levee as water repeatedly threatened to break through and flood the surrounding neighborhoods.

Beyond the flood risk, the overbanking prevented some of the water flowing through the valley from reaching downstream, resulting in less water for communities in southern New Mexico, Texas, and Mexico and creating a risk that the Middle Valley's debt would rise.

Upstream, Cochiti Dam was doing the job the US Army Corps of Engineers intended when they built it a half century before, holding water back to prevent flooding of communities on the valley floor—but in the process, flooding sacred Cochiti Pueblo land. The beach at the dam's recreational area was closed, its docks swamped by the rising water. But in the strange world of Middle Rio Grande water management, things were about to change. Irrigators, Marken explained to her board, should expect good water supplies into July, but after that there was risk.

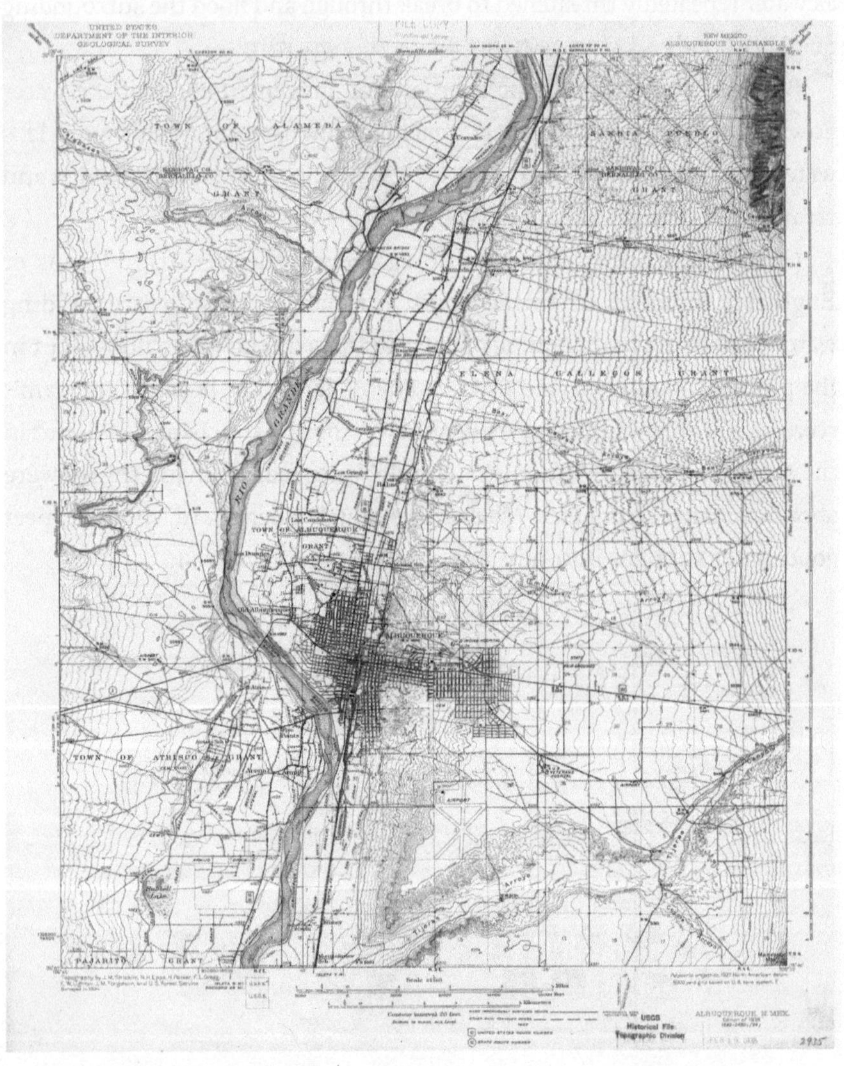

Figure 18. Albuquerque before the floods. USGS Topographical Map, 1938.

CHAPTER 5

TRANSITIONS

Cometh the Floods, Cometh the Feds

The year 1941 was, by far, New Mexico's wettest year since record-keeping began in the late 1800s.[1] "In the higher altitudes heavy snows added to the state's water storage for the coming summer, with the runoff for the Rio Grande predicted to be 25 percent greater than normal and the largest probably since 1920," the Associated Press reported in late March.[2] Community leaders were confident in the previous decade's investment in river management tools. As late as May 1, the *Albuquerque Journal* confidently told its readers that, while the Rio Grande was "running full," there was "no threat of floods in the Middle Rio Grande valley." Conservancy District chief engineer Stanley Phillippi credited the district with protecting the valley, saying, "There was little danger of a flood."[3]

Phillippi was wrong.

The flood of 1941, and a smaller but also extreme event the following year, played a crucial role in shaping the evolution of the institutions greater Albuquerque was trying to build to manage its relationship with the Rio Grande. One of Elinor Ostrom's crucial design principles involves the capability of institutions to adapt to changing circumstances. The floods of 1941 and 1942 offered a crisp answer for Albuquerque: poorly. The levees thrown up by the Conservancy District in the first burst of river rearrangement of the 1930s were not up to the task for which they were built. And the financial tools needed to improve them were an abject failure.

By May 10, 1941, hundreds of men were "battling the suddenly-maddened Rio Grande in the 150-mile stretch from Pena Blanca to San Antonio to keep the once lazy stream captive in its banks," and Phillippi was warning of the risk that the Conservancy District's levees might not hold.[4] Phillippi's threats were well taken. The river broke through levees up and down the river. "Three hundred years ago the Spaniards named it El Rio Bravo del Norte—The Savage River of the North—and Tuesday it was living up to its name," a nameless *Albuquerque Journal* reporter wrote on May 14 after an aerial tour of the flooded valley with federal surveyors.[5] While the translation was questionable, the point was clear: El Rio Bravo del Norte still could wreak havoc. By mid-May, the flood force had risen from hundreds to thousands, working around the clock to shore up weak levees. Rio Grande flows into the valley on May 16, 1941, reaching 22,000 cubic feet per second, were the highest ever recorded.[6] Some 50,000 acres of valley land the levees were meant to protect were flooded.[7]

While 1941 was the largest flood, it was not the only one. In the early 1930s, not long after the draglines threw up the valley's first continuous levees, flows breached them and flooded areas of the valley north of Albuquerque. In 1937 farm fields and crops were damaged up and down the valley. In 1939 flooding from the east, off the mountains, left the old yazoo north of downtown Albuquerque underwater. And it happened again in 1942.[8]

Pursuing Federal Help

Recognizing that the Conservancy District's efforts were insufficient, New Mexicans pushed for federal help. In 1941 even before the risk from the winter snowpack had become apparent, the New Mexico State House of Representatives unanimously approved a memorial urging Congress to send $2.5 million to the Middle Rio Grande Conservancy District to reimburse the district for flood control levees in the valley. It was "unjust and unfair," the memorial's authors wrote, for the district residents to pay their own flood-control expenses "since most of the other flood control work of the nation was Federally financed."[9]

All that spring of 1941 there was talk of the possibility of a federal takeover of the valley's river management system by the Army Corps of Engineers and the Bureau of Reclamation. There was nothing unusual about that. Dating to the Smith-McNary bill in the early 1920s and even earlier, valley residents advocated for the federal government, not residents, to underwrite Albuquerque's relationship with the Rio Grande.[10]

As the floodwaters subsided in July 1941, surveyors scouted a possible site for a main stem dam on the Rio Grande in White Rock Canyon: the land of Cochiti Pueblo. As we will see, this portended one of the most dramatic episodes in the evolving relationship between New Mexico's Indigenous Pueblo nations and the colonial city builders. But at the time, the focus remained financial, and New Mexicans embraced an idea they had repeatedly turned to—federal funding for the project. "Given complete flood control in the Upper Rio Grande Valley and cheap power, together with a solution to the financial problems of the Middle Rio Grande Valley, the northern and Middle Rio Grande valleys would be ready for their greatest period of development," an observer reported.[11]

In 1942 the question of a federal bailout for the Conservancy District became a campaign issue. Las Cruces Republican W. A. Sutherland, who had represented Max Gutierrez during the struggles over how to pay for and manage the Conservancy District, ran unsuccessfully against Clinton P. Anderson, one of the Conservancy District's founding fathers, for New Mexico's single seat in Congress. Sutherland explained that his twofold goal in working with Gutierrez a decade earlier remained—a federal takeover of the project in cooperation with a Conservancy District run by an elected board.[12] Sutherland lost to Anderson, and the Conservancy District remained as it was, locally financed and managed, with a non-elected board. But the problems continued to worsen. The next major step toward federal action came two years later. The Flood Control Act of 1944 authorized a federal study, and the conclusions three years later passed sharp judgment on New Mexico's attempt to manage its relationship with the Rio Grande.[13]

Drawn up jointly by the Bureau of Reclamation and the US Army Corps of Engineers, the *Plan for Development of the Middle Rio Grande Project* concluded that the Conservancy District project had failed. Aggradation—the rise in the Rio Grande's bed from sediment deposition—continued. Weak levees, often little more than heaps of sand thrown up by the Conservancy District's draglines as they gouged drains across the valley floor, were eroding. "The present levee system is no longer adequate to protect against floods of magnitude common to the area because of their inadequate height," the report concluded.[14]

Sediment was blocking the Middle Rio Grande Conservancy District's headings, and land was once again being lost to irrigation. The sediment problem also made it hard to get water downstream, as required by the Rio Grande Compact and the US treaty with Mexico.[15]

The federal investigation found that the root cause was not hydrological but institutional. Farmers who were taxed on the presumed benefits of reclamation of their lands could not pay their assessments. Repeated efforts by the state to avoid dispossessing landowners who could not pay their assessments had succeeded in keeping farmers on their land. However, this left the Conservancy District needing help financing the work that needed to be done.

The Bureau of Reclamation report concluded that the answer was a federal bailout of the Conservancy District's bonds and a restructuring of the assessments to keep farmers on their land.

Reclamation's Plan

In its 1947 plan, Reclamation recognized something the boosters had seen two decades before about Albuquerque's relationship with the Rio Grande. Managing the river was about more than hydrology. It was about city building, enabling Albuquerque to make peace with the ribbons of green that both threatened and defined the city, "to improve and stabilize the economy of the Middle Valley," in the language of the report's authors.[16] In an important foreshadowing of the changes to come, the Reclamation report also emphasized the changing nature of the community's relationship with its river. "Additional development of fish and wildlife values and recreation facilities is needed through the Middle Rio Grande Valley to satisfy the increasing demand by the large number of out-of-state visitors, together with the local demand for such facilities," it found.[17] But the funding path through the US Congress was anything but straightforward.

Within Albuquerque, once again, a civic organization, the Middle Rio Grande Flood Control Association, emerged in the late 1940s to push for federal funding for flood-control improvements. Greater Albuquerque was in the middle of a boom that would see its population grow more than tenfold from 1920 to 1960, spurred by its role in national defense. The association's roster of participants reads like a Who's Who of post–World War II Albuquerque civic and business leaders.[18] Different this time around was the focus on flood protection for growing national interests in Albuquerque's post-wartime role as a connecting rail transportation hub, including to the Los Alamos Atomic Laboratories, the Sandia Atomic Laboratories, and Kirtland Air Force Base.[19] Supporting letters concerning vital national interests were collected from dignitaries like David E. Lilienthal of the Atomic Energy Commission.[20]

Congress initially balked at the project, with the House of Representatives cutting its funding from a vast 1948 legislative package providing federal authorization for flood control, river management, and harbors. But in June 1948 the Senate put $3.5 million back into the legislation. Championed by New Mexico Senator Dennis Chavez, the House agreed to a conference committee action, and President Harry Truman signed the bill. "Things definitely are looking up for the Middle Valley," said the *Albuquerque Tribune*.[21]

As we will see, this would be the first step toward transforming the institutional structure underlying the Middle Valley's river management. The wobbling financial foundation of the river management system, made so evident by the community's inability to respond to the floods of 1941 and 1942, was headed toward a federal takeover. It came with a significant injection of federal funding. With some persistence, a federal 1956 bailout of the remaining balance of original MRGCD bonds would also happen as part of that process.[22] Albuquerque's desperation to protect itself from the flood menace would also lead to the tragedy of Cochiti Dam.

Interlude: July

By early July of 2023, managing the Rio Grande through New Mexico's Middle Valley had become a tangled web. The river's runoff forecast, 50 percent above average because of a big mountain snowpack the previous winter, had held up.[23] But the path between snowpack, snowmelt, and water in the river and the ditches had grown increasingly complex.

The challenge remained the conflict between conflicting goals: a) a desire for more water for irrigators and the ecosystem, b) the risk of flood damage to the levees in Valencia County downstream of Albuquerque, and c) the state of New Mexico's obligation to pass water downstream communities in southern New Mexico, Texas, and Mexico.

Under the rules, flood control was the highest priority. Assigned the job of flood protection, the US Army Corps of Engineers had continued through May and June to throttle down releases from its two big flood-control dams upstream—Abiquiu on the Rio Chama, and Cochiti on the Rio Grande's main stem at the head of the Middle Valley. This created a paradox: Because of the risk of flooding, the Army Corps of Engineers had held back a large quantity of water in its flood-control dams. But under the Rio Grande Compact rules, the Conservancy District couldn't touch it.

Figure 19. Water flows in the Alameda Lateral, an incongruous green belt briefly confined to a culvert beneath Albuquerque's juvenile detention center as it threads through a light industrial neighborhood on the valley's eastern edge. Photograph by John Fleck.

It would have to sit there until fall, when it would be moved downstream after the irrigation season was over.

In the heart of Albuquerque the river, for much of the spring, had risen out of the 600-foot-wide main channel built by the Bureau of Reclamation. The river spread quietly out through the bosque. This caused some consternation for bicycle riders and walkers who found their favorite trails inundated but delighted the city's nature-loving bosque fans, seeing the first episode of overbanking since 2019. It was the closest the Rio Grande was allowed to get to the sort of floodplain wandering from the time before levees constrained its path nearly a century before.

With the flood menace forgotten, it was a joyful event to see water flowing through the strip of woods between the river's levees. Beyond the levees, water flowed through the shaded irrigation ditches of the valley. But in the last week of June, the Army Corps of Engineers began throttling back releases from Cochiti Dam. Whatever water remained in Abiquiu would have to stay there until fall. The valley began drying out just as the heat of summer settled over the Middle Valley. With high temperatures, irrigation demand was up, as was the demand the riverside bosque was placing on the river. Through the center of Albuquerque, sandbars began emerging as the Rio Grande's flows dropped quickly.

Anne Marken repeated what had become a familiar refrain in her water supply briefings at the Conservancy District board's monthly meeting: "I encourage you all to continue praying for rain."

CHAPTER 6

PUEBLO SOVEREIGNTY

In creating new tools to manage their growing city's relationship with the Rio Grande, the public entrepreneurs who built the Middle Rio Grande Conservancy District had to accommodate an institution that had existed on the valley floor since time immemorial—Pueblo sovereignty. Flowing rivers create interdependencies between communities. The newly emerging metropolis was already bumping into Pueblo land upstream and downstream, and the shared river made conflict, collaboration—or both—inevitable.

The multiple meanings of the word "Pueblo" itself embody the tensions. Originally coined by Spanish colonizers, the word and with its multiple related meanings is embraced by the people and communities who self-identify as Pueblo. As explained by their Pueblo Cultural Center: "A pueblo is a tribal nation; a body of land under a tribal governmental structure; and a community made up of related people who have similar beliefs, spirituality, and lifestyle." When the federal government responded to massive flooding in 1941 and 1942 by looking for a place to build a flood-control dam at the head of the Albuquerque reach of the Rio Grande, proponents argued that the dam would benefit all valley residents, including the six Native American Pueblo communities that had made the valley home from time immemorial. Cochiti Gov. Jose Alcario Montoya, whose community sat at the valley's upstream end seventy-five miles above Albuquerque, was skeptical. Speaking at a multi-day congressional hearing, he said:

> And so I have heard yesterday here that we are in very great danger from flood and that we are losing land. I do not think it is so that we have lost any land. Suppose the land is on one side of the river and the river cuts over and cuts part of that land away. While it is doing that it is making new land on the other side and so we never lose any. When the river gets down, we use that land again for cultivation.[1]

It turned out that the danger to Cochiti Pueblo would not come from flooding but rather from the dam intended to stop that flooding. The convergence of the Puebloans' struggle to retain their sovereignty with the pressures of a growing city attempting to manage a river led to an awkward compromise: the participation of the Pueblo communities in the task of flood control, drainage, and irrigation in return for Albuquerque's support in their political struggles to defend their sovereignty.

But in the end, one piece of sovereignty was lost—the integrity of Cochiti land and water, as a great dam was built through the Pueblo's heart.

The Struggle for Sovereignty

New Mexico's Puebloans have an observation frequently shared with their colonizing Hispanic and Anglo neighbors: We were here before you came, and we will be here after you're gone. Resistance, resilience, and adaptation to the changes wrought by modernity are hallmarks of Pueblo culture. As the institutional arrangements to manage growing Albuquerque's relationship with the Rio Grande were being crafted, the Puebloans insisted on keeping their place on the land and maintaining what they could of their relationship with the river. Thus, we see Isleta's Pablo Abeita and other Pueblo leaders alongside people like Aldo Leopold and Max Gutierrez, the early public entrepreneurs who shaped the collective action tools being created to manage the river. But though the sovereign Pueblo nations endured, the changes driven by colonialism and modernity were profound and painful—but nowhere was as painful as at Cochiti Pueblo.

The village of Cochiti, with a twenty-first-century population of some five hundred people, sits on high ground above a bend in the Rio Grande as the river emerges from the canyons to the north and begins spreading out across a widening valley floor.

Its name comes from the Keres word "K'úutìim'é," "people from the mountains," a reference to the community's heritage on the mesa lands above the Rio Grande.[2]

It is the first community the Rio Grande visits on its trek through New Mexico's Middle Rio Grande Valley. Today, green farm fields, primarily planted in alfalfa, fill the floodplain on both sides of the river down the hill from the village. Today's fields are straight-edged rectangles crisscrossed with roads and modern culverts on land that has provided sustenance to the community for time immemorial.

Looming over the village is Cochiti Dam, rising 250 feet above the Rio Grande. Built in the 1960s and 1970s, the earthen dam's mass is breathtaking. Its crest is five miles long, damming the Rio Grande before making a dogleg turn to dam the Santa Fe River, a half day's walk from one end to the other and back again. It has caught the most significant floods that either the Rio Grande, the Santa Fe River, or both have thrown at it in the half century since its construction, protecting the city built downstream.

Look at the boundaries of modern Cochiti's land, and the dam appears as a slash through its heart.

Cochiti and the other Rio Grande Valley Pueblos have been buffeted for centuries by the institutions that define modernity's relationship with the Rio Grande. The bloody first contact with Spanish conquistadors in search of gold was followed by waves of physical and cultural violence that imposed Spanish ideas about religion and a new economic structure of agricultural production—evolving notions of property rights culminating in the twentieth-century desire of downstream communities for irrigation, drainage, and flood control. Cochiti and the other five Middle Rio Grande

Figure 20. A stereoscopic image of Cochiti Pueblo, circa 1880–1890. The image represents the cultural appropriation of stylized Native American imagery typical of the day, which created a cultural current that Pueblo communities were adept at harnessing in their political struggle for sovereignty. Courtesy of the Library of Congress.

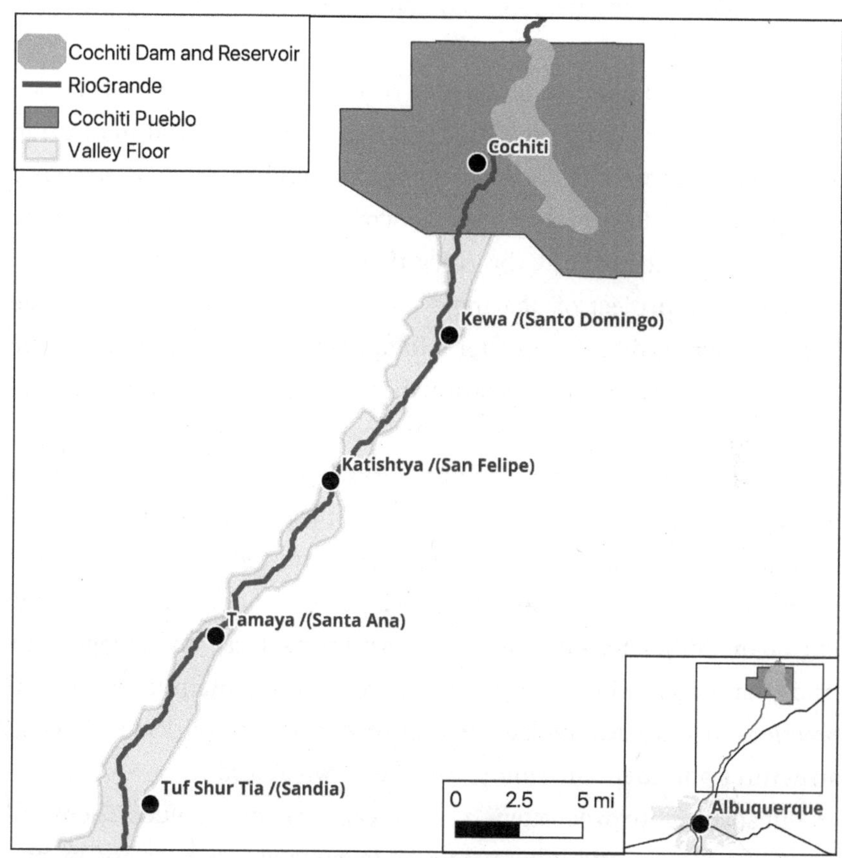

Map 8. A scar across Cochiti's heart. Map by John Fleck.

Pueblos living astride the river have endured but have been profoundly changed.

If the institutions that govern our relationship with the Rio Grande have shaped our landscape, there may be no more critical institution to understand than Pueblo sovereignty. Sovereignty offers a profound example of the deep meaning of the word "institutions"—not merely government agencies, but the rules themselves that both enable and constrain the project of sharing a river. The six Middle Rio Grande Pueblos surrounding the greater Albuquerque metropolitan area have existed for centuries in a relationship of ongoing resistance to the colonizers' attempts to push them aside or assimilate them into the dominant culture. Roughly half of the Rio Grande's miles flow through the core of the valley's metropolitan area through the land of the six Pueblo nations. This land has been legally contested since the arrival of the Spanish more than four centuries ago. Sovereignty here means the Puebloans' inherent authority to govern themselves—to manage their lands, have some control over their water, and maintain their cultural practices. It is an acknowledgment of their distinct political and social structures and their autonomy over their own affairs.

But sovereignty over water—a river—can never be absolute. There will always be communities upstream and downstream, and actions by one sovereign will impact those around them. There was no way to build a great city on the Rio Grande Valley floor without coming to terms with Pueblo sovereignty, by either pushing the Puebloans out or bringing them in. The flood control, drainage, and irrigation systems the city wanted to build had to cross through the Pueblos' lands. The Pueblo nations' sovereignty over that land and water and the cultural foundations on which that sovereignty lay were thus central to the work ahead. By the early twentieth century, the Albuquerque boosters' struggle to bring an integrated system of flood control, drainage, and irrigation to the Middle Rio Grande was caught up in the Puebloans' existential battle not only for control of land and water but for their very cultural survival.

By the 1920s, the Puebloans had become skilled at playing the Americans' political game, with masterful public relations campaigns that built the political alliances needed to kill two pieces of federal legislation that would have robbed them of their sovereignty. Their success was a harbinger of an enduring struggle extending beyond land and water, including deep religious and cultural issues. In the end, they settled for a bargain—support for the protection of their sovereignty in return for joining in the development of flood control, drainage, and irrigation systems in the Middle Rio Grande.

The cost was high. Expanding irrigation to the south required ever-larger canals crisscrossing the land of Cochiti and its Pueblo neighbors, forever changing their ancestral lands. This led to a fight over water quality, as pollution from Albuquerque threatened Isleta downstream from the big city. But Albuquerque's push for flood control had the most important impact on the Pueblos. In the 1960s and early 1970s, the boosters built a massive earthen dam that sliced through the heart of Cochiti's world.

Of the many who might be named,[3] two Pueblo leaders in particular played crucial roles: Pablo Abeita of Isleta Pueblo and Jose Alcario Montoya of Cochiti Pueblo. Both were educated in schools established to teach Native American children the languages and cultural ways of the dominant culture. Both learned the language and ways of the dominant culture but returned home with a multicultural fluency, which they used to defend Pueblo culture rather than assimilating. The two understood that defending their sovereignty was tied to the struggle of shared management of the Rio Grande.

Jose Alcario Montoya

Described by the Pueblo writer and historian Joe Sando as an unpretentious, noble leader, Jose Alcario Montoya was a prominent, lifelong citizen of Cochiti Pueblo in New Mexico. He was born in the late 1870s (there is uncertainty about the date) and died in 1966.[4] His life thus spanned a period of monumental change for his people and the valley in which he lived, from the railroad's arrival in his childhood to the first earth movers beginning work on the great dam that would overshadow his community and nearly tear it apart. He represented traditional, conservative Pueblo perspectives that would have to find their way as they interacted with a more progressive faction that began in the 1920s. Simultaneously, his collaborative efforts to protect all Pueblo nations' land rights and cultural traditions extended far beyond his own small village.

Montoya, whose Keres name was "Ã-põtch,"[5] first attended his village school (taught in Spanish), then the Albuquerque Indian School (taught in English), and then St. Catherine's Industrial Indian School in Santa Fe, New Mexico.[6] These Indian schools of the times were intended to assimilate Native American youth into non–Native American society.[7] Jose Alcario learned the schools' languages but kept his culture. His role as a linguistic and cultural translator would be a central feature of his role throughout his life.

Pablo Abeita

Downstream sits Isleta Pueblo, on the opposite end of the Middle Rio Grande's Pueblo landscape from Cochiti. Its community proudly maintains its Tiwa language and heritage,[8] including a long history of irrigating the Rio Grande Valley floor. But by the early twentieth century, Isletans were increasingly struggling to maintain their way of life in the face of the burdens imposed by a growing Albuquerque fifteen miles upstream.

Pablo Abeita led their struggle. Like Cochiti's Montoya, Abeita was educated in the dominant culture's schools. Like Montoya, Abeita learned the dominant culture's language and developed a bicultural fluency. "The ability to thrive in two worlds—that of Isleta and the wider New Mexico and national communities—characterized Abeita from an early age," write

Figure 21. Isleta Pueblo Leader Pablo Abeita, 1913. Courtesy of the Albuquerque Museum Archives, PA2003.009.002.

his biographers. Abeita also used it in service not of assimilation but as a tool to help his community preserve its culture.[9]

A master of public relations, Abeita stood before a congressional committee in 1920 and offered a lesson in the complexity of the interplay between the colonialists' dominant culture, enduring Pueblo cultures, sovereignty, and the challenge of making peace with the Rio Grande. The occasion was an Albuquerque hearing before the House Committee on Indian Affairs to consider legislation that Pueblo leaders saw as an assault on their sovereignty. In the speech, one of the most consequential in the evolving relationship among the Pueblos, Albuquerque, and the river, Abeita sketched out the terms of a bargain. Albuquerque needed the Pueblo nations' help in overcoming the challenges of managing an increasingly troublesome relationship with the Rio Grande. Isleta needed the colonizers' help overcoming problems caused by their wholesale alteration of the river. At the same time, the Puebloans needed help fighting off efforts to rob them of their sovereignty.

> Gentlemen, your time is limited, you don't belong to yourself you belong to that great invincible onrush called progress and hurry, so I will not take too much of that valuable time of yours. . . . If we run short of water in this valley it is all on account of you who came and if we are flooded with alkali it is on account of you who came. If we run short of water for irrigation it is because of you who came are gobbling up all the water and if we are flooded with it, it is because you who came are dikeing and damming the river thereby causing the water under the ground to raise, thereby when we sow wheat we raise alkali; all this is done or caused because of you who came. But as I said before we were ready to do our part. . . . Drain the land and not the Indian—if you drain our lands you will only be repairing a loss which came upon us by your coming upon us.[10]

Colliding Forces 1918–1921

By the end of World War I in 1918, Albuquerque was emerging as New Mexico's economic center—the largest concentration of financial and human-made capital in the state but still interconnected along the 160 miles of the Middle Rio Grande Valley's ribbons of green with much older Hispanic and Puebloan villages. The railroad had brought a mix of opportunity and disruptive change. The railroad builders had shown little care for the Pueblo land as they tore down the Rio Grande Valley—blocking or ripping out irrigation canals with little regard for the communities whose land the canals irrigated. The railroad engineers diverted arroyos, flooded farm fields, and even rearranged the Rio Grande itself as it flowed through the Pueblo nations' lands. The resulting economic boom among the colonizers created a push for expanded irrigation, with repeated efforts to run irrigation canals through Pueblo land, generally without permission or support of the Pueblo communities themselves.[11]

But the Pueblo nations endured. The immediate post–World War I years were a time of colliding social and biophysical forces in Albuquerque, and its connected river reaches. Responding to and sorting through those intersecting forces would eventually require considerable collective action.

Ranchers, Pueblos, and "the Pueblo Flood"

These colliding forces can be glimpsed in a bundle of seemingly disconnected page 3 news stories in the *Albuquerque Morning Journal* on June 22, 1921.

Near the center of the page came news of US Senator Holm O. Bursum's push to make more loan money available to ranchers and cattlemen, struggling under the weight of drought, which made access to the narrow ribbons of green along New Mexico's rivers critical. One of the problems the ranchers faced was the need for land titles to back the loans. The landmark US Supreme Court case, United States v. Sandoval, complicated

Figure 22. The railroad changed Isleta Pueblo forever by slicing through the community's heart on its route through the Rio Grande Valley. Photograph by Jack Delano, US Office of War Information, 1943. Courtesy of the Library of Congress.

their situation in 1913, which confirmed Pueblo lands as tribal lands, acknowledging their unique status.[12]

Bursum's pursuit of this question would play a crucial role in the following years as efforts to clarify land titles along the Rio Grande were swept up in the struggle to bring flood control, drainage, and irrigation to the valley floor.

At the top of page 3 of the *Journal* that Wednesday was a large grainy picture labeled and explained only as "First Photographs of Pueblo Flood." Deep floodwaters overtake a car "at Main and Fourth street" in an urban setting. Throwing off a modern reader, it involved neither a New Mexico Pueblo nor Albuquerque. On June 3, 1921, the city of Pueblo, Colorado, several hundred miles to the north and on the Arkansas River, was devastated by a flood of historical significance. Several weeks later, the first pictures made their way to Albuquerque newspapers. The image would have likely captured attention by showing one of the closest major railroad connections to Albuquerque. Was this to be Albuquerque's fate?

Where the ranches Bursum was trying to help faced a problem of too little water, this was a problem of too much. With its growing urban area around a steel-producing industry and prominent rail yards, Pueblo, Colorado, would soon seek professional advice on the best recent Progressive Era solutions to preventing future flood catastrophes. Ambitious Albuquerque civic leaders were watching.

The final piece of the convergence on that Wednesday's *Albuquerque Morning Journal* was a short item about the governors of four Pueblo nations visiting Washington, DC, for a meeting with the officials at the US Department of Interior to discuss conflicts then going on about the Pueblos' legal sovereignty—their powers and rights to provide governance on their own lands. Among them was Jose Alcario Montoya of Cochiti Pueblo.

Keres Pueblos

Cochiti is one of four Indigenous communities in the Rio Grande Valley upstream of Albuquerque rooted in the Keres language and culture and having lived on the valley floor for, in the language of the colonizers' law, "time immemorial."[13] Theirs are cultures far more deeply rooted in place than the Spanish and American newcomers—"Kastera" and "Merikaana," in the language used by Keres historians. Their modern incarnations are a resilient blend of resistance and adaptation—in their relationship with the river and the dominant culture.[14]

The four communities—Cochiti, Kewa (also known by its Spanish name, Santo Domingo), Katishtya (San Felipe), and Tamaya (Santa Ana)—were the first the old Rio Grande encountered as it emerged from the steep-sided canyon country of what is now northern New Mexico into the broad, flat valley where Albuquerque now resides.

Cochiti is the northernmost of the four, built in the fashion of the valley's earliest inhabitants, on high ground adjacent to the river, close enough to take advantage of its floodplain for farming, but safely above the river's spring snowmelt rise. The river's presence defined the human geography. While the village, built on some of the best high ground west of the Rio Grande, was never at risk, jetties were built in 1911 and 1912 to protect farmland on the valley floor. It was modest in size but productive as farmland. While communities downstream struggled with rising water tables, by the time of the founding of the Middle Rio Grande Conservancy District to provide drainage farther down the valley, the Cochiti community's farms were "excellent land, well drained and constantly fertilized by the siltage in the river irrigation water."[15]

Similarly, Cochiti's Keres neighbors to the south struggled with the Rio Grande. Mobility in the face of a river that moved across the floodplain was a fact of life for Kewa Pueblo (Santo Domingo) immediately downstream of Cochiti. Living and farming on both sides of the Rio Grande, the Kewa people had been flooded and forced to move four times since the early

1700s. In 1886 the Kewa community lost both its churches and a third of its houses.[16]

The primary village of the Tamayame people, Santa Ana, is located on the Rio Grande Valley floor on land the Pueblo community bought from Spanish colonizers adjacent to their homelands. They irrigated their five hundred acres from a ditch with its heading four miles to the north, on the land of their neighbors, Katishtya (San Felipe) Pueblo. The Tamayame struggled with the Rio Grande eating into their farmland. In 1915 they built ten jetties into the river, "capped with heavy timber, and planked with three-inch planking on the upper side."[17] But while the Pueblos wrestled with the river around their farms and relatively small villages, the struggles of building a major city around the Rio Grande were of another scale entirely.

The people of New Mexico's Middle Rio Grande Pueblos had not asked to have their communities incorporated into the central New Mexico population center growing around them. But the collective actions needed to manage the Rio Grande were confronting one of the central questions raised by Elinor Ostrom: How will the collective action institutions created by the public entrepreneurs confront the question of scale? Where will the boundaries around the system be drawn?[18] On the Rio Grande, the answer to redrawing the institutional hydrology included the lands of the Pueblos.

A Historical Puzzle

In understanding the history of Albuquerque's relationship with the Rio Grande, the question of including the Pueblos' land within the boundaries of the integrated flood control, drainage, and irrigation system of the Middle Rio Grande Conservancy District requires explanation. There is little evidence that the northern Pueblos, upstream from Albuquerque, actively advocated for their inclusion in the newly engineered hydraulic system. While the challenges they faced in making peace with the river were real, they were far more modest in scope than the swamping and flooding that stood in the way of Albuquerque's growth as a city. The swampland that dominated the valley floor was rare in the narrow upper reaches of Cochiti, Kewa, Katishtya, and Tamaya.[19] The Pueblos' flooding and drainage issues were far less pronounced than Albuquerque's. So why were the boosters behind creating what would become the Middle Rio Grande Conservancy District so eager to spread the district's costs and benefits to Pueblo lands?

The explanation of the Pueblos' inclusion is twofold. The first piece of the answer can be found in the engineering reality of the hydraulic system needed to transform the valley's land. Early dam-building proposals repeatedly identified sites in this reach of the river. From an engineering standpoint, Pueblo lands in the valley's upstream reach offered the best sites for diversion dams to run irrigation water down the valley floor. There were several places where the river narrowed in a way that was ideal for the construction of irrigation diversions, which could then flow down the valley floor, parallel to the river, to deliver water to farmland. In addition, there was no way to build the levee and drainage system Albuquerque thought it needed without integrating it across the Pueblo nations' land. To work, the levees and drains needed to be continuous. "[T]he Indian lands are so interspersed with the white lands that it would be impossible to drain or reclaim any of this area without treating it as a unit. The Indian lands cut right across certain areas, and then come the white lands. Then come more Indian lands," Pearce C. Rodey, the Conservancy District's attorney, told Congress in 1927.[20]

The second and more important reason was money. While the Pueblos were not particularly affluent themselves in the framework of the urbanizing economy, their inclusion would provide access to federal government money needed to help get the Conservancy District off the ground. "Indians Ready to Aid," the *Albuquerque Journal* explained in 1920. Federal legislation in 1920 created a framework the boosters needed via the federal Indian Irrigation Service (predecessor of the modern Bureau of Indian Affairs) to integrate a valley-long drainage system, flood control, and irrigation and access federal funding to help pay for it. "This section of the bill will enable the secretary of the Interior to provide for the drainage of the Pueblo land in New Mexico *in connection with the land in white ownership*" (emphasis added).[21]

The Boosters' Quid Pro Quo

The two great forces shaping the Rio Grande and the communities around it—the Pueblo nations' struggle to maintain self-determination and protect their land against intrusion by non-Natives and the Albuquerque boosters' struggle to bring flood control, drainage, and modern irrigation to the Rio Grande Valley floor—converged in the decade after New Mexico's statehood in 1912. For the Puebloans, it was the most recent example of a long struggle to maintain sovereignty and self-determination over their land and water. For New Mexico's non-Natives, it was a struggle to clarify property rights in a way that would enable the growth of a modern economy. For the boosters, it was a struggle to act on their choice to build a city in the floodplain of a river.

The need for drainage and flood control had become a central focus for the ambitions of Albuquerque's boosters. The Commercial Club, the predecessor to Albuquerque's Chamber of Commerce, in 1915 touted its goal to double its population—"50,000 by 1920."[22] To make that possible, they believed they needed an integrated flood control and drainage system running the Middle Rio Grande Valley's entire length, anchored by a dam at the mouth of White Rock Canyon forty-five miles upstream of Albuquerque, down to San Marcial more than a hundred miles downstream.[23]

Repeated attempts to manage the river faltered on one of Elinor Ostrom's crucial design principles: How does a community draw the boundaries around the resource? For village life, the boundary was small, but as Albuquerque struggled with its growth into a metropolitan area, the question of scale became central. Flood control and drainage in pieces would not work. But with six Middle Rio Grande Pueblos astride the river, the need for the Pueblo communities' cooperation in the development of flood control, drainage, and irrigation became inextricably entwined with the Native American communities' struggle for their right to self-government and sovereignty over their land and water. The *Albuquerque Morning Journal* in 1920 frankly sketched out the terms of a bargain, a quid pro quo that would define the formation of the Middle Rio Grande Conservancy District.

A 1920 bill before Congress that would have stripped the Puebloans of sovereignty was "a grave injustice to the Indians," the *Morning Journal* wrote. "However, having in mind justice to the white population as well, this paper refused to join in an effort to defeat the bill unless the Puebloans affected, would enter into what deemed to be necessary agreements with regard to the drainage of the valley."[24]

Albuquerque would help the Pueblo nations defend their sovereignty if they helped Albuquerque manage the river needed to build a city on the valley floor.

Pueblo Sovereignty—a Political, Legal, and Cultural Struggle

The struggle over clarifying and codifying the legal structure of Pueblo sovereignty had, by 1920, become a crucial unresolved question in the development of New Mexico. Unlike many other Native American tribes, whose relationship with the United States was governed by treaties, the Pueblo people's rights to their lands were affirmed through Spanish and Mexican land grants and later acknowledged by the United States following the Treaty of Guadalupe Hidalgo in 1848. This treaty ended the Mexican-American War and resulted in the cession of a large portion of Mexico's northern territory, including modern-day New Mexico, to the United States. The Pueblo nations' lands were not held in trust by the US government, as is common with other Native American tribes. Instead, they were acknowledged as property owned by the Puebloans based on the land grants they had received from prior Spanish and Mexican rule.

The land was theirs under the law because of their tenancy on it from, in the legal phrase, *time immemorial*.

The law, for a time, was a jumble. The United States Supreme Court, in its 1877 decision in the case of United States v. Joseph, set out a unique legal status for the Puebloans, ruling that Pueblo nations were not "Indian tribes" under the law and could sell their land.[25] This distinct legal character of Pueblo land was then complicated by the landmark US Supreme Court 1913 Sandoval decision, which essentially said the opposite—that under US law, the Pueblo nations did have the status of Native tribes.

This unique legal status has led to a complex and often fraught legal landscape for the people of the Pueblo nations. On the one hand, it gave them greater ownership and control over their lands than other tribes. On the other hand, it made Pueblo lands more vulnerable to encroachment and legal disputes.

The Carter Bill

This was the context when Oklahoma Congressman Charles Carter, a member of the Chickasaw Nation and an advocate for Native American rights, attempted in 1920 to clarify the legal status of all Native Americans with "a bill for the purpose of conferring citizenship upon Indians." "There is no one within the boundaries of the United States who is more entitled to citizenship than the aborigines of this country," Carter explained. "Yet we have gone along, during more than a century of this Government, excluding them from those rights."[26]

What seemed a simple call for justice and equality was, from the perspective of members of New Mexico's Pueblo communities' perspective, anything but. Citizens of the Pueblo nations had not asked to join the dominant culture through the act of US citizenship, Isleta Pueblo's Pablo Abeita told Carter and a group of visiting members of Congress during a 1920 meeting at Albuquerque's YMCA. For the legislation's critics, led by the leaders of New Mexico's Pueblos, Carter's bill was a call for assimilation—a loss of their cultural sovereignty. Aligned with the Haudenosaunee (commonly known as "Iroquois") and the pan-Native Society of American Indians, the Puebloans helped kill Carter's bill.[27]

While the boosters sided with their Pueblo neighbors in opposing the Carter bill, it is important not to overstate their role. The fight against the Carter bill was a national crusade, the impact on Albuquerque's aspirations an afterthought. But in striking their deal with the Puebloans, the boosters had started down a path toward collective river management.

The Bursum Bill

Killing the Carter bill did not end the Pueblo nations' struggle for self-determination. Pablo Abeita, Jose Alcario Montoya, and the other Pueblo leaders confronted a fresh challenge in 1922 with another congressional bill that would have handed over significant portions of their homelands to non-Natives, encroaching on their lands while removing their cultural sovereignty. Again, they demonstrated their political skills, mobilizing a notable national collection of activists, women's clubs, Franciscan priests, and artistic communities.[28] Again, the linkage of the valley's need for flood control and drainage to the Pueblo nations' struggle for sovereignty over their homelands played a crucial role.

New Mexico US Senator Holm Bursum introduced the legislation to clarify who owned long-contested lands in and around New Mexico's Pueblos—the Pueblo nations or colonizers living on and often within their borders. But while much of the debate focused on the bill's land rights elements, it went further in ways that threatened the Pueblo nations' cultural sovereignty. It would have robbed them of powers to govern their own community affairs. "This bill will destroy our common life and will rob us of everything which we hold dear—our lands, our customs, our traditions," the Council of All the New Mexico Pueblos[29] wrote in a November 1922 public appeal.[30]

Across the pages of *The New York Times* and *Sunset Magazine*, the Bursum bill was portrayed as a land grab from peaceful people. The novelist D. H. Lawrence described Bursum's legislation as an attempt to favor "the hungry, unscrupulous frontier population squatting" on Pueblo land. The bill, Lawrence wrote, would take the Pueblo nations' water and destroy their communities. "The squatters . . . openly declare that the Pueblos will be finished in ten years," he wrote in *The New York Times*.[31]

Cochiti Pueblo's John Dixon echoed the claim, saying the non-Indians encroaching on Pueblo land amounted to squatters.[32] But as Isleta's Pablo Abeita pointedly noted, in the political process underway to sort out the question, the Puebloans had no democratic representation because they could not vote. "We have worlds of protest to make," Abeita wrote, "but the trouble is that we cannot go to see our congressman (we have none)."[33] In opposing the Carter bill, the leaders of the Pueblo nations had opposed a particular brand of citizenship they viewed as robbing them of their cultural sovereignty. But the fact remained that they lacked the political power that came with the vote.

Pueblo leaders of a century ago, like Pablo Abeita and Jose Alcario Montoya in midlife, emerged as multilingual and multicultural translators. They were connected to their autonomous land communities and individual Pueblo traditions. They were also well-traveled compared to most New Mexicans of the time and shown to cooperate in a successful political confederation, active regionally and nationally, in asserting the Pueblo nations' rights and values and helping place those arguments persuasively in the English-language media. They were thus deeply embedded in the tradition of public entrepreneurship at the heart of the efforts to remake valley communities' relationship with the Rio Grande.

For Abeita, Montoya, and their colleagues, the battle against the Bursum bill was one of many sovereignty issues they adroitly and collaboratively navigated at various governance scales.[34] In the winter of

1922 two issues were again linked: the settlement of the Pueblo nations' claims of encroachment on their lands and cultural integrity and the development of valley-wide river management. Albuquerque's Rotary Club passed a resolution calling Bursum's legislation "unfair and unjust to the Indians." The Club backed an alternative that linked the settlement of the land disputes to a coordinated river management system created by the connection of flood control, drainage, and irrigation systems across Native and non-Native land.[35]

Under the weight of the same sort of national critique that killed the Carter bill, the Bursum bill soon died even as the boosters' plans converged on the concept of an integrated middle valley river management system across Pueblo and non-Pueblo land. Eschewing any earlier sentiments to break up the Pueblo grants or lands,[36] the Albuquerque boosters focused on federal support. It did not go unnoticed that with roughly half of the irrigable lands in the northern half of the valley, the Pueblos—and their intact lands—represented a significant federal funding avenue.

Federal Support for Pueblo Participation in Conservancy

While the general shape of the grand bargain, protecting the Pueblo nations' sovereignty in exchange for participation in the conservancy project, had been evident since the early 1920s, working out details remained challenging. Despite the defeat of the Carter and Bursum bills, the persistent threats to Pueblo sovereignty had not gone away, nor had the complex question of how to include Pueblo lands in the Middle Rio Grande Valley project.

Meeting at Kewa (Santo Domingo) Pueblo in December 1927, eleven New Mexico Pueblos formally joined to incorporate the Council of All New Mexico Pueblos, successor to the group that had challenged the Carter and Bursum bills. At the top of their agenda that day was an insistence on the terms of the Conservancy deal: Native lands already under cultivation should be kept free of charges for improvements, and their priority rights to water in times of scarcity must be protected.[37]

Soon after, Congress passed a bill authorizing federal help for the Conservancy project in the form of $1.6 million ($28 million in inflation-adjusted 2023 dollars) to pay for Conservancy work on Pueblo land.[38] But the legislation immediately became entangled once again in a question of sovereignty. Critics complained that it had been structured so that Puebloans could lose their land to foreclosure under the repayment terms included in the bill.[39]

In public, the debate played out in a way not uncommon for the time, as Anglo surrogates for the Pueblos worked the political levers to protect the Native American communities' sovereignty as the final institutional pieces of the Conservancy were being assembled. The challenge, the attorney for the Pueblo nations explained, was not unlike that faced by the Hispanic farmers—an expectation that repayment for the Conservancy's costs would come from converting land devoted to subsistence farming to commercial agriculture. "Many of them do not see how they can ever pay," the attorney explained. "Most of them grow only enough crops for their own use." The resulting debt "will give the Indian department a whip hand over them which might be used to their detriment," he explained.[40]

After months of negotiation and debate, the final details reflected a crucial compromise that would fundamentally influence the relationship of Albuquerque and the surrounding communities with the Rio Grande. First, and perhaps most importantly, the legislation not only provided financing for the Pueblos' share of the project. It also included a commitment legally acknowledging something obvious—that the Puebloans were the valley's first people. A total of 8,346 acres of Pueblo farmland was declared to have a "prior and paramount" right to water. In times of shortage, Pueblo farmers could still irrigate that land while non-Native farmers were cut off. Beyond that land, another 15,000 acres of Pueblo land could also be "reclaimed"—brought into irrigation with the benefit of the valley's new water management infrastructure.[41]

Chapter 6

The Dam Site

For dam builders, the late 1800s in the western United States was a time of promise. The early use of science to inform policy at national scales was beginning to take shape in the land and water surveys led by the US Geological Survey under a Civil War veteran, explorer, and scientist named John Wesley Powell.[42] But for Native American communities the results were far more threat than promise.[43]

Powell first noted the potential of a dam in White Rock Canyon. "The canyon walls are hundreds of feet, and in some cases more than a thousand feet, above the waters," he wrote in an 1890 report to Congress. "White Rock Canyon empties below into a valley which I shall call the Albuquerque Valley. In it lie Bernalillo, Albuquerque, Los Lunas, Socorro, and other towns. Now, all the water that comes out of White Rock Canyon can be used in the Albuquerque Valley."[44]

Given what followed, Powell's description of the narrows at the downstream end of White Rock Canyon was grimly prophetic: "Whoever has control of that point owns that dam site and has the right to take the water out of its natural channel and carry it into canals—has command of all the agriculture of that great district."[45] It was an explicit recognition of the hydrologic reality: that the upper reaches of New Mexico's Middle Rio Grande Valley were the best place, from a purely engineering standpoint, to build the dam or dams needed to divert Rio Grande water to irrigate the valley downstream. In its recognition of the importance of property rights—"whoever has control of that point"—it also foreshadowed a century of conflict.

Albuquerque took note of Powell's words. "Albuquerque is to be the first point in the United States to receive the benefit of the work of irrigation now being undertaken by the United States government," the *Albuquerque Journal* wrote after a reporter sat down with Powell at an 1889 meeting in Santa Fe. Powell believed a dam at the site would make possible "homes in that vicinity for more people than constitute the entire present population of New Mexico and make Albuquerque a greater city than has ever been dreamed of by its most sanguine friends."[46] Neither Powell nor the Albuquerque boosters seem to have taken notice the fact that the dam site sat on the land of the people of Cochiti Pueblo.

Dam Boosters Try, and Try, and Try

The first formal proposal for a White Rock Dam came in 1894, and a long series of attempts followed, buoyed by the promise of hydroelectricity that could be generated from a canyon dam. Early experimentation in developing water management efforts frequently focused on private endeavors. Still, those private efforts failed at White Rock Canyon (as across much of the western United States). By the early twentieth century the emphasis shifted back to the institutional arrangement that Powell had advocated more than a decade before: a dam built by the federal government. In 1901 the US Geological Survey recommended not one but two dams on that stretch of the river, one at the upstream end of White Rock Canyon and a second fifteen miles downstream toward Albuquerque on the land of the Katishtya people at the Pueblo of San Felipe. The US Geological Survey waved off the fact that native land on which communities had lived for time immemorial would be lost to the dams: "[T]he submergence of the pueblo could be properly handled only by the Government."[47] It would take three-quarters of a century for the dream of the dam builders and the Puebloans' nightmare to be made real in White Rock Canyon.

Moving with the River

A half century after Powell endorsed the site, the Rio Grande at the mouth of White Rock Canyon remained undammed, save for a modest irrigation diversion built in the 1930s by the Middle Rio Grande Conservancy

District. But after the Middle Rio Grande Valley flooding in 1941–1942, the pressure to build there had grown. Montana Congressman James O'Connor pressed Jose Alcario Montoya during that 1943 congressional hearing, claiming evidence that the land available to the Cochiti community had been shrinking.

Montoya: "The land that we cultivated we never lose; we always cultivate it."

O'Connor: "There has been no shrinkage, then, of your agricultural land?"

Montoya: "No, it comes back on the other side."

Was Montoya being deliberately obtuse? Not exactly. While Cochiti did struggle in the early twentieth century as the river whipsawed across the valley floor, encroaching on Cochiti farmland, Montoya's response speaks to a deeper issue. "Considerable damage has been done to the lands (of Cochiti Pueblo) by erosion by flood waters in the Rio Grande," H. F. Robinson of the US Indian Service wrote in 1913. "To protect the land from further river encroachment in 1911–12, jetties were built to throw the main current to the center of the channel where it belonged."[48]

The actions described in Robinson's report and Montoya's testimony three decades later illustrate a fundamental change in the relationship between human communities and the Rio Grande. When colonizers arrived, bringing their legal structures with them—first Spanish law, then Mexican, then American—they brought a notion of property that challenged the Pueblo way of life. No longer was it possible for communities to adapt to the river's changes by moving. The institution of property—"This patch of land is mine"—created a need to keep the river in a single channel. What was once the river's natural wandering across a fertile floodplain open to community use was conceptually transformed into a "flood," and the need for flood protection emerged.

The historical record clearly shows Cochiti Pueblo and the other Indigenous villages along the Rio Grande struggling by the twentieth century with the same challenges the Rio Grande posed to the colonizers—flooding, drainage, and irrigation. But Montoya's view was not wrong when considering the more profound history of the Puebloans' life on this land. The native communities' past ways of adapting to a changing river had been taken away from them by the institution of "property." The need to protect or benefit one community's property in one place required changes to other people's property in other areas, whether it was through agricultural diversions and canals to get water to dry land or a flood-control dam to keep water away. This wave of change would have fateful consequences for the Pueblo of Cochiti.

Tragedy

In hindsight, there is a tragic inevitability in what happened to the Keres people of Cochiti Pueblo and their place. The tragedy here is in two senses of the word: a terrible outcome, but also in what the philosopher Alfred North Whitehead called "the solemnity of the remorseless working of things."[49] The construction of Cochiti Dam was a tragedy for the people of Cochiti and the other Middle Rio Grande Pueblos in the sense of a terrible outcome. But Whitehead's inexorable forces were also at work. One can imagine a different political world in which Cochiti's cultural sovereignty trumped Albuquerque's desire for flood control. But we do not live in that world.

For Cochiti and the other Rio Grande Pueblos for whom White Rock Canyon above Cochiti Pueblo was sacred, the tragedy in the first sense was the destruction of a cultural foundation. Completed in 1975, Cochiti Dam provided New Mexico's Middle Rio Grande Valley with a flood-control dam on the river's main stem. It came at the cost of inundating Cochiti Pueblo farmland—both above and below the dam—and, perhaps more importantly, destroying sacred cultural sites, not only for Cochiti but for all Middle Rio Grande Pueblo people.[50]

The tragedy in the second sense was the remorseless working of modernity's wave across the Rio Grande Valley floor: a desire for flood control to build a modern city; a canyon that was, from the perspective of nineteenth- and twentieth-century hydraulic engineering, an ideal dam site; and a tangled institutional tale that ironically depended on the valley's Native American communities to help fund the entire enterprise of flood control, drainage, and irrigation. The floods of 1941 and 1942 demonstrated how vulnerable the growing metropolitan area was. By the 1950s, the political world in which Cochiti sat, dominated by the growing city, renewed its drive to build a flood-control dam at the head of the valley. The bargain struck in the 1920s—a compromise to preserve what Pueblo sovereignty remained at the time in return for incorporation of the land of both Pueblo nations and colonizers in the great project of reclamation—placed Cochiti squarely in the path of modernity's juggernaut.

In pursuing the flood-control dam, boosters offered another bargain between traditional culture and modernity—opportunities for developing recreation areas and a housing project that they argued would bring economic development to Cochiti. The resulting struggle over the dam and the community's future pitted "brother against brother, brother against sister, and father against grandfather," former Cochiti Gov. Regis Pecos recalled. Pecos recalled the agony as Cochiti elders agreed to the construction but pleaded to preserve the community's most sacred site. Many in Cochiti saw no choice but to acquiesce in the dam's construction.[51]

"This land is the only homeland we have ever known . . .," Pecos said. "This was not supposed to happen. The Indian wars were over. . . . To see this construction proceed before our eyes; sacred space and place defined by all those who had gone before violated before our eyes was very hurtful. Unimaginable pain."[52] "Every day, on my way to school, we saw the earth ravaged by bulldozers," Pecos recalled of his childhood. "We went to sleep hearing the destruction of our heartlands."[53]

Among those who also presumably heard it was an aging Jose Alcario Montoya, who died in 1966 as the sound of the bulldozers was changing Cochiti forever.[54]

The spirit of Jose Alcario Montoya's life is still felt. When Deb Haaland, a member of Laguna Pueblo, was sworn in as one of the first two Native American women elected to Congress, New Mexico state archivist Diane Bird reflected:

> When I was a child growing up at Santo Domingo, I would listen to my uncle John Bird (Santo Domingo Pueblo) and great-grandfather Jose Alcario Montoya (Cochiti Pueblo) talk about solutions to maintaining Pueblo land and water rights, their plans to visit Washington, DC to testify against the damming of the Rio Grande, and their participation in the All Indian Pueblo Council activities. Last January, I imagined them proudly standing in the U.S. Capitol Statuary Hall, alongside the statue of Popé, as Deb Haaland and Sharice Davids took their oaths.[55]

In 2021 Haaland was appointed Secretary of the Interior, the first Native American to hold the post.

Interlude: August

By early August 2023 the incantations offered in response to Conservancy District water operations manager Anne Marken's prayer calls were failing. It had not rained since the middle of June, the hottest and driest summer in Albuquerque since record-keeping began in the late 1800s. The Rio Grande was paying the price as the flow of water down the Rio Grande's main channel dropped. After a bounteous runoff, by early July, previously submerged sandbars were appearing in the river's main channel. The river's flow at Albuquerque's Central Avenue Bridge kept dropping.

Yet the Rio Grande kept doing the quiet work of keeping the valley green. Shaded by leafy trees, including one of the valley's most magnificent

Figure 23. Even as flows in the Rio Grande's main channel dropped to near nothing, the shallow groundwater—every bit as much a part of the river—kept Albuquerque's valley floor lush and green in the summer of 2023. Photograph by John Fleck.

old cottonwoods, and popular with the valley's ditch walkers, the Griegos Lateral through Max Gutierrez's old neighborhood kept flowing. If you were an endangered Rio Grande silvery minnow, life in the main river channel was growing increasingly difficult. But in the landscape beyond the levees, the alteration of the Rio Grande's hydrology was once again proving resilient. The shade endured, the ditches still flowed, and irrigators still got at least some water—not as much as they wanted, but some. The shallow aquifer, so closely connected to the Rio Grande that it rightly should be considered a part of the river, continued to pass water to deep-rooted trees. The ribbons remained green.

For one brief afternoon on August 8, the dry spell broke with a vengeance. Heavy monsoon rains swept across the city, spiking flows through the city's main flood-control channel to their highest level in a decade and nearly washing out lanes of the interstate as huge pieces of concrete tore loose under the pressure of the flood water. It *felt* like enough to break the flash drought. But by the time it had spread out and dissipated into the Rio Grande's drying bed south of Albuquerque, the flood flow had dwindled to near nothing. The Conservancy District's water managers were able to skim off a bit of the water at their diversion dams at Isleta and San Acacia downstream of Albuquerque, sending it toward farm fields. But none of the storm's water made it through the river's dry southern reaches to Elephant Butte Reservoir.

At the Conservancy District's board meeting a week after the storm, Marken laid out the dire scenario the district faced. The bounty of winter snow had melted off, and the rules governing New Mexico's debt under the interstate Rio Grande Compact had prevented the Conservancy District from storing any water as a hedge against a dry summer. With dwindling supplies upstream, there once again was a risk that the ditches might go dry. The Middle Rio Grande's altered hydrologic system was once again on the brink of breaking down. Again, Marken urged: pray for rain.

Figure 24. Looking across the Country Club neighborhood to the Rio Grande, as the newly developed Conservancy District levees and drains turned swampland into a city in the making, circa 1930. Courtesy of the Albuquerque Museum, PA1968.001.293.

CHAPTER 7

THE FINANCIAL MODEL UNRAVELS

The 1930 aerial photo of Conservancy Beach (now known as Tingley Beach) and the newly reclaimed neighborhoods around it suggest a promise of tidiness and hope. The long, linear swimming pond of Conservancy Beach, with its neatly sculpted islands and lifeguard station, parallels the Rio Grande. Newly graded streets lead toward a river now pinned between levees, flanked by drains. In a single year, Albuquerque's swamps and floodplains had been transformed into some of the most desirable residential real estate in the Middle Rio Grande Valley, a garden spot in the making. Or so it was hoped.

But while flood control and drainage benefits quickly spread to large areas of the valley floor, the tidiness and hope did not. For the four decades after Max Gutierrez lost in court and the first draglines began digging the drains and building the levees to disconnect Albuquerque's floodplain from the menace of the Rio Grande, the Conservancy District was a civic project that remained chaotically uncompleted. As we saw in the failures of the community's response to the large floods of 1941–1942, the Conservancy District physical infrastructure was inadequate, a problem compounded by the financial engineers' failures to develop an institutional structure capable of fixing the problem.

The boosters' naïve misunderstanding of the valley's agricultural potential left the Conservancy District with no way to pay for the river's reengineering. From the beginning, many of the predominantly Hispanic subsistence farmers of the old villages on the valley floor could not pay the tax assessments demanded by those pushing to create a twentieth-century metropolis. The draglines cut ditches, the levees and irrigation dams went up, the irrigation water continued to spread through the valley each spring as the snow melted, and the debts continued to rise.

The menace of swamps and flooding that had dominated public discussions about Albuquerque's relationship with the Rio Grande in the 1920s had faded by the 1930s. In their place emerged the financial menace Max Gutierrez had warned of, as tax delinquencies and the risk of losing their land loomed over farmers on the valley floor unable to pay their new Conservancy taxes. Farmers on the valley floor had traded one menace for another. The inclusion of the Pueblo nations' lands and the accompanying federal funding helped get the project off the ground, but the rest of the financial structure was a disaster.

Behind it all was a fierce and unresolved question rooted in the principles for success (or failure) of collection action natural resource governance regimes: Who has a say? Who should govern this project, appointed "experts" or a board elected by the people? It would take more than two decades, into the 1950s, to sort out the financial question, then another two decades, into the 1970s, to sort out for good the question of who should choose the members of the Conservancy District board.

The Enduring Struggle to Pay for Bringing the Rio Grande to Heel

The question of "Who has to pay?" plagued the Conservancy District from the beginning.[1] The original financing and tax structure devised in the late 1920s envisioned a roughly fifty-fifty split between agricultural and nonagricultural lands.[2] Agricultural lands included Pueblo farmland, which had already brought crucial federal funding to the project.[3] All non-Native lands in the District would be taxed, but the expectation placed on farmlands was the cause of the problems. If your land was unsuitable for commercial farming—swampy or covered by bosque forest—the financing mechanism presumed you would benefit the most from the improvements by converting the land to commercial farming. It would, therefore, have to pay the most in taxes. From a commercial perspective, lands in the worst shape would be taxed at the highest rate.

In 1927 only about 46,000 acres were in irrigation. District planners projected that another 77,000 acres would be convertible to crop production. An early farm economics study noted, "The construction of canals, drainage ditches, and dams is an expensive undertaking and the farmlands of the District are expected to pay approximately one-half the costs of reclamation."[4] That was the plan. The reality was very different. In some cases, taxes on the worst land were up to two and a half times higher than those on the best agricultural lands. Farmers had to pay whether they had the money *or* the intention to clear, level, and plow that land.[5] Notably, early versions of federal farm loans (crucial for commercial agriculture) weren't available in the Middle Rio Grande Valley throughout the 1920s and 1930s, as evaluations of loan repayment success were too low, Conservancy District liens too high, and water rights unadjudicated.[6] This left the valley's many subsistence and noncommercial farmers bearing unrealistic upfront labor and capital costs for turning what amounted to an old floodplain into a farmable ring around the growing city. They were expected to expand acreage—clear the bosque, level slopes, build on-farm ditches, flush the alkali salts, and amend the soils, all of which would involve substantial upfront investment.[7] It all combined into an unrealistic burden on the valley's thousands of predominantly Hispanic small farmers. Max Gutierrez lost every 1920s Conservancy District court case attached to his name, but this was the scenario he saw coming.

If the engineers' plans for repaying the Conservancy District's construction bonds in the initial financing model were risky at inception, this became more problematic when they almost immediately ran into the Great Depression. Given this shaky financial foundation, the District had difficulty selling the bonds to raise the capital needed for the flood control, drainage, and irrigation work contemplated in Joseph Burkholder's ambitious engineering plan. Almost immediately, the federal government stepped in with one of the early Depression-era New Deal tools. In 1932 the newly formed Reconstruction Finance Corporation (RFC) bought up most of the Conservancy District's construction bonds, which had yet to be sold.[8] It was cause for community celebration.[9] But the bonds still had to be repaid. The valley communities would have to raise the money somehow.

The Cloud of Tax Delinquencies

The escalating failures of the Conservancy District exposed the blind spots of the Progressive Era expertise employed to remake Albuquerque's relationship with its river. The failure was laid bare by a report by sociologist Hugh Calkins entitled *Reconnaissance Survey of Human Dependency on Resources in the Rio Grande Watershed*:

> When any agency or group of agencies undertakes a program of watershed conservation, a series of complex problems arise. Any such program necessarily involves an adjustment of two sets of relationships—those among soil and water and plant life, and those between all of these relationships and human activity.[10]

Calkins, working for the US Department of Agriculture, did something Burkholder, Rodey, and the rest of the boosters had not, making a careful study of the agricultural productivity and potential of the land and communities on the valley floor.

Calkins documented the seismic change that had come over the predominantly Hispanic subsistence farming culture on the valley floor with the creation of the Conservancy District. Families that had owned their land for generations, small subsistence plots, were being forced to change their relationship with the land and the river: "With the establishment of the Conservancy District in 1928, much of the rural population was rather precipitously injected into a commercial situation demanding a new type of adjustment in the use of irrigated land, a type which would be productive of high cash returns to meet new cash costs."[11]

The means of the force was the Conservancy District tax. It was not the only tax imposed to fund building a city. Roads and schools also imposed burdens, and tax delinquency related to a range of public services provided by the state and county (not solely the Conservancy District) significantly touched many Middle Valley groups in the Great Depression. But the Conservancy District levy especially hit small farmers. Calkins's economic analysis in 1936, when the Conservancy District was still in its infancy, was already stark in projecting sustained insolvency absent significant change. He found total delinquency of 42 percent for all tax levies (combined construction bond and maintenance levies) in 1936 for all dollar payments due, but 70 percent were due for private agricultural landowners.[12]

A year after Calkins's report, the threat to valley farmers came to a head as a December deadline for state action on the unpaid taxes loomed. Led by Liga Obrero, a Hispanic community organization, community leaders made their case in November 1937 to Gov. Clyde Tingley. Participants included the Middle Rio Grande Farmers Association, the Committee on Spanish American Affairs, the Middle Rio Grande Small Landowners Association, the Farm Bureau, and nine district ditch groups. Their petition was a poignant restatement of the economic and social reality Max Gutierrez had so clearly understood:[13]

> There are 9,349 tracts delinquent in Conservancy Taxes. These are owned by 4663 owners; 4190 of them are Spanish Americans and 473 are Anglo-Americans. Of the delinquent tracts, 85% of them are under 10 acres. Studies have shown that small 5- to 10-acre farms are the main source of livelihood for

> the farmers owning them. The farms are too small to produce the surplus crops which can be sold for cash, but they do supply the larger part of the food needs of the farmers, and in some cases a little cash. Such farms cannot pay taxes to the Conservancy District of $6 an acre. It was known at the time the Conservancy District was established these farms would never be able to pay the tax. The owners of these farms protested at the time, but their protests were ignored. No opportunity was given to vote on the Conservancy District or its financial obligations.

The following weeks saw a frenzy of litigation and negotiation as a December 6 tax sale loomed for many properties. On December 3, the Friday before the tax sale deadline, a District Court judge put the process on hold as state and federal officials scrambled to find a durable solution.[14] "Everything possible will be done to save the homes and farms of residents of the Middle Rio Grande Conservancy District," said Gov. Clyde Tingley.[15] While Conservancy District taxes, and therefore tax delinquencies, were found to be legal, the court blocked the convoluted process by which such delinquencies could lead to actual loss of land.[16] Thus, farmers could stay on their land, but with tax delinquency looming, the threat of dispossession and loss of title was always present.

As the 1930s closed, it was clear that a financing model based on the presumed benefits of reclaimed agricultural land would never achieve the needed acreage or revenue. The farmer and taxpayer protest movement pushed for change at the federal, state, and local levels. At the Conservancy District level, while the protestors' request for a change to an elected board didn't happen, maintenance assessments were reappraised in 1941. By then, suburban growth was emerging. From 1941 onward, annual Conservancy District reports began discussing increasing suburbanization pressures.[17] For those nearest to the metropolitan area's core, urban growth came with upward pressure on land values. But while farmers were not losing their land, tax delinquencies left a lien on their property and lingering uncertainty over land titles.

Initial state efforts to wash away tax debts were unsuccessful. Those efforts in 1940, under Gov. John Miles, included a request to Congress for federal relief for tax-delinquent farmers,[18] and a state legislative relief act to eliminate any further Conservancy District delinquency burden on uncultivated lands.[19] The state cooperated with the federal Reconstruction Finance Corporation to create a 1940s redemption and rehabilitation program for reestablishing clear titles.[20] With federal relief funds for land rehabilitation and loans to pay off back taxes, in addition to favorable delinquency relief terms on state and county taxes owed, thousands of Conservancy District landowners were able to remove the cloud hanging over their land. From 1939 to 1944, the RFC provided $585,000 in direct grants to over 3,000 participating Conservancy District landowners and $750,000 in loans to help pay back taxes. As part of the deal the state cut the landowners' state and county debt obligations by 50 percent. By 1944 clear title was redeemed on nearly 30,000 acres of land.[21] The program worked well, and variants remained in place for another decade.[22] The success helped keep small farmers on their land while allowing others the freedom to sell with clear titles. Importantly, since the growing hope was for the federal government to re-work the financing of the Conservancy District, it cleared the way for an even larger federal role in the valley.[23]

The Federal Presence Grows

Sorting the delinquency issues and avoiding confiscations cleared an essential obstacle for the federal takeover to come.[24] On the heels of floods in 1941 and 1942, the region's role in the World War II military effort helped underpin the drive for federal help. Seizing momentum, the Albuquerque boosters, with their Middle Rio Grande Flood Control Association, were lobbying for federal funding. The boosters produced glossy-for-the-times publications in the years following World War II, emphasizing the risks to New Mexico's atomic installations and noting that "interruption of these facilities by flood might mean a national disaster."[25]

Pushed by all these forces, the result, codified in the federal Flood Control Acts of 1944, 1948, and 1950, was the federal Middle Rio Grande Project, which brought together the US Bureau of Reclamation and the US Army Corps of Engineers. Still operational today, it was initially an estimated $95 million project, with the expectation that only about $16 million to $18 million would be reimbursable locally. The bailout was both physical and financial. A still ill-behaved Rio Grande would be further channelized, with improved levees and upstream dams to further reduce Middle Valley flood risk.

In the early 1950s, the federal government and local officials agreed that the Bureau of Reclamation would assume all Conservancy District debt obligations, with almost $6 million outstanding, and issue new debt obligations for additional levee and flood-control works and ditch system rehabilitation. In 1955 the US Congress appropriated money to pay off the Conservancy District's outstanding original bonds.[26] This federal rescue, born of the physical failures made so evident by the floods of 1941–1942 and the financial shortcomings of the institutional tools needed to fix them, would reshape the management of Albuquerque's Rio Grande through the twentieth century and beyond. Even with waves of federal projects and funding, the work of establishing a stable financial and governance structure remained unfinished. To make the financial structure work required taxing the urban residents of the valley floor. Over time, the aggregate local burden on the *non*-agricultural lands was raised significantly above 50 percent to make the financing work. This led to a new political struggle, as city residents wondered what they were getting for all that money. With increasing insistence, they asked for a democratic say in the Conservancy District's operations.

An Urban Burden

By the 1970s, the tension between the Conservancy District's historic irrigation system and a growing city was reaching a breaking point. The conflict came to a head in a rash of drownings in the irrigation ditches flowing through the city's midst. The Rio Grande, this time distributed in irrigation ditches rather than spilling out of its main channel, had again become a menace. That led to a deeper question: In urbanizing Albuquerque, what was the purpose of the Middle Rio Grande Conservancy District? Who should decide?

By the 1970s, urban property owners felt a fundamental unfairness in the financing structure, which left non-irrigators paying the largest share of the Conservancy District's costs. Farmers weren't happy either, feeling that non-irrigators didn't widely recognize flood protection provided by the Conservancy District and its federal partners. Further, while the aggregate financial burden on agricultural lands may have been roughly 25 percent of the Conservancy District's revenue, a smaller number of remaining farmers was increasingly bearing it, their rates rising as others left agriculture or converted their lands.[27]

The changing nature of the city played a role. Between the start of World War II and 1970, the population of urbanizing Albuquerque had more than quadrupled as the military-industrial complex, in the form of nuclear weapons research, design, and manufacturing, expanded at Kirtland Air Force Base and Sandia National Laboratories. If early acequia irrigation marked the first major reshaping of the river and its floodplain by growing communities, and the formation of the Conservancy District marked the second, by the 1970s, urban growth was reshaping Albuquerque's relationship with the Rio Grande for a third time. Subdivisions and homes were increasingly encroaching on the old ditches, changing the uses and values of the river and its distribution system.

While Albuquerque boomed, the rural counties that made up the rest of the Middle Rio Grande Conservancy District's valley terrain did not. The population of Socorro County, at the downstream end of the Middle Rio Grande Valley, shrank by 15 percent from 1940 to 1970. Geographically, the result was increasingly unbalanced. Albuquerque, with the bulk of the population but an ever-shrinking share of the valley's irrigated land, was responsible for roughly three-fourths of the Conservancy District's funding, most of which came from non-irrigators. Arguments concerning who had to pay, which had gone on in various ways since the 1920s, were stacked on top of questions of "Who has a say?" A Conservancy District board appointed by Second Judicial District judges rather than elected by voters left a lack of accountability.

Into that simmering conflict came two fundamental changes associated with Albuquerque's growing and changing urbanity. Community members increasingly valued the ditch network as an urban amenity, as green space in a hot, dry city. On the other hand, in some parts of the city, youngsters kept falling into the ditches and drowning.

City Edges

The value of the ditches and their peril was made clear in *The Rio Grande in the Albuquerque Metropolis*, commonly called the *City Edges* study, a community-driven report published in 1975.[28] *City Edges* argued, based on community surveys, that the valley's irrigation ditches should be embraced as community pathways. The river management, both the narrow strip between the levees and the wider ribbons of green created by the spiderweb of mains, drains, laterals, and old acequias, should be managed for recreation and nature preservation, not simply flood control and irrigation.[29]

The *City Edges* study described a city disconnected from its river. Gone was the flood menace and swamped landscape that had been a defining characteristic of Albuquerque's relationship with the Rio Grande as late as the 1920s. "Most people know the Rio Grande as something you look

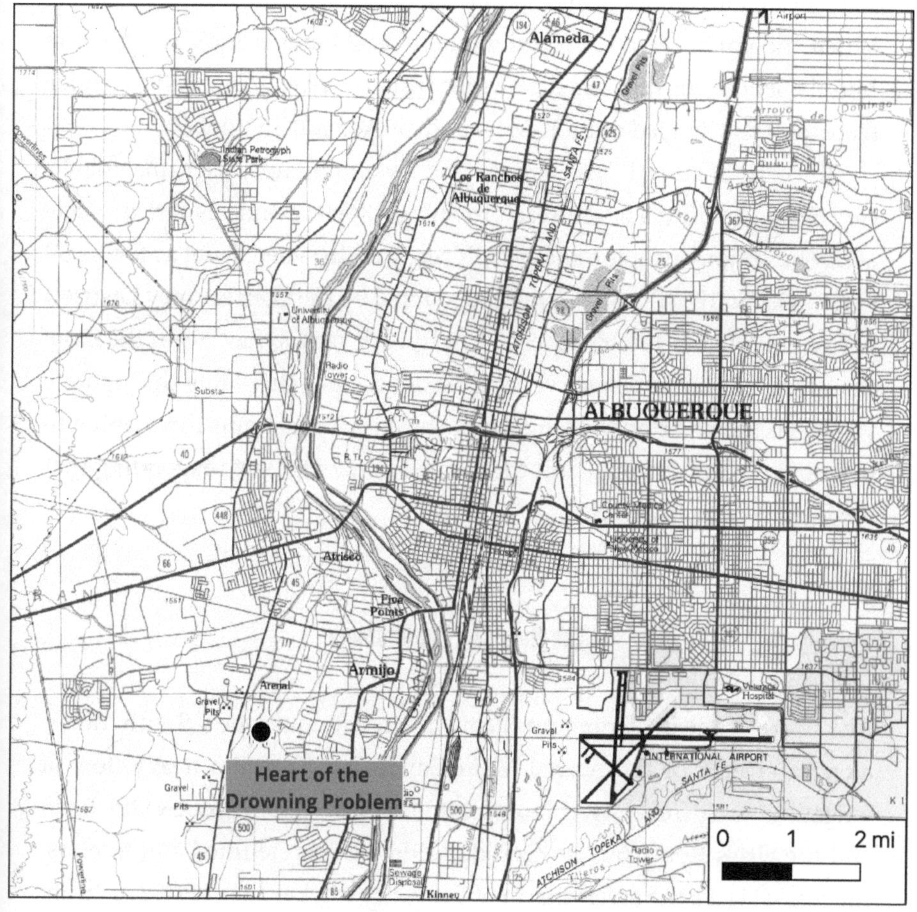

Map 9. Drowning in old irrigation ditches was a growing problem as Albuquerque's suburbs spread across the Rio Grande Valley floor. Base map by USGS, adapted by John Fleck.

at from inside a moving automobile on a bridge," the study concluded. When the study team surveyed students at Albuquerque's Washington Middle School, located less than a mile from the river, to identify riverside features, they singled out a K-Mart and an Ace Auto Supply.[30]

But with flood risk largely gone and swamping no longer imaginable, *City Edges* identified a new threat: drowning. Official estimates varied widely about how many people, mostly children, had drowned, from as few as 39 since 1959[31] to 110 (the official number offered by the Conservancy District) between 1959 and 1983.[32] Fences went up, but far too few, given the more than 1,000 miles of Conservancy District ditches threading through the valley. Politicians traded blame, with the city at one point threatening to put up fences on its own and the Conservancy District responding that it would tear them down.[33]

The Heart of the Problem

The heart of the drowning problem was in Albuquerque's South Valley, along a stretch of the Arenal Main Canal that carried a heavy flow of irrigation water from a river crossing adjacent to Albuquerque's Old Town and the city's Route 66 Rio Grande bridge. Concrete-lined and treeless, the Arenal lacks the green charm of the valley ditches the *City Edges* study discussed. But time and again, it was attractive to valley kids looking for a place to cool off in the summer heat.

In the summer of 1972, Albino Escamilla, who lived just 800 feet from one of the ditches fed by the Arenal, filed a class-action lawsuit trying to force the Middle Rio Grande Conservancy District to fence ditches through residential areas. Escamilla told the story of an infant falling from an unprotected bridge into a ditch and being swept downstream for fifty feet before being rescued and given mouth-to-mouth resuscitation.[34] In addition to fencing, Escamilla's lawsuit contained a second demand. He challenged the governance structure of the Conservancy District, calling

Figure 25. Concrete-lined, treeless, and far from the scenic postcard ditches of Albuquerque, the Arenal Canal in Albuquerque's South Valley was at the heart of the drowning controversy of the 1960s and 1970s. Photograph by John Fleck.

for an elected rather than an appointed board "on the one-man, one-vote principle."[35]

The neighborhood at the heart of the controversy offers a case study in the rural-to-suburban transition made possible by the creation of the Middle Rio Grande Conservancy District and Albuquerque's changing relationship with the Rio Grande. In the early decades of the twentieth century, it was a mix of sand, sagebrush, and alkali near a secondary Rio Grande flood channel. It was one of the areas of the valley floor vastly improved by the remaking of the Rio Grande's hydrologic system. Procopio Armijo, a farmer, stockman, and one of the area's political leaders, had actively advocated for flood control, drainage, and reclamation a half century before. In 1918 he joined Aldo Leopold, Max Gutierrez, and other community leaders in one of the first major political pushes to create the Middle Rio Grande Conservancy District.[36]

The land in the area can be counted as successfully "reclaimed" by the arrival of flood control, drainage, and more reliable irrigation water, transitioning to farmland through the 1930s and into the 1940s. But from the beginning, it was becoming clear that the land, close to the city and connected by two bridges, would be more valuable as housing. Public records show parcels quickly being turned over for subdivision, even in the 1930s.

In the years after World War II, as the federal Bureau of Reclamation took over the Conservancy District, Albuquerque's population boomed, and the tempo of suburbanization quickened. The predominantly Hispanic farming families who had been eking out a living farming while they worked jobs in town began selling some of their lands, and subdivisions spread. Five and ten houses at a time, old farm fields became smaller plots and tiny housing tracts. In the mid-1930s, right before Conservancy District assessments came due after the initial moratorium, Procopio Armijo's neighbors sold a thirty-one-acre agricultural plot that the buyer split into seven smaller ones.[37] Entering the 1950s, Procopio Armijo was still irrigating land in the area. By 1958 he and his wife were selling lots in the Procopio Armijo Addition.[38]

From the neighborhood around those tracts, the youngsters Albino Escamilla was trying to protect in the 1960s and 1970s were heading out to play in the ditches.

Drownings, Fences, and the Push for Change

The 1967 request from Raymond Garcia, a rookie Democratic state representative, was modest. Could the state conduct a study about the possibility of creating a state park in Albuquerque's South Valley for its 65,000 residents? Garcia asked in a June letter to Gov. David Cargo. Perhaps something along the river somewhere between Old Town Bridge and Isleta Pueblo? He noted the absence of public recreation in the area and said he would support state funding.[39]

Born in Albuquerque, educated in Albuquerque schools and the Western Business College, and a thirty-five-year-old father of five, the energetic and ambitious Garcia worked for the Sandia Corporation and was the owner-operator of a South Valley print shop with his wife. He was a public entrepreneur in the tradition of Aldo Leopold, Max Gutierrez, and Pablo Abeita, seeing his community's needs and proposing institutional innovations to meet them. As a rookie state legislator he introduced a sweeping civil rights bill. In addition to working as a civil rights advocate, he would go on to promote drug abuse education, economic development, and funding the movie industry, of which he was an early supporter.[40]

Garcia's push for a park was his first step toward changing the community's relationship with the Rio Grande. But his lasting impact on Albuquerque was a change he pushed for in the structure of the institutions—the rules—governing the community's relationship with the Rio Grande. With Garcia as a prime mover, a legislative caucus soon formed to push for a vast park along the river.[41] Garcia introduced a funding proposal for the initial study.[42] The park Garcia first advocated for in 1967 was finally created in the 1980s. But more important was the change of the governance of the Middle Rio Grande Conservancy District, the agency formed to manage Albuquerque's relationship with the river, from an appointed to an elected board.

Max Gutierrez's 1920s plea that the people on the valley floor, who paid for the Conservancy District and lived with the consequences of its work, have a direct say on how the agency was governed, had found a champion in Garcia. And Garcia's advocacy started, in significant measure, with his response to the concerns of South Valley residents about a growing urban problem—neighborhood kids drowning in the valley's irrigation ditches.

In April 1967 it was sixteen-month-old Bobby Scott. Scott lived in a subdivision built near the river on land reclaimed from an old swamp after the Conservancy District's construction of the riverside drain. Scott was playing on the banks of the riverside drain when he fell in. Rescuers found him a half hour later, a mile downstream, floating face down in the water.[43] Two days later, elected officials pleaded with community leaders to pressure the Conservancy District's appointed board to fence the ditches. "The Conservancy District has the authority to cooperate if this board will act," the county's Democratic Party chairman said at a community meeting. The Conservancy District's board did nothing and District officials insisted drownings and fencing to prevent them were not the government agency's responsibility.[44]

The following year, the question of drowning and fencing emerged in the legislature during a debate over the latest in a long series of attempts to switch to an elected rather than appointed board for the Conservancy District.[45] The bill's backers pointed to the District's failure to fence ditches. "What do fences have to do with whether the board is appointed or elected?" asked Max Coll, a Republican representative from rural Chaves County. "What we are discussing is the responsiveness of appointed officials rather than elected officials," responded Bernalillo County Democrat Richard B. Edwards.[46]

Raymond Garcia's Successful Push

The following year, 1968, Garcia stepped up his parks push, calling for horse and bicycle trails, along with tennis courts, baseball fields, and barbecue pits along a forty-mile stretch of the Rio Grande. "This would be one of the most attractive scenes in the whole southwest," he said when he unveiled the plan.[47] As with the drowning problem, the park discussion quickly devolved into an argument about Conservancy District governance. In pushing the park proposal, Garcia and his legislative allies also suggested another crucial step—legislation requiring elections for the Conservancy District's board members.[48]

Garcia got $50,000 in the 1968 legislative session to study the park, and its pursuit became the centerpiece of his reelection campaign.[49] Legislation to mandate elections for the Middle Rio Grande Conservancy District's board died in 1973, but in 1974 Garcia finally found a formula to pull off a political feat that had seemed out of reach for half a century.

For a proposal that had failed many times before, shifting from an appointed to an elected board faced surprisingly little opposition in 1974. Raymond Garcia and the other backers of the shift had built the necessary political support and used a novel tactic. Rather than direct action by the legislature to change the Conservancy Act and require elections, Garcia proposed a constitutional amendment requiring any government agency with taxing authority to be governed by a board elected by those being taxed. The amendment's wording was general: "No tax or assessment of any kind shall be levied by any political subdivision whose enabling legislation does not provide for an elected governing authority." But as the debate commenced, it was understood that the Middle Rio Grande Conservancy District was the only government agency to which the change applied.

This approach showed a mastery of New Mexico laws and legislative process. In even-number years such as 1974, the legislature is only permitted to act on the state budget and specific items on a list submitted to them by the governor. The only exception is constitutional amendments, which the legislature can consider without being on the governor's list. Unable to convince Gov. Bruce King to include their proposal on his list of approved projects, which suggested the rural Democratic governor's opposition to the idea, a legislative change in the statute, the path that had failed time and time again, was no longer open to them. So, they structured it as a constitutional amendment.[50] This shifted responsibility for any change from legislators to the voters of the entire state of New Mexico. But it also created a risk. Once they got it through the legislative gauntlet, they had to go before the voters. Thus, Albuquerque's relationship with the Rio Grande and the river's flow was again filtered through law, politics, and rules.

While Raymond Garcia may have been motivated by a desire to help his constituents deal with drownings, the need for ditch safety, and his desire to rethink the community's relationship with the Rio Grande by creating a park, the constitutional question landed in a far more fertile field. The evocative phrase "taxation without representation" came up repeatedly. "Elected groups," he said on the day he introduced the bill, "are more responsive to the people."[51] Garcia's bill swiftly passed the state House of Representatives in early February on a 54–5 vote.[52] Within a week, the full Senate overrode opposition from the Senate Conservation Committee and approved the bill 28–11. With that, Gov. Bruce King's opposition was rendered irrelevant. Unlike statutory legislation, proposed constitutional amendments don't need the governor's signature. They go straight to the people.

The question was placed on the statewide ballot for November 1974: Should the Middle Rio Grande Conservancy District board be directly elected? Less than a month after the Senate approved sending the measure to the state's voters, Garcia announced his candidacy for the statewide office of lieutenant governor, noting the Conservancy District bill as one of his most important legislative accomplishments.[53]

Who Has a Say, and Who Has to Pay?

At the debate's heart was the question of benefit. With flood control and drainage in New Mexico's Middle Rio Grande seen by many as a solved problem by the 1970s, urban critics thought they were being asked to subsidize irrigation in the rural areas outside the city's core. Bill Hume, an *Albuquerque Journal* reporter who served decades later as a water policy advisor to New Mexico Gov. Bill Richardson, put it this way in early 1974 as the legislature was considering the question: "The system of assessments amounts to a farm subsidy program visited directly on the non-farm landowners in the Conservancy District. The farmers doubtless need the subsidy, and it's probably in the public interest that it should continue, but its burden should be more widely spread."[54]

In a newspaper photo, longtime Conservancy District critic Joseph Gallegos, standing beside Raymond Garcia, points to a poster board with a large pie chart. His finger lands on the number "68%"—the share of the Conservancy District's tax burden falling on the residents of Bernalillo County. The most urban of the district's counties, receiving the least benefit from the Conservancy District's irrigation works, was paying two-thirds of the costs.[55] Since 1959 a two-tiered tax structure funded the Conservancy District's operations.[56] Larger landowners, those who irrigated five acres or more, were appropriately called "Class A" property owners. They paid a flat per-acre rate calibrated by the district to provide 25 percent of its revenue. Smaller landowners—"Class B"—paid the rest via an ad valorem tax proportionate to the property's assessed value. Class A properties, paying just a quarter of the cost, were predominantly rural and agricultural. Class B properties, generally urban, footed three-quarters of the bill.

But while the tax structure placed the bulk of the costs on the urban property owners, the governance was flipped. The rules required four of the seven judicially appointed board members (resident landowners) to earn 75 percent of their livelihood from agriculture. The rules explicitly gave farmers the legal authority to tax non-farmers to subsidize agriculture. Those being taxed had little say. Critics called the whole structure profoundly unfair. At its heart, it was an argument about the relationship between the Rio Grande, the city that had grown up astride it, and the government agency—the Conservancy District—that had made that city possible. "With the taming of the Rio Grande," one valley resident argued, "the Conservancy District can no longer use 'flood control' as an excuse for an exorbitant tax assessment." "Reclamation," the goal set out half a century before, had been accomplished, he argued. "This leaves irrigation as the only excuse for many small landowners to foot the bill for a few large landowners. This small landowner is subsidizing the large farmers and landowners."[57]

For the Conservancy District's defenders, it appeared to be an existential threat. They looked to the history of the Sandia Conservancy District, where a shift from an appointed to an elected board in the late 1950s had caused the agency's collapse.[58] The Sandia Conservancy District was a post–World War II aborted attempt to protect Albuquerque from floods caused by summer rains across the city's rapidly developing uplands. Much like the Middle Rio Grande Conservancy District in the 1920s, the Sandia Conservancy District was created to support the community's pursuit of federal water funding. Urban flooding across the heights posed an entirely different hydrologic problem for the growing city, necessitating a new governance structure to manage it. But much like its older sibling, the Middle Rio Grande Conservancy District, the newborn Sandia Conservancy District immediately became embroiled in the same arguments over governance and taxation?[59]

Interlocking lawsuits and legislation in 1958–1959 led to the disbanding of the Sandia Conservancy District's appointed board to be replaced by an elected board.[60] The agency's opponents won all five seats on its newly created board, and governance quickly devolved into chaos. By 1962 the Sandia Conservancy District had been dissolved, never to participate in building any actual flood control works.[61]

The *Albuquerque Journal*, voice of the establishment, fulminated about the proposed constitutional amendment, accusing its backers of attempting to "torpedo the operations of the Middle Rio Grande Conservancy District, which embraces the fruitful valley areas of Sandoval, Bernalillo, Valencia and Socorro Counties." The *Journal* falsely claimed the Conservancy District "has restored 80,000 acres of water-logged lands to full agricultural production."[62] The *Journal*'s argument did not sit well with one resident of the South Valley neighborhood at the center of the wave of drownings:

> "Politically motivated disaster," "pernicious danger," "subversive motive," and more one would think you were writing about revolution instead of elective government.[63]

On November 5, 1974, the voters of New Mexico spoke, but barely. After fifty years of near-continuous efforts by various parties pursuing such a change, Constitutional Amendment 2 passed by a vote of 62,103 to 62,083. Just twenty votes—less than one-fiftieth of a percent of those cast—determined who would have a say over managing New Mexico's most important river.

One Person, One Vote, and Exceptions

Special water districts come in all shapes and sizes, governed by a dizzying array of rules. The Middle Rio Grande Conservancy District is just one. If climate change is writ large in water, then if we want to understand our capacity for adaptation, there is justification for focusing on such districts. While water governance agencies have often operated behind the scenes, increasing water scarcity may change that. One significant trend is the movement toward greater *direct democracy* in our water governance agencies,[64] and the 1970s brought that to the Middle Valley. Sort of.

In a variety of landmark rulings, the US Supreme Court has consistently applied the principle of one person, one vote, at all levels of government,[65] albeit with limited exceptions. The basis for one person, one vote, in United States law is the equal protection clause of the Fourteenth Amendment to the US Constitution, as passed and ratified in the aftermath of the Civil War. When challenged, the courts have ruled that there is no presumption of an exception and that a state political subdivision must have a compelling interest to justify any discriminatory classification. The burden of proof is on defending the exception. Courts have recognized a notable strand of exceptions for the case of special district water resource agencies (e.g., irrigation, drainage, watershed, and conservancy districts). As one legal scholar summarizes:

> Decisions that apply or refuse to apply the one person, one vote rule to special purpose units of government raise major policy problems. For example, while democratic government demands equal representation for all voters, local governments need flexibility to include only concerned voters on changing local issues. Another problem arises because special purpose units are often related to natural resource management; the government of special purpose units may greatly impact environmental and agricultural units.[66]

Of special interest, then, are justifications for deviation from the principal in the case of multipurpose special water districts, where the beneficial purposes and their relative weights have significantly changed through time, both statutorily and on the landscape. Climate change and its effects on a river system only exacerbate such questions. Beyond scholarly abstraction, the Middle Rio Grande Conservancy District in 1974 raised all these questions.

"It Is Difficult to Develop Economically in a Marsh"

With state voter approval of the 1974 constitutional amendment, backers of elections for the Conservancy District faced what has been called the paradox of success. Like the proverbial dog that caught the car, they had to figure out what to do with it. They quickly learned that democracy is never easy. While the amendment required a shift to elections for the Middle Rio Grande Conservancy District, the details were left to the New Mexico legislature to answer two critical questions. How would the seats on the newly elected board be geographically distributed among the Middle Valley's urban and rural residents? And who would be eligible to vote—property owners or all registered voters? These were crucial changes to the rules by which the communities of New Mexico's Middle Rio Grande Valley would manage their relationship with the river flowing through their midst.

If the first half century of the Middle Rio Grande Conservancy District's existence had been about the existential struggle to manage flood control, drainage, and irrigation to enable the growth of a city—and to figure out how to pay for it—the next half century would be about the community agreeing to the desired future conditions of its relationship with the river. The problems that brought the original advocacy coalition together, however uneasily, in the early years of the twentieth century, had been solved. With the infrastructure in place the challenges of flood control, drainage, and irrigation were shifting by the mid-1970s from the creation of infrastructure to its maintenance. But that left Albuquerque and the surrounding communities with new and evolving questions. Was the Rio Grande no longer a menace, now simply a water supply canal? Were the irrigation ditches meant to supply water for commercial agriculture, or should the ditches be recreational amenities—walking and cycling trails, long linear parks threading through the city? Should the Rio Grande between the levees be an urban amenity like a community park? Should the river be kept as a sort of wild nature in the city's midst?

And what should be the relationship between the city and the rural expanse beyond it, up and down the valley? Was it reasonable for urban residents to continue disproportionately subsidizing irrigation water for their rural neighbors?[67] For what goals, and to what end? The objectives of those public entrepreneurs who gathered at the Commercial Club in 1919 (Pablo Abeita, Max Gutierrez, Aldo Leopold, and the others) had largely been met. But the community continued to wrestle with a central *evolutionary* question of the type laid out by the institutional scholar Elinor Ostrom: How would the Rio Grande management regime evolve in the face of a changing river and a changing community?

The 1975 legislative debates over details of Conservancy District board representation and elections started from the premise that the urban residents paying most of the Conservancy District's total costs would also hold most of the power. Bernalillo County, the heart of the Albuquerque metropolitan area, was given three of the seven seats on the board, with the rural counties of Sandoval, Valencia, and Socorro getting one seat each. The seventh seat was to be held by an "at large" representative from any of the four counties. It was presumed that urban candidates would have the best chance at winning that seat, meaning that under the new system, the urban areas could potentially control the Conservancy District, a shift from the old rules that required four of the seven seats to be held by commercial farmers.

Raymond Garcia, no longer in the legislature, pushed for giving all registered voters a say in the election of a Conservancy District board[68] but lost to those who argued that the "taxation without representation" argument meant voting should be restricted to the people paying the taxes: the property owners. The resulting framework passed the legislature with little debate, and Gov. Jerry Apodaca signed it in April 1975.[69]

What followed confirmed the worst fears of election opponents. Far from settling on a path forward for the Conservancy District in response to the changes sweeping the valley, the democratic process created a new forum for bitter battles over the same questions that had dogged the management of the community's relationship with its river. The drowning problem, despite little action by the newly elected board other than public education, waned. A widespread community public education effort and changes in how youngsters played seem to have stemmed the tide. By the 1980s, drownings were declining. Videos, school presentations, and the ever-present drumbeat of the slogan "Ditches are Deadly" had their effect.[70] But while drownings declined, the tension over who would pay the Conservancy District's costs merely shifted to a new forum. No longer guaranteed seats on the board through the rules of its members' appointment, commercial-farming interests turned to the electoral process and won seats that way instead. Flood control and drainage were abstractions to a democratic process, while irrigation water was a tangible motivator to get candidates to run and voters to the polls.[71] "The only people who were elected were those who used water or had a vested interest in the district," explained Jim Baca,[72] who served as the District's general manager for less than a year, pushed for reform, and was fired.[73]

Baca's brief tenure, from October 1988 to July 1989, illustrates the chaos of an agency the press labeled "trouble-plagued."[74] Scandals included two board members being improperly compensated $5,000 each by the District for their legal fees when they sued their own agency and another board member charged with having Conservancy District employees install a culvert on his property so his daughter could move a mobile home.[75] Amid the chaos, the basic work of flood control, drainage, and irrigation continued. Farmers and non-farmers benefited from the levees and drainage ditches; farmers still got their water, "and to outdoor enthusiasts, the banks of the district's ditches serve as horse riding trails and walkways through the tangled maze of cottonwood trees."[76]

But despite one of the key motivations behind the push for elections fifteen years before, by 1989 the share paid by non-farmers for the Conservancy District's operations had risen to 85 percent. The farmers, led by Socorro County alfalfa grower Corky Herkenhoff, an elected district board member, defended the arrangement. "The perception is that the farmer is getting rich at the expense of the other ratepayers," Herkenhoff said. "As profit margins go, we make about one-half to 1 percent profit a year. That's pretty skinny."[77] Farmers weren't happy with evolving payment terms, including a charge for irrigation water service. For what appears to be the first time in the district's history, irrigators were charged a toll per acre for irrigation water service beginning in 1987.[78] It would take nearly another decade of battling over financing and more legislative change before the modern structure of a per-acre water service charge and more standardized ad valorem property tax assessments for all parcels in the district were in place.[79]

But amid the late 1980s debates and legislative hearings over financing the future of the Conservancy District, New Mexico's longtime top state water official, Steve Reynolds, hearkened back to the reason for the District creation in defending the heavy urban share. In providing flood control and drainage, keeping the Rio Grande's menaces away, the Conservancy District provided crucial but largely invisible benefits to Albuquerque's continued management of its relationship with the Rio Grande. "A number of those within the district do not fully understand they are benefited by drainage and flood protection. The district may have some difficulty convincing them that they should have some interest in that," Reynolds said. "But it is difficult to develop economically in a marsh."[80]

Interlude: September

In early September 2023 the rains seemed to arrive on cue as the Middle Rio Grande Conservancy District board of directors listened to Anne Marken's monthly report. Inside the district's Barelas headquarters building, Marken again urged prayers for rain, while outside, showers danced across the Middle Valley.

The combination of rain and some clever use of the water management rules had kept the Rio Grande's main channel flowing intact—but

Figure 26. In a riverbed left dry by Rio Grande management decisions, opportunistic plants wasted no time colonizing the river's sandy remains. Photograph by Brennan Davis.

barely—through Albuquerque despite the hot, dry summer. The Conservancy District took water saved by paying irrigators to fallow fields and added it to the river at crucial points where wasteways returned irrigation flows to the river. Water managers nervously monitored conditions, hiring college students on bicycles to make daily surveys of areas most at risk of drying. With the targeted addition of water imported via the San Juan-Chama Project from the Colorado River Basin, the river continued to flow.

While the river limped by in its main channel, the valley's irrigators struggled. You could see it on the alfalfa fields of the old Tobacco Farms area in Albuquerque's South Valley—still noticeably green, but satellite data showed them drier than any September in recent years.

A bonus supply of water imported from the Colorado River Basin through the San Juan-Chama Project's diversion dams and tunnels had helped through the summer, but that water had run out in late August, Marken explained to the Conservancy District's board. She promised that the Conservancy District's crews would grab any runoff they could from September rains, diverting it to provide at least a little water for irrigators. "I will encourage everyone," she said, "to continue praying for rain."

CHAPTER 8

THE OXBOW

"Slopped upon your reception room floor is a broth containing catfish, bass, carp, crayfish, muskrats, and ducks," the 1976 note to the Middle Rio Grande Conservancy District said. "This action serves to inform you and your bureaucracy exactly how the entire Oxbow area now smells as a result of your arrogant decision to interrupt the life-waters of the last sweet-water marsh remaining in the Albuquerque area." The note was signed "Eco Warrior."[1]

The "arrogant decision" to which Eco Warrior referred was the Middle Rio Grande Conservancy District's action days earlier to divert water from its Corrales Drain, which had been flowing into what had come to be known as the Oxbow, a fifty-acre remnant wetland at the foot of a bluff on the Rio Grande's west bank in the heart of Albuquerque. Oxbows were once common in New Mexico's Middle Rio Grande Valley. But by the mid-1970s, this oxbow was Albuquerque's last. It had become *the Oxbow*, and a growing environmental consciousness in the community converged there as the Middle Rio Grande Conservancy District tried to begin draining it in service of water management "efficiency."

At the heart of the conflict was a question of community values. To water managers, water flowing into the Oxbow was wasted, lost to the "beneficial use" that characterized water use in New Mexico law and practice. They planned to drain it once and for all. To many members of the community, that plan represented values gone astray. As found in the Oxbow, nature was beneficial in and of itself.

Figure 27. A view from the Oxbow. Photograph by John Fleck.

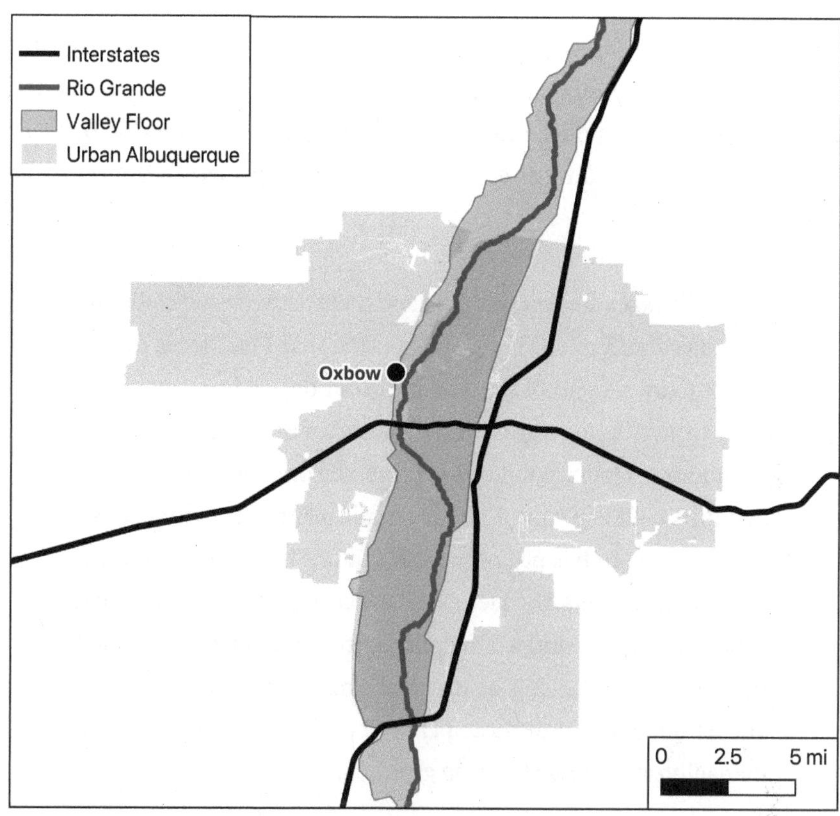

Map 10. The Oxbow: nature in the heart of a city. Map by John Fleck.

Throughout the twentieth century, environmental consciousness had been a part of Albuquerque's struggle with a sometimes unmanageable Rio Grande. For a young Aldo Leopold, writing in 1919, "environmental consciousness" meant duck hunting, and he recognized the tension between then-current ideas about the environment and the project of drainage and flood control:

> Petty squabbles are reported here and there between gun clubs and drainage districts. . . . The only solution that I can see is for the public to own a part of the ducking grounds—at least enough of them to give the average citizen a chance for a reasonable amount of shooting. Under public ownership, the drainage question, for instance, could be solved on the simple principle of highest use. If a certain marsh is not needed as a public hunting ground, but is needed for farms, then let it be drained. On the other hand, if it is near a large city and will furnish more citizens with recreation than hogs or corn, let it be excluded from the drainage district, and let the public bear the expense of acquiring, developing and managing as a public hunting grounds.[2]

Those conflicts did not disappear as the Middle Rio Grande Conservancy District transformed the river and its floodplain in the following decades. Leopold's "principle of highest use" was primarily settled in favor of agriculture and urban growth. What ducking grounds remained were relegated to state game and fish reserves and federal wildlife areas in the southern reach of the Middle Rio Grande, far downstream from the city.

In the heart of Albuquerque levees and drains created a sharp boundary between city and river. The urban water park of Conservancy Beach, developed in the early 1930s, replaced the old swimming holes at the Rio Grande's edge. City parks—including those Leopold helped create—became the dominant public green space. Among them is the City of Albuquerque's Rio Grande Park, which grew out of a 1917 proposal by Leopold and came to be even as the Conservancy District was remaking the city's relationship with the river. But by the 1970s, the community's understanding of the "principle of highest use" was evolving. The political struggle over the future of the Oxbow embodied that evolution.

The amount of water was negligible. Evaporation off the Oxbow's open water, and the transpiration from its plants, was likely less than two hundred acre-feet per year, a bit more than a similar-sized alfalfa field, and about the same as the water used for the trees and lawns of just fifty homes in the Village of Los Ranchos, the affluent neighborhood just across the river.[3]

Two days after Eco Warrior dumped the slop bucket, environmental groups converged on the Oxbow to take a stand. They "camped in the right of way," blocking bulldozers and draglines—the same kind of ditch-digging equipment that forty-five years before had dug the great drains that completely reorganized the hydrologic system of the Middle Rio Grande Valley floor. This time, the draglines represented a Conservancy District attempt to drain the valley's last swamp.

Just as had happened when Max Gutierrez and the other farmers blocked draglines in Los Chavez, Duranes, and Sandia Pueblo, the environmental activists represented a community objecting to the Conservancy District's attempt to remake the Rio Grande and the communities' relationship with it without their consent. In both cases, the draglines were severing the Rio Grande from communities and landscapes around it about which people cared. It was a clear example of how the Rio Grande is not merely a hydrologic system but a social-hydrologic one. Human connections to the river, through community irrigation ditches in the 1930s and a rare remaining "natural" wetland in the 1970s, were crucial.

In the 1930s, it was farmers angry that their water, land, and therefore their lives were being reorganized by a political machine bent on changing their relationship with the Rio Grande without their permission—and then, to compound the hurt, sticking them with the bill. In the 1970s, a parallel problem was taking shape. By then, it had long become clear that irrigated agriculture could never pay for the Conservancy District system draining farmers' land and providing them with water. By then, property taxes from non-irrigators supported a supermajority of the District's budget. Again, the question of who would foot the bill and how those people's values might be represented was central to Albuquerque's relationship with the Rio Grande.

Rising environmental consciousness and a booming population drove the change in the 1970s. Greater Albuquerque's population grew sevenfold, from about 45,000 when the Conservancy District was formed in 1930 to more than 300,000 in the 1970s. The flood risk, the swamping, and the belief in the need for a belt of commercial agriculture around the growing city were largely gone. The Conservancy District—the institutional arrangement created to mediate that relationship—would have to adapt.

Marjorie Van Cleave and the Path to the Oxbow

To understand the story of the Oxbow in the 1970s, we must return to the enthusiasm of the 1930s, as Albuquerque's relationship with the Rio Grande was changed quickly and dramatically as the levees and drains went in.

The change in the ecosystem was little noticed at the time. But it was noticed. It would be a mistake to think about the natural system of New Mexico's Middle Rio Grande Valley as a stable tabula rasa upon which human changes were applied. Ecosystems are constantly changing, and humans have been a significant part of that change for millennia.[4] Beginning long before Spanish colonizers arrived with their ideas about irrigation, farming, and community, Pueblo Native communities cleared land, planted crops, and manipulated water to grow food.[5] The ecological and hydrological alteration accelerated with the arrival of a Spanish agricultural political economy, emphasizing more intensive cropping. Increased irrigation upstream, overgrazing of upland watersheds, and deforestation as early communities cut trees for timber and fuel added to the changes by the 1700s, leading to a shallowing and widening of the river's increasingly meandering path through the Middle Rio Grande Valley.[6]

While noteworthy, those changes were modest compared to what happened with the construction of levees and drains by the Middle Rio Grande Conservancy District in the early 1930s. The lakes and swamps that were such a problem for city builders hosted rich and dynamic wetland ecosystems—cattails, sedges, rush, and watercress, all fringed by willows, cottonwoods, salt cedar, and Russian olives (the latter two non-native plants long established in the valley). Wet meadows and marshes dotting the valley provided the valley's richest and most extensive plant communities.

Much of what we know about those changes results from remarkable work in the 1930s by a young University of New Mexico graduate student named Marjorie Van Cleave. Her thesis, "Vegetative Changes in the Middle Rio Grande Conservancy District,"[7] languished for six decades after its publication. In the gendered roles of Van Cleave's day, the young scientist worked briefly as an Albuquerque schoolteacher, married in an elaborate society wedding, and disappeared from the public stage.[8] She was a child of the urban elite of modernizing Albuquerque: her father played bridge with Aldo Leopold, and the two invested in the Home Building and Loan Association, a vital piece of the financial infrastructure of the growing city the public entrepreneurs like Leopold had helped create. Between her duties organizing Alpha Chi Omega sorority dances while a UNM student, the ecological fieldwork she accomplished was some of the most consequential for our understanding of the changes to the hydrological and ecological systems of the Rio Grande as Albuquerque remade the river.[9]

Rediscovered in the 1990s by environmental scientists trying to make sense of the changes they saw in the Rio Grande ecosystem, Van Cleave's thesis was a careful attempt to catalog—from the perspective of an ecosystem rather than a city—what happened when the Conservancy District drained Albuquerque's swamps. Van Cleave meticulously cataloged the ecosystem across a range of wetland habitats maintained by flooding and the shallow aquifer: small lakes, marshes, wet meadows, grass-woodland bosque on the meadows' high spots, and the cottonwood-willow forest. While the soggy landscape may have been unsuitable for human use, plants like cattails, sedges, watercress, duckweed, watermilfoil, and salt grass happily took up residence in the rich and complex ecosystem. With drainage, the lakes and swamps disappeared almost immediately, Van Cleave found, and the riverside vegetation quickly declined.[10]

The drains and levees not only disconnected the human community from the river. They also wholly remade, in an instant, the water-dependent ecosystem of the valley floor.

Jetty Jacks

In the decades that followed, as we have seen, the failings of the project of flood control, drainage, and irrigation became increasingly apparent. The first failing was institutional—the community's inability to settle on a financial structure to fund the work needed to manage its relationship with the Rio Grande. The second failure, which flowed from the first, was hydrologic. Two years of flooding in 1941 and 1942, the result of huge snowpacks and rapid spring melts, tested to the breaking point the levees the Conservancy District's draglines had thrown up flanking the river's main channel a decade before and swamped the District's irrigation canals.

In the 1950s, the hydrologic failure was drought. As the Rio Grande slowed to a trickle through Albuquerque, there was too little water for farmers in the Middle Valley and too little to send downstream to meet New Mexico's obligations under the interstate Rio Grande Compact to farmers in Southern New Mexico and Texas.

As we have seen, the federal government, primarily the Bureau of Reclamation, focused on two things when it stepped in to provide the influx of money and hydrologic management the valley so desperately needed. Financially, it offered a way to permanently end the threat that valley farmers would lose their land because of Conservancy taxes. On the hydrologic side, it planned to remake the Rio Grande again.

Figure 28. Jetty jacks, installed in the 1950s to contain the Rio Grande, remind us of a river channel that was contained by engineering. Photograph by John Fleck.

The language the Bureau of Reclamation used to describe its proposed plan for the Rio Grande provides insight into their thinking. In the 1947 report laying the groundwork for the federal government's Middle Rio Grande Project, the agency's engineers outlined the construction of a flood-control dam network on the major upstream tributaries of the Middle Rio Grande. They proposed a plan for what they labeled "channel rectification." To "rectify" is to "restore to a normal or proper condition; to set right."[11] Much like the agency's name—"Reclamation," or to "reclaim"—the language implies a vision of nature where human engineering corrects the flaws of the natural world. The agency viewed the meander of an old oxbow, which slows down the Rio Grande, allows sediments to drop out and raise the riverbed, and spreads the water out to evaporate, as a mistake to be corrected. It took more than a decade of politics and planning, but by the spring of 1959 the Bureau of Reclamation was ready to open bids on the project. Its engineers explained that they proposed to "train" the river to follow the "right" path; "to follow a set channel . . . instead of meandering almost at will."[12]

Their plan involved carving out a straightened channel six hundred feet wide, laying lines of "jetty jacks" along its bank lines—tangles of sixteen-foot steel beams so named because they look like children's toy jacks—to capture sediment and anchor the river's banks.[13] Aerial photos from late summer of 1959 show the result in the river stretch adjacent to the oxbow. Reclamation crews had dug a new channel through what had once been bosque and sand flats. The old meander was stranded, with lines of jetty jacks crossing the old oxbow to help ensure the river would never reclaim its old path.[14]

The project, especially the installation of the jetty jacks, completed the hydrologic and ecological alteration ably documented by Marjorie Van Cleave when the Middle Rio Grande Conservancy District began remaking the Rio Grande a quarter-century before. Angling through the floodplain between the levees and the narrow central river channel, the lines of jacks slowed water, allowing sediments to drop out. The resulting changes in the narrow riparian corridor alongside the Rio Grande were dramatic. Large areas of newly stabilized soil were ideal habitats for trees that once struggled against the river's annual floods. The strip of land was rapidly colonized by trees, including native cottonwoods, willows, and non-native salt cedar and Russian olive, similar in some respects to the old valley floor ecosystem Van Cleave had documented, but now concentrated along the narrow human-made river channel rather than spread out across the valley floor.[15] The Bureau of Reclamation's plan also included improvements to the main Conservancy District irrigation canals so that in low-flow years, managers could move water through the ditches "and the water-wasting bed of the Rio Grande can be dried up during the periods of low water."[16] The replacement of a natural floodplain with an artificial distribution system of irrigation canals crisscrossing the landscape grew in importance.

At the old Oxbow, "channel rectification" transformed a simple bend in the river into something new and unrecognizable. Yet it would take decades for the community to reach a consensus on the identity and purpose of this "something else."

A Riverside Park

From the beginning, the idea of the Rio Grande as an urban amenity, an environmental and recreational benefit, had hovered at the edges of the city's relationship with the Rio Grande. The primary challenges of flood control, drainage, and irrigation had long dominated the growing Albuquerque metropolitan area's relationship with the river. The twin menaces of flooding and swamps and the elusive pursuit of commercial agriculture broadly defined that relationship. As a result, the task of meeting those challenges and managing that relationship fell to water management agencies—the Middle Rio Grande Conservancy District, the Bureau of Reclamation, and the Army Corps of Engineers.

Outside the levees, the river's manifestation in the spiderweb of ditches crisscrossing the valley floor was thriving—not as commercially successful agriculture, perhaps, but as something deeply valued by the community. The result was an increasingly tidy garden on the valley floor, as subdivisions filled in around the ditches, some with backyard gardens irrigated from ditches, many benefiting from trees rooted in the shallow aquifer fed by dirt-lined acequias. While some commercial farmers still irrigated in the Pueblos and rural non-Native lands beyond the city, in Albuquerque itself, the ditches were no longer performing the agricultural task for which village residents had built them centuries before. But they still were performing an important job, providing the ribbons of green that made Albuquerque a well-tended garden.

As one scholar put it, "When rivers didn't flood every year, people figured they, not the rivers, owned the floodplain."[17] Albuquerque's robust levees and drains were increasingly successful at making it possible to turn that floodplain into a city. But the Rio Grande itself, pinned between those levees and largely disconnected from the community by riverside drains that acted as impassable moats, seemed forgotten.

The 1976 fight to save the Oxbow represented a change in Albuquerque's relationship with the Rio Grande. The shift happened as the community's evolving values were changing its institutional relationships with the river. The Rio Grande as a community amenity rather than simply a menace had been a part of the discussion since the early twentieth century. Aldo Leopold, then with the Forest Service, captured it in a 1917 talk to the Game Protective Association, when Albuquerque had just two small city parks. "It would be a safe bet to say that on a pretty Sunday afternoon there are twice as many people hanging over the rail of the Barelas bridge, and tramping under the cottonwoods along the Rio Grande between Barelas and Old Albuquerque, as there are in both of the city parks put together," he said.[18]

Leopold was both a gardener and a naturalist, and his idea carried elements of both—"herons, beaver, muskrats, song birds, . . . ducks, snipe and other wild life" but also walking trails and picnic tables. By

1918 Leopold's idea had evolved into a plan for a levee and "foot paths, benches and other improvements on the banks of the Rio Grande between Old Albuquerque and Barelas."[19] Presuming landowner donations of their undeveloped riverside bosque, city and county governments would split the operational costs evenly.[20] The institutional arrangement was vital. Two missions, recreation and flood control, would be joined in a single project. And the general taxpayers, not merely those who would specifically benefit, would share the cost.

In a sense, Leopold's vision of parkland and recreational access was a mindful gardener's approach to something that had long existed organically. Palmer's Slough, a mile west of Old Town, had long been a popular swimming hole, a side channel of clear water popular with Albuquerque teenagers for picnics and Boy Scouts for hikes. It had its dangers. Fifteen-year-old Louise Umbrage and a friend, picnicking in May 1923, were wading in the water when they "stepped into a hole and were gripped by the undertow." The unnamed friend got out. Louise did not.[21]

It was not the dangers that doomed Palmer's Slough but rather the community's changing relationship with the Rio Grande. In 1936 it had been singled out as the source of malarial mosquitoes, and the "once popular swimming and fishing hole with Albuquerque's youth, has been drained and a large area of land reclaimed for cultivation."[22] In its place was a purpose-built park. Much of what was eventually built, incorporating the first stretch of the Conservancy District's levees in the early 1930s, was more urban park than natural space. It had ballfields, a zoo, and an artificial swimming beach, mainly *outside* the levees. Leopold's 1917 dream of a city embracing its river remained partially unrealized for another half century.

The original Rio Grande Park story reflects how urban development and recreation were intertwined with Albuquerque boosterism, the Conservancy District, and Albuquerque's relationship with the Rio Grande from the beginning. In Leopold's original 1917–1918 vision focusing on the Rio Grande's edge near the city core, riverside landowners from Old Town Bridge south to Barelas Bridge would all be convinced to donate part of their lands to the city as a "public gift." The nascent Albuquerque Chamber of Commerce quickly picked up the park idea in concert with the group's push for development via drainage.[23] Leopold and the Chamber's Civic Bureau noted how the park would provide civic beauty, and its levee would "add to the value of farmland throughout the whole valley below the park."[24] Much of the land ownership pattern was in thin strips connected to the river at their undeveloped bosque end. Many small landowners did donate relatively quickly, but several held out, some until later condemnation proceedings.[25] As land accumulated, Albuquerque's first recognized riverside park was formally dedicated in 1929, fittingly at the same time as the country club and adjacent housing development. Political luminaries gushed with pride before an "immense crowd," and one speaker made explicit the connections between the park and the broader effort to remake Albuquerque's relationship with the river: "Development of Rio Grande Park has been a forerunner of the Conservancy as it brought about the successful drainage of a large tract."[26]

The river channel itself, the space between the levees, would remain the province of water management agencies. The water for the artificial swimming beach came from a drain through the old Palmer Slough, an artificial swimming hole for Albuquerque's youth replacing the natural one.[27]

Rio Grande State Park

For the half century following the Conservancy District's creation, Albuquerque's relationship with the Rio Grande was shaped by levees and drains that acted as barriers between the community and the river. The 1976 fight to save the Oxbow bears the hallmarks of a turning point, but like most such historical events, it is better seen as a point in a continuum. Oxbow advocates had been working on saving the accidental wetland for at least five years before Eco Warrior dumped their bucket of dead fish in Conservancy District's offices. Most importantly for that process, advocates had worked with the city government to get a grant from the National Endowment for the Humanities that led to the 1975 publication of the *City Edges* study, which found widespread community support for the preservation of the environment of the Rio Grande and the surrounding bosque forests.[28]

Understanding the institutional framework here matters. The space between the levees was controlled by what Rex Funk years later described as "a long list of State and Federal Agencies whose acronyms read like a bowl of alphabet soup." Floating at the top of the bowl was the Middle Rio Grande Conservancy District, the local government agency created by the state legislature to manage flood control, drainage, and irrigation. Funk, the veteran of the Oxbow battle who had become a city open space planner in 1982, began advocating from the inside for the establishment of a Rio Grande Valley State Park—a formal designation of the river, the space between the levees that the community had abandoned to the water management agencies, as a public space of value to all for its own sake. Funk's argument was rooted in fairness. Property owners who didn't irrigate were paying the bulk of the cost of running the Conservancy District without receiving much in the way of benefits.[29]

In a continuing thread of public entrepreneurship, linking back to Aldo Leopold and others, Funk and the other open space advocates prevailed. In 1983 the New Mexico legislature declared 4,000 acres of riverside bosque a state park and placed the City of Albuquerque, not the Conservancy District, in charge of managing it. This artificial river landscape—created as a narrow strip of land disconnected from the broader floodplain by the construction of the Conservancy District's levees and drains in the 1930s, made permanent by the Bureau of Reclamation's "channel rectification," jetty jacks, and the subsequent establishment of a riverside forest—was becoming Albuquerque's beloved "natural" park.

The Silvery Minnow

In exploring Albuquerque's evolving relationship to the Rio Grande, it is valuable to understand how the word "conservancy" was used in the early 1920s and the creation of the Conservancy District. For Aldo Leopold's Progressive Era mentor, Gifford Pinchot, conservation meant developing and using natural resources and avoiding the waste of neglect.[30] Such neglect might be the failure to control a flood-menacing river and solve attendant drainage problems. Thus, the creation of the Middle Rio Grande Conservancy District involved a sustained focus on conservation *as* development. With time, this set up an almost inevitable conflict with growing national sentiment around notions of preservation, including as expressed legislatively in the Endangered Species Act of 1973.[31] This collided together in the form of a tiny silvery minnow.

The announcement in the August 19, 1994, *Albuquerque Journal* heralding the next phase in incorporating environmental values into the management of Albuquerque's Rio Grande would have been easy to miss. It was buried on page C6 of the paper, at the tail end of the outdoor columnist's weekly fishing notes:

> The Rio Grande Silvery Minnow will officially become an endangered species today, reports the Fish and Wildlife Service.
>
> The minnow is found in the Rio Grande between Cochiti Dam and the headwaters of Elephant Butte Reservoir, says Hans Stuart, public affairs officer for the service.
>
> The listing means the agency will be working with water-management agencies to ensure the survival of the minnow is a consideration in their activities, Stuart says.
>
> Anglers who use minnows from the Rio Grande for bait will need to recognize the species and return them to the river. Under the Endangered Species Act, the minnow is protected from collecting or harming.[32]

First formally described by western scientists in 1856 based on a fish found on the Rio Grande in Texas, the Rio Grande silvery minnow once lived from the Española Valley of northern New Mexico to the Gulf of Mexico. But with the dams blocking its path up and down the river and the reduction of flows, by the time of its Endangered Species Act listing in 1994, the minnow's range had been reduced to the Middle Rio Grande Valley.[33]

Three-quarters of a century before, Aldo Leopold's advocacy for parks and hunting grounds was rooted in the creation of environmental amenities for the use of humans. It was a recognition that community values toward the river extended beyond mere protection (from flooding and swamps) and extraction of resources. But it was still about gardening, bending the landscape to human values.

The battle over the Oxbow suggested something more: a community asserting an interest in the natural spaces themselves—an "existence value" independent of whether people were actually going to the Oxbow to look at the cattails, birds, and fish.

The creation of Rio Grande State Park straddled those two ways of thinking about the community's relationship with the environment. Yes, people wanted to go there and enjoy it. But in preserving the vast stretch of bosque, large portions were protected extending beyond the areas with walking paths, bike trails, birdwatching, and the human enjoyment of lovely fall colors. Creating the park suggested that those lovely fall colors and birds mattered even where no human was there to see them. As unnatural as the bosque may have been, given the way it emerged in its modern form after dams and levees and channelization made those ribbons of green possible, it was nature now, to be protected and nurtured, the community was saying.

In focusing on intrinsic environmental values, the minnow looked more like the Oxbow—an attempt to preserve a thing of value for its own sake. But the process surrounding the minnow bore a crucial difference. It did not emerge from local political processes grounded in community values, as had the parks and hunting grounds of Leopold's day and the Oxbow and Rio Grande State Park. Here was the federal government reaching down with the long arm of the US Fish and Wildlife Service and imposing a national value on Albuquerque's management of the Rio Grande. By linking federally subsidized Middle Rio Grande water management to the fate of the minnow, the action made it clear that with other people's money comes other people's values.

There is little evidence, beyond a single episode in the early 1990s when the residents of Los Ranchos opportunistically invoked the minnow in their fight against a roadway and bridge they opposed, that the people of Albuquerque in the mid-1990s knew or cared about the tiny fish. Scientists and environmental activists had been paying attention, but not the public.

But the legal and policy framework around the Endangered Species Act meant that community values were not the issue. It didn't matter whether the people of New Mexico's Middle Rio Grande Valley cared about the minnow. Unlike saving the Oxbow or creating Rio Grande State Park, preserving the minnow did not require building public support and political coalitions. Once the Endangered Species Act listing elevated the minnow into the public consciousness, scholars looking for it found evidence that the public valued the minnow and a flowing river to keep it alive.[34] Still, it was not public support that drove the resulting management process; instead, the legal ins and outs of the Endangered Species Act and the web of federal funding and authorities became the arena of action.

By 1998 the US Bureau of Reclamation, whose infrastructure had played a key role in pushing the minnow to the brink, began using water imported from the Colorado River Basin via the San Juan-Chama Project to keep the fish alive.[35]

A series of lawsuits followed, and the minnow hovered on the brink of extinction. In 2003 the Fish and Wildlife Service formally ruled that the actions of the valley's water managers on behalf of their communities' water use endangered the fish. The ruling was the first in a series of mandates that required water managers to leave water in the river's main channel for the minnow rather than take it out for human use.

It was work forever in process, never done, with the minnow continuing to hover at the edge of extinction as water managers struggled to keep a small population alive in a river fundamentally different from the Rio Grande in which the fish had evolved. By the third decade of the twenty-first century, there were times when the only thing keeping the river's main channel from drying was water imported via the San Juan-Chama Project from another basin entirely, through dams and tunnels, an artificial supply injected into the Rio Grande to make good on the water requirements to provide federal legal protection for a tiny fish.

Interlude: October

By October of 2023, rules established a century before favoring irrigation supplies for the Middle Rio Grande Valley's Native American Pueblos over non-Native communities were on full display. With available water dwindling, the entire Middle Rio Grande Conservancy District plumbing system was being operated to bring water to the Native American farmers. Only after their needs were met, district water manager Anne Marken explained in her monthly report to the agency's Boards of Directors, would non-Pueblo farmers get any water. Ditches carrying water across the Pueblo nations' "prior and paramount" lands were fat and full. Ditches across the rest of the Conservancy District's 1,200 miles of canals were hit and miss—drains still carried water, including to farmers in Valencia and Socorro County downstream of Pueblo irrigators. But many of the irrigation canals were puddled and teeming with thriving mosquitoes or cracked, weedy mud.

The Middle Valley's cottonwood gallery forest, though, seemed to be taking the water shortfalls in stride. Whether along the ditch banks or lining the river between the levees, the cottonwoods were well adapted to the late summer and fall scarcity of a desert river, dipping their roots down into the shallow groundwater, the subsurface manifestation of a river with little flow. The near-dry riverbed, though, was about to get wet again, Marken explained. Water that had been stored in upstream flood control dams during the summer to avoid risks posed by Valencia County's weak levees would, come early November, be moved downstream in a hurry to meet the Middle Valley's water delivery obligations to its downstream neighbors. Once again, rules were driving the hydrology of the Middle Rio Grande.

The good news, Marken said, was the onset of El Niño, a climate pattern triggered by warm waters in the equatorial Pacific Ocean that tend to steer the North American winter storm track toward the southwest, increasing the odds of a wet winter: "I guess it's that time of year when we start to pray for snow instead of rain."

Figure 29. Tracks in the sand of a nearly dry Rio Grande. Photograph by L. Heineman.

CHAPTER 9

CITY WATER

Connecting to the Rio

The challenges of flood control, drainage, and irrigation were not the only collective action problem to be solved in the evolution of growing Albuquerque's relationship with the Rio Grande. Rivers also constrain and thus define the structure of communities through two most basic human needs: water to drink and a place to dispose of waste. Thus it was in Albuquerque, where from the community's earliest days the Rio Grande was the source of drinking water. Then, as the city grew, its river soon became a place to dump the city's sewage.

While the struggle with flood control, drainage, and irrigation was the most obvious manifestation of Albuquerque's relationship with the Rio Grande, the project of providing drinking water and sewage disposal also played a crucial role. From the early days of hauling barrels of water from the Rio Grande one at a time to a twenty-first-century complex of physical and institutional plumbing that included Colorado water from across the Continental Divide, water and wastewater services represented another critical path in the collective action challenge water posed to building the modern community of Albuquerque.

Barrels

For drinking water, Albuquerque's earliest residents would haul barrels of water from the river, letting the mud in the cloudy water settle before using it. The community's switch to the aquifer—the water underground—came early. The first pumped well for municipal water was sunk in 1875 in Old Albuquerque's plaza, a half decade before the arrival of the Atchison, Topeka, and Santa Fe. "The gushing stream of clear, cold water which came out of that green iron monstrosity was the wonder of the town," Erna Fergusson described nostalgically a half century later. "People made long, all day journeys to see it, coming from as far away as Los Lunas in their buck-boards, buggies, and family carriages." It was the only pump in town, with a tin can for priming, available to anyone who brought their own bucket.[1]

While it makes for a quaint story about early village life, the "green monstrosity" was more novelty than city water supply, far too modest compared to the scale of the needs of a growing city. By the 1880s it was clear that Albuquerque needed a water supply *system*. Such systems had become central to an urbanizing nation—important in practical terms and symbols of modernity and collective identity. "The water supply to a great city is necessarily one of the most important and interesting features, upon which depends, to a greater extent, possibly, than any of its other advantages, either natural or artificial, its ultimate growth and prosperity," the city of Philadelphia's water system designers explained in 1860.[2] Alongside a water system, it became apparent within a few years of the arrival of the railroad and the early growth of New Town that the old waste disposal model—outhouses and chamber pots and ditches—could no longer meet the scale and aspirations of a modern city.

But like the struggle to find the proper governance structure for managing the flood control, drainage, and irrigation needed to build a city on the Rio Grande Valley floor, it was not obvious what sort of institutional arrangement should be used to solve the problem of ensuring a reliable supply of municipal water for drinking, cooking, bathing, watering a bit of lawn in the yard, providing enough pressure in hydrants to fight fires, or disposing of waste. From the perspective of technology, Albuquerque was pursuing a well-worn path. The transition from rural to urban in the eastern United States had long been underway. Cities confronted the technological challenges of pumping and treating water and plumbing a city's streets to get water to homes and businesses and carry away their sewage. It was a crucial step in building community, as one historian explained: "To go on the urban water grid was to connect one's human body to that of the so-called body of the city."[3]

But watching Albuquerque's community leaders in the 1880s struggle with the details of how to approach the problem provides a window into a community's struggle to find and act on its identity. This struggle once again required public entrepreneurs.

The Pursuit of City Water

"Water Works," the *Albuquerque Journal* headlined in August 1882: "A Company Organized to Furnish Albuquerque with Water." It was a commercial enterprise with a capital stock of $500,000—a vast fortune in the day.[4] The scheme, a dam on the Rio Grande upstream from Albuquerque with a canal carrying the water along the mesa to a reservoir east of the city, never came to be. But the attempt illustrated the challenge of sorting out how, both technologically and institutionally, to solve the problem of municipal water for the developing city.

The Atchison, Topeka, and Santa Fe had arrived two years earlier, and the rapidly growing commercial center and rail yards needed water. The need was not entirely commercial. From the beginning of Albuquerque's city-building era, water for parks played a role. The railroad "needs water to supply its buildings," an observer explained in the winter of 1882, "and early in the spring will need water to irrigate the several neat little parks that it has just laid out."[5] As was often the case in the 1800s, Albuquerque turned to the private sector for the task, but in this case, with a public-private model. Municipal governments in their modern form, with the ability to tax and provide broad collective public services like roads, water, and sewer service, did not yet exist in New Mexico. Instead, going back to the early toll bridges, many public services were provided by civic-minded entrepreneurs investing capital to both make money and provide city-building services. This was the form the earliest water companies took. A private company would provide water service, operating under a municipal franchise governing issues like rates and the provision of public services (fire hydrants, parks, and the like). Efforts quickly settled on the aquifer, rather than the river, as the water source. But the challenge was formidable, marked in the 1880s by a series of false starts that left Albuquerque struggling to meet its water needs.

At first, Albuquerque Water Works Co. struggled to deliver on the promise of a reliable municipal water supply. But with Albuquerque's incorporation as a town in 1885, the community settled on an approach to provide reliable municipal water. Prompted by recognition of collective issues such as the need for "drainage of the town" and correcting the "stagnant sewers," a mass meeting of Albuquerque residents was called on July 28, 1884, to consider incorporation as a town under the Territorial Laws of New Mexico.[6] The 27th ordinance of the newly formed town Board of Trustees granted the Albuquerque Water Company an exclusive franchise, tax-free for twenty years, "to establish, construct, maintain and operate in and adjacent to the town of Albuquerque, or within the Albuquerque grant, water works to receive, take, store, purify, conduct and distribute in and throughout the said town of Albuquerque, water. . . ."[7]

The following year, in the spring of 1886, Albuquerque's first municipal water system began serving customers from a well and reservoir east of downtown.[8] "Water vs. Dust," Solon Rose advertised in the morning paper. "Call and examine my large stock of hose, lawn-sprinklers, hose carriages and hydrants." The greening of Albuquerque had begun.[9] The company drilled a second well in 1888 to meet summer demand, and the following year, the original well was deepened another one hundred feet. By 1891 the system's Gaskill Compound Duplex Pump could deliver two million gallons of water per day to the reservoir, located a mile and a half east of the railroad depot. By pumping the water to a 4-million-gallon reservoir 210 feet above the valley floor, the new system ensured 95 pounds per square inch of water pressure to the city's 64 fire hydrants.[10] Albuquerque had passed an important milestone on its path to modernity.

The Private Versus Public Conundrum

The idea of a private water company was not universally popular, with ongoing arguments over private versus public institutional models. The topic of the 1915 debate team contest between the Albuquerque-based University of New Mexico and the "state college"—then New Mexico A&M College, to become New Mexico State University in Las Cruces—was "the municipal ownership question": "Resolved, That Municipalities Should Own and Operate Plants for Supplying Light, Water, and Transportation."[11]

By the early twentieth century 113 of the 154 US cities with populations greater than 30,000 owned or operated their water systems. It would be a few years before Albuquerque crossed that population threshold. Still, it had its eye on the goal of growth when judge and civic leader Bernard Rodey stood before the newly formed "Municipal Water League," quoting the work of Progressive Era reformer Frederic Howe.[12] Howe, from Ohio, was a follower of the work of Henry George, a nineteenth-century journalist, political economist, and reformer who opposed private monopolies hoarding natural resources for profit rather than the public good. A century before Elinor Ostrom, Henry George touched on important questions about governing the commons and managing resources to achieve broad public goods.[13] Much of the debate in Albuquerque was more prosaic, involving water customers angry at the private municipal water company's rates. But at its root was a more profound philosophical question rooted in the progressive politics of the day: What is the role of government in providing public services and regulating private industry for the public good?

Clyde Tingley Enters the Stage

Clyde Tingley looms large over Albuquerque's history. In nearly four decades of political life, which began with his 1916 election to city council, led to the New Mexico governor's office, and then back to his position as the chairman of the city commission—effectively the mayor—he helped shape modern Albuquerque more than any other elected official. The issue that first propelled him to prominence was municipal ownership of Albuquerque's water system.

Like many of Albuquerque's important nineteenth- and early twentieth-century immigrants, tuberculosis brought him here. In Tingley's case, it was the illness of his wife, Carrie. Her Ohio doctors had urged her to move to Albuquerque's warm, dry air. He dabbled in Democratic Party politics early, but the debates in 1915 over municipal water system ownership marked his entry onto the public stage. Every Thursday night during May and June 1915, the city council hosted meetings to discuss "the Water Supply Question." Tingley took out an advertisement in the *Evening Herald* encouraging community members to attend. "Are you satisfied with the present rates? Do you want the Franchise as proposed by the Water Supply Co. to be submitted to the vote of the people *or do you want Municipal Ownership*?" (emphasis added).[14]

Tingley, then a lawyer in his early thirties, was joining a civic chorus pushing to buy out the private water company, arguing that excessive monopoly rates were hindering Albuquerque's growth. Tingley's stance aligned him with other civic-minded local luminaries. They crossed the political spectrum, including Bernard S. Rodey and his son, the young

Harvard-trained lawyer Pearce C. Rodey, an early specialist in water issues who, as we have seen, played a vital role in the establishment of the Middle Rio Grande Conservancy District, and the banker / real-estate developer and "prominent as a socialist" William P. Metcalf.[15]

Tingley and other advocates of municipal ownership had powerful foes. "Municipal ownership usually spells inefficiency," the politically powerful *Albuquerque Journal* railed. "Usually municipal ownership means scandal, higher taxes, jobs for the inefficient, poor service."[16] Perhaps more important was the owner of the company that owned the water franchise: Alonzo Bertram McMillen. Like Tingley, McMillen came from a farming family in Ohio. A lawyer and entrepreneur, McMillen represented the established business community. But it was, in significant measure, a civic-minded capitalism. In the first decades of the twentieth century, he had amassed a business empire that included banks, insurance, media, and extensive real-estate holdings in the valley. This included buying the private water company in 1905. While complicated if not befouled in his legacy of Land Grant lands acquisition,[17] he was elected the first president of the newly formed Albuquerque Chamber of Commerce in 1918.[18] Shortly thereafter, he hired the thirty-one-year-old Aldo Leopold as managing secretary to help move his city visions forward. McMillen was a part of the Albuquerque establishment, involved in civic affairs like good roads, sanitation, valley drainage, and economic development for decades. When Tingley pushed for the municipal acquisition of McMillen's water company, it highlighted not just a policy debate but a clash between old-guard private interests personified by McMillen and a different version of a public-focused leader in the person of Tingley.

The question was turned over to the voters, who in April 1916 sided with Tingley and the progressives, approving the sale of municipal bonds to buy out McMillen. While the political arguments were fierce, there was reason to believe McMillen was happy to hand off the water system to the expanding city[19] if he was compensated for his past investments.[20] Working out the details took more than two years, but in July 1918 the

New Mexico courts approved the sale of the water system by McMillen to the City of Albuquerque for $400,000—equivalent to $9 million in 2020s-era dollars. Albuquerque had joined the modern cities providing municipal water service.[21]

"Offal, Filth, and Garbage"

In addition to drinking water, Albuquerque's drive to become a city in the 1880s quickly confronted a common urban problem on the system's back end. Sewage also was a collective action problem. No one person could solve it for themselves. "Several drains and sewers have been constructed, emptying into what is commonly known as the 'Albuquerque ditch,' and also . . . parties have been in the habit of depositing offal, filth and garbage therein," William Hazeldine, one of the city's earliest urban developers, reported to the city's Board of Trade in 1883.[22]

Hazeldine asked for the prosecution of the miscreants. But prosecution could only solve the problem if there was an alternative way to get rid of the waste. Albuquerque had initially turned to its existing infrastructure, dumping sewage into the main ditch flowing through town. Eventually, the "stench of the foul matter"[23] led the city to pursue its first sewers, with the idea of discharging the rapidly growing city's waste directly into the Rio Grande.[24] Those early efforts ran headlong into a classic collective action problem. In 1888 residents voted down a bond issue to pay for a sewer system, leaving the city with a pestilent ditch flowing through its midst instead, and many simply dumping waste beneath their homes, creating significant health risks.[25] In 1890 voters finally agreed to the sale of bonds and the tax increases needed to repay them, and ten miles of sewer pipe were built, dumping the resulting effluent directly into the Rio Grande downstream from Barelas.[26]

By the early 1900s, the system was failing the rapidly growing city. "I believe the people of Albuquerque are willing to pay a substantial increase in taxes if it will mean a more sanitary city," declared one city alderman.[27] Pipes laid in sandy soil were breaking, and the system built across the valley floor was so flat that the sewage "failed to produce self-cleansing velocities," in the words of the engineer brought to Albuquerque in 1906 to diagnose the problems. The outlet was often underwater, leaving sewage backed up all over town. It was one more challenge created by the decision to build a city on the flat, swampy Rio Grande Valley floor, which in the area downstream of the new downtown had effectively become one big, interconnected cesspool.[28]

It took several years for the community to address the problems identified by the engineer. Town aldermen recruited their own young city engineer, James N. Gladding, direct from the Boston Institute of Technology (now the Massachusetts Institute of Technology) in 1907 to begin the formal planning.[29] By 1909 the city's residents again were willing to sell bonds and tax themselves to pay for the improvements. The notorious "city ditch" running through New Town was "abolished."[30] By 1911 twenty-five miles of new sewer were built, along with a pump station to solve the problem the flat valley bottom had posed for moving sewage from the city's residents to the Rio Grande.[31] The new system was built to handle a growing city, though it was dumping directly into the river. As declared by a consulting engineer, "Question of disposal of sewage at Albuquerque at present time is not a serious one, as it can be discharged into the Rio Grande river near the present outlet without causing a nuisance to the city or anyone upon the river below the city."[32]

By the 1920s, four decades after the railroad's arrival spurred Albuquerque's urban boom, the county population had more than tripled to 30,000 people. The community had finally built a sewer system capable of moving waste out of the urbanizing city core. But it was still dumping untreated waste into the Rio Grande, flowing past communities downstream like the nearby Isleta Pueblo. Ten years into statehood, New Mexico now had a State Board of Health, which said enough was enough and told the city to build a sewer disposal plant to treat the sewage before dumping it into the river.

In agreeing with the requirement the city engineer's report recognized the emerging metropolitan area's changing relationship with the Rio Grande:

> Such a plant will greatly increase the sanitary conditions along the river. The proposed Rio Grande park fronts entirely on the river and is only about one-half mile above the present sewer outlet. Strictly sanitary conditions should exist for a considerable distance on either side of the proposed park as well as in the park itself.[33]

The decision to build the plant, completed in 1923, marked a turning point in Albuquerque's relationship with the river. No longer merely a flood menace, a source of irrigation water, and a place to dump the city's waste, the Rio Grande had become a thing of value for its own sake.

Isleta

"Albuquerque is upstream from us," former Isleta Pueblo governor Verna Williamson-Teller wrote in 2008, "so we get everything that comes out of the city of Albuquerque, including bad air and bad water and many times, bad people."[34] In building its sewage treatment plant at the downstream edge of the metropolitan area, Albuquerque was effectively dumping its waste at Isleta's doorstep. In 1987 the United States Congress gave Isleta the legal authority to do something about it.

The people of Isleta lived and farmed in the Rio Grande Valley long before the arrival of Europeans, with homes on high ground adjacent to the Rio Grande above the floodplain and farm fields on the river's edges. Pablo Abeita, Isleta Pueblo community leader in the early twentieth century, was instrumental in the political alliance between Pueblo and colonizing cultures that helped fight off federal legislation threatening Pueblo sovereignty and ensured Pueblo participation in the valley-wide efforts at flood control, drainage, and irrigation.

The federal Indian Irrigation Service built the first pieces of what would become the Middle Rio Grande Conservancy District's irrigation and drainage network at Isleta in the early 1920s, before the District's formation. Isleta's participation was central to Albuquerque's city-building project. However, the accommodation between the Indigenous community living in the valley since time immemorial and the upstart twentieth-century urban area upstream has always been complicated.

When Albuquerque's consulting engineer said in 1908 that the young city could dump its sewage untreated into the Rio Grande "without causing a nuisance to . . . anyone upon the river below the city," it may or may not have been accurate at the time. But nearly a century later, even with the addition of wastewater treatment, it was no longer true. By the end of the twentieth century, Albuquerque's wastewater treatment plant had become the largest Rio Grande tributary between the Rio Chama and the New Mexico-Texas-Mexico border. It was causing "mayhem to the river." The state cautioned people not to swim in the Rio Grande because of the contamination. But, amazingly, the gray, foamy discharge complied with state and federal water quality rules.[35]

This was unacceptable to the people of the profoundly religious, river-based Isleta. Every September, the community performed a month-long harvest ceremony that culminated with "cleansing and bathing in the river, and also ingesting river water," Williamson-Teller explained.[36] In 1987 Congress offered a new tool—an amendment to the federal Clean Water Act that gave Native American communities the legal authority to set their own water quality standards that were tougher than state and federal rules. Led by Williamson-Teller, Isleta went through the arduous process laid out by the new federal regulations, and in 1992 the US Environmental Protection Agency approved the Pueblo's tough new water quality standards, based on "primary contact ceremonial use and primary contact recreational use."[37] To a community so profoundly tied to the Rio Grande, the state's caution that people stay out of the river was not an option.

Isleta won widespread support from neighboring communities but not from Albuquerque. Complaining about the cost of sewage treatment plant upgrades, Albuquerque sued not its downstream neighbors but the federal Environmental Protection Agency, charging that the federal government had overstepped its authority in approving Isleta's stricter standards. In its ruling in Isleta's favor, a federal judge sided with Isleta, effectively upholding the principles of sovereignty for which Pablo Abeita had fought so hard nearly a century before. What Isleta did in protecting the Rio Grande, the federal court ruled, "is in accord with powers inherent in Indian tribal sovereignty."[38]

Steve Reynolds Declares the Basin

In much the same way it took the better part of a century to sort out the handling of Albuquerque's sewage, the relationship between groundwater and surface water, once thought settled, continued to bedevil the growing city. Drilling wells deep into the aquifer, Albuquerque seemed to have disconnected its municipal water supply from the Rio Grande. For decades, it worked. But by the 1950s, hydrologic science, Albuquerque's booming population, law, and politics were converging in a way the community could no longer ignore.

The science came from a young US Geological Survey Engineer named C. V. Theis, who in 1935 published a brief, equation-heavy paper in the *Transactions of the American Geophysical Union* entitled "The Relation between the Lowering of the Piezometric Surface and the Rate and Duration of Discharge of a Well Using Ground-Water Storage."[39]

That Theis was based at the USGS's Albuquerque office was a coincidence. He could have lived and worked anywhere, and the impact of his science on Albuquerque's relationship with the Rio Grande would have been the same. The research was based on his studies of groundwater in eastern New Mexico. The impact of the research was global because of its implications for water management. While it took years for scientists to work out the details and even longer for law and policy to catch up with the science, the implication was straightforward: groundwater and surface water are hydrologically connected. Pump water from the aquifer beneath Albuquerque, and sooner or later, depending on how far the pumping is from the river, water will seep from the bed of the Rio Grande to fill the hole created by the pumping.

By the 1950s, Albuquerque was booming. Its population doubled from 1940 to 1950 and was on a path to nearly double again from 1950 to 1960, driven by the twin World War II economic booms of transportation hub and military research and development center. To meet the demands, the city water department was drilling wells across the city as fast as possible—in the Rio Grande Valley floor and eastward across the heights between the river and the Sandia Mountains. Thus, for example, the city in 1954 began work on a well field, water lines, and a huge storage tank on the edge of Los Griegos, adjacent to the intersection of the old Barelas and Los Griegos irrigation ditches that had irrigated Max Gutierrez's alfalfa field three decades before.[40]

By the late 1950s, that push rang headlong into a young Steve Reynolds, appointed the state's top water official—the title was State Engineer—in 1955 by Gov. John Simms. Reynolds was a brash young former University of New Mexico assistant football coach at the start of a career that, over nearly four decades, would help shape New Mexico's relationship with the Rio Grande. One of his earliest challenges was to confront the implications of Theis's scientific findings for the rapid expansion of Albuquerque's groundwater pumping. According to a formal legal declaration by Reynolds, any new groundwater pumping would have to be offset by a reduction in surface water use. Albuquerque couldn't just pump the groundwater for free, as if it sat on a bottomless lake.

Under New Mexico law, older users had first dibs on the Rio Grande's water, and Albuquerque couldn't just take it from them by arguing that the aquifer was different. The implications were profound. To continue its pumping spree Albuquerque would have to buy out senior water users, reduce their demand on the Rio Grande to offset any new pumping, or find a new water source. That would mean that, in the short run, Albuquerque would have to buy out and retire some irrigated acreage, Reynolds explained. In the long run, water imported from the Colorado River Basin would provide the bulk of Albuquerque's supply.[41]

In explaining his decision, Reynolds made clear his vision of Albuquerque's future. Water used by agricultural irrigation on the valley floor would inevitably have to give way to urban growth. Retired water rights would be the key to the transition. Legal historian Em Hall, who once worked as a young attorney for Reynolds, described his views of water management this way: "Natural processes were good in his view only by virtue of what they could do for man. Water that was left in a stream helped no one and water that was left in the ground remained hidden. Steve Reynolds fought the increasingly popular notion that water in rivers—'instream flows'—deserved legal protection because he believed so fundamentally that the operative term in 'beneficial use' was 'use.'"[42] In other words, in confronting the impact of all that new groundwater pumping on the Rio Grande, Reynolds's concern was not for the Rio Grande as a natural system. It was for people downstream who needed its water.

The city sued, reaching in its legal approach back to the beginnings of Albuquerque's relationship with the Rio Grande. Tracing its municipal lineage to the 1706 Pueblo de Alburquerque y San Francisco Xavier land grant, the very modern, very twentieth-century city asserted that "it had the absolute right to the use of all waters, both ground and surface within its limits, for the use and benefit of its inhabitants." The city argued that the King of Spain said in 1706 that it was okay. Reynolds disagreed, as did the New Mexico Supreme Court.[43]

Twenty-four years after losing the lawsuit, the City of Albuquerque purchased its first water right, entitling it to the water once used to irrigate twenty-nine acres off the Chical Lateral in Valencia County downstream from the city. The deal allowed Albuquerque to end water use on the land and pump an equivalent amount of water from the city's groundwater wells.[44] In the following years, Albuquerque bought more water rights, taking some land out of production and leasing the water rights back to farmers in other cases to allow the land to stay in production until Albuquerque needed the water. But the city's approach quickly turned to the second option made clear by Reynolds's initial declaration. It would find the water somewhere else.

San Juan-Chama

At the heart of Albuquerque's complex relationship with the Rio Grande lies a paradox—the river's inherent variability has brought both too much and too little water. Swamping and floods require collective action for drainage and flood control, while water scarcity during dry years profoundly shapes the community's reliance on the river.

While river flood control and drainage dominated Albuquerque's efforts in the early twentieth century to manage the river, scarcity was never far from view. The Middle Rio Grande Conservancy District addressed water scarcity by building El Vado Reservoir in the mid-1930s. Its storage capacity was modest compared to massive dams on other western rivers. But El Vado helped smooth fluctuations by storing high spring runoff in spring for irrigation in summer and fall. That helped valley farmers, giving the old acequia communities a new tool for managing late-year shortages. Still, it was never meant for the kind of demands posed by Albuquerque's rapid postwar urbanization.

For that, Albuquerque's leaders looked across the Continental Divide to northwestern New Mexico. The San Juan River meandered through sparsely populated desert communities, flowing toward its confluence with the Colorado River and the downstream states of Utah, Nevada, Arizona, and California. The river is one of three primary tributaries in the Colorado River's Upper Basin, but most of the water originates in Colorado, flowing through the rocky deserts of what has long been Navajo country. From the beginning of large-scale water development in the Western United States, and before final interstate compacts on allocating the Rio Grande were in place, Albuquerque's boosters had cast a covetous eye on the San Juan.

What would eventually become the San Juan-Chama Project originated in the early 1900s, when surveyor Jay Turley developed an early scheme to use San Juan's water on agricultural land in the San Juan and Chaco valleys.[45] Over several decades, Turley could never persuade private investors or the federal government to pursue it. Still, the idea that the San Juan's water might somehow be used in New Mexico was planted.

By the 1920s, attention shifted eastward across the Continental Divide toward diverting the San Juan River's water through the mountains to the water-short Middle Rio Grande. Even as the Conservancy District works were being built in the 1930s, federal surveyors were sketching plans for a San Juan-Chama Project to divert water from the San Juan to the Rio Chama, the same tributary on which El Vado Dam was taking shape.

Concurrently, the federal government and the states of Colorado, New Mexico, and Texas were negotiating what would become the Rio Grande Compact, a water-sharing agreement. Technical analysis indicated that New Mexico could be at a disadvantage without augmenting its water supply, so the San Juan-Chama Project seemed inevitable.

As Albuquerque's population boomed, more than doubling from the 1940s to 1950, fueled by federal spending on the state's newest industry—the military-industrial complex—the push for the project grew. The boom continued, Albuquerque nearly doubled again from 1950 to 1960, and a deep drought in the 1950s collided with the city's urban aspirations. These postwar realities led to the approval of what would become the San Juan-Chama Project. Completed in 1971, the project includes twenty-six miles of tunnels and the Heron Dam, a storage reservoir on Willow Creek, a tributary of the San Juan.[46]

While the San Juan-Chama Project and the Middle Rio Grande Project are formally separate projects, they are inextricably linked. By adding supplemental water to the Rio Grande, the San Juan-Chama Project fundamentally changed Albuquerque's water management. In 1977, for example, the City of Albuquerque agreed to let the Middle Rio Grande Conservancy District borrow some of the city's allocation to help irrigators cope with drought.

Until 2008 Albuquerque's municipal use of San Juan-Chama water was indirect. Albuquerque would pump groundwater for use by city residents, then make up the harm to the river (water leaking out of the Rio Grande's bed to fill the hole left in the aquifer by groundwater pumping) by releasing San Juan-Chama water down the main river channel. In 2008 Albuquerque transitioned to direct use of the water, completing a $400 million diversion and water treatment plant paid for locally with dedicated rate increases. The project channeled the water directly to customers' homes, with the imported water making up the bulk of Albuquerque's water consumption.[47] Thus, while the ribbons of green alongside the Rio Grande on Albuquerque's valley floor were primarily fed by the river itself, the blanket of green landscaping spread across the community's higher ground was primarily provided by water imported from the San Juan River basin. While such use of transmountain diversion annually contributes to the distribution of green in the Middle Rio Grande Valley, it pushes against the boundaries of how one might think about sustainability in a watershed.

The San Juan-Chama Project has also adapted over time to serve evolving environmental priorities, notably protecting endangered species. For example, beginning in the 1990s, San Juan-Chama water was used to supplement instream flows in the Rio Grande to support dwindling populations of the endangered Rio Grande silvery minnow. This reflected emerging societal values about preserving biodiversity and threatened species, a priority never contemplated by government agencies when the project was first implemented solely for agricultural and municipal supply, even if some New Mexico scholars were already beginning to consider future needs.[48] With time, the flexibility of the imported San Juan-Chama water enabled managers to dedicate some portion to keeping the river wet even as traditional demands continued to grow. Thus, the project has incrementally aligned with the original aims of boosting supply for human uses and newer environmental goals.[49]

Interlude: November

In early November, things got weird on Albuquerque's Rio Grande. Early on the morning of November 3, what had been a narrow, tenuous ribbon of water snaking through the near-dry riverbed through Albuquerque began rising. Over the next six hours the water level rose a foot and a half as a pulse of water made its way downstream.

This was an institutional hydrograph at its most explicit. The flow was happening at the intersection of physical infrastructure—the upstream dams—and rules. Water had been held behind flood-control dams during the spring's high runoff, stored under the web of rules until the end of the irrigation season. The water was out of reach of the irrigators, who had struggled all summer, and also out of reach of any environmental and community benefits a flowing river during the hot, dry summer might have provided. The rules prioritized efficiency, where efficiency was defined as providing the maximum supply of water to the communities in southern New Mexico, Texas, and Mexico.

To move the water, the US Army Corps of Engineers waited until irrigation season was largely over before cranking open the gates of Cochiti Dam. Over a period of three hours on the morning of November 1, the flow from the dam went from modest to gushing. Twenty-four hours later, as the rising front of the pulse flow reached Albuquerque, the Rio Grande was a marvel. It started as a trickle as the wetting front of the gently rising river crept across the dry sand, spreading out into the tracks left behind by frolicking canines (neighborhood dogs or bosque coyotes—both are

Figure 30. A baby cottonwood, which had taken advantage of low Rio Grande flows through Albuquerque, lives its last hours as flows on the river rise. Photograph by John Fleck.

common sights). The water filled the tracks slowly, one footprint at a time. The water found easy paths along tire tracks left by off-roaders who had turned the sandy riverbed into a playground during the hot, dry summer of 2023, cutting and running through old channels that had been left dry when the river had begun dropping four months before.

Beyond the river's main channel, the ditches that had spread the Rio Grande out across its old valley floodplain through the spring and summer were largely dry. The only exception was a few that carried the last of the year's irrigation water downstream to provide to the crops at Isleta Pueblo, the community whose struggle for sovereignty a century before had ensured that it would forever have the highest priority to irrigation water in times of scarcity. The cottonwoods flanking the Rio Grande and the valley ditches beyond still held their fall colors, turning the ribbons of green for a few weeks in fall to ribbons of gold.

At her monthly report to the Middle Rio Grande Conservancy District board, Anne Marken reviewed the rules driving the strange high autumn flow after a dry summer. And then, turning her attention to next year, she shifted her prayer call from the short-term benefit of rains to a long-term hope for a good season of winter snows.

CHAPTER 10

BRIDGES

Crossing the Rio

Few things better capture Albuquerque's complicated relationship with the Rio Grande at the end of the twentieth century than the December 1995 death of a massive century-old cottonwood named Naomi. Naomi stood along Rio Grande Boulevard, which was one branch of El Camino Real before Albuquerque became a modern metropolis. The old highway here followed the high ground past the old villages of Los Candelarias and Los Griegos, upstream of the Villa de *Alburquerque*. At the moment of New Mexico's statehood in 1912, Naomi would have stood to the west as improvements were made to El Camino Real—which became the north–south backbone of a state highway system.

These highway efforts were led by the bridge-building first state engineer, James E. French. In the twenty-first century, the job of the "state engineer" was focused entirely on water management. But in its earliest incarnation the job was broader: not only focused on water but on road building as well. The Good Roads movement for automobile travel was every bit as important at the time.[1] French and colleagues followed quickly with the first extensive mapping of valley drainage needs in 1917 and 1918. Water and roads were intertwined from the start. If the railroad marks the beginning of modern Albuquerque, it didn't take long for the automobile to transform its geography.

We can surmise that Aldo Leopold drove the file miles north of Albuquerque when the Chamber of Commerce's new secretary went for a bit of

Figure 31. Moonset over Albuquerque's Central Avenue bridge. Photograph by John Fleck.

bird hunting by himself ("22 rifle only," jotted in his journal) in the swampy slough and bosque past the western end of Los Griegos road on a hot August day in 1918.[7] It wouldn't have been far from Max Gutierrez's farm. Leopold reported the bosque was full of nesting birds. Naomi would have been part of that swath of cottonwoods, slightly upriver. We can then jump to the last decade of the twentieth century, where Naomi stood watch over a quiet country lane with a largely obeyed twenty-five-mile-per-hour speed limit past country estates. But by then, Naomi stood in the east–west path of the proposed Montaño Bridge, an attempt by urbanizing Albuquerque to overcome the obstacle the Rio Grande presented to the transportation network of a growing city.

Naomi was a creature of a floodplain once washed in high water years by a Rio Grande swollen by melting snows. She stood at the southern edge of the Village of Los Ranchos, a rural enclave of affluent homes made possible by the dams and levees that had narrowed the Rio Grande in the half century before her death. Before the intervention of large-scale human infrastructure, the river had steadily raised the water table, creating lush wetlands that made an ideal habitat for non-humans but which drew the pejorative label of "swamp."

In modern terms, "wetland" carries positive emotional and environmental policy connotations, describing places that provide vital habitat for a range of species, improving water quality, and providing a buffer to dissipate rising flood waters, a place for the water to go. "Swamp" carries the opposite emotional baggage—murky, mosquito-infested places hostile to human habitation. Stopping the floods that once lapped at Naomi's feet and draining the swamps around her, and many like her standing in the way of Albuquerque's development as a city, were the central motivations for creating the Middle Rio Grande Conservancy District.

For more than six decades Naomi lived with the results. Naomi was born in a flood—a tuft of cottony seed falling on soils moistened by high spring flows in the late 1800s. But the Conservancy District levees cut her off from the river that enabled her birth. The Griegos Drain, built in 1930 a thousand feet to the east, drained the swamp that once made much of the Village of Los Ranchos unhospitable terrain. While her age at the moment of her death in December 1995 was debated, it seems possible that a young Max Gutierrez could see her one hundred yards upstream from the Griegos ditch bank as the flood waters swamped the old village of Los Ranchos in 1904 and lazed comfortably around Naomi's then-young roots. Eighteen-year-old Max was some years away from becoming involved in politics in 1904, but his recently deceased oldest brother Emiliano had already served in the Territorial Legislature before his untimely death. Among the issues Emiliano worked on was legislative funding for bridges.[3]

Naomi was estimated to have been 125 years old at the time of her death. Naomi may have pre-dated the railroad's arrival in this stretch of the Rio Grande Valley, watching over its transition from rural subsistence farming to a major American metropolitan area.

Making peace with the Rio Grande across the twentieth century required levees and drains, and the floodplain edge on which Naomi grew was profoundly changed. Its neighborhood was lower ground, among the areas adjacent to the growing city most vulnerable to spring snowmelt floods and a rising water table. A few hundred yards to the east, the land of a farmer named Melquiades Montaño had become a shallow lake as a rising water table flooded the valley's lowlands. Large stretches of the valley upstream had been taken over by alkali, the white salty residue left behind when the water table lay just below the ground's surface.

Across the twentieth century, Naomi stood sentinel as the land around her, freed from the risk of flooding, transitioned from alkali, swamp, and the occasional subsistence farm to a community of country estates. There were better roads, paved, and more of them. Naomi was there standing lookout in 1918–1922 as Max Gutierrez was serving as Bernalillo County Commissioner, joining Aldo Leopold in endorsing drainage, working on issues like funding flood control and bridge repair, and personally spear-heading efforts to lead increased county paving efforts for an expanding urban area.[4] Upstream and down, patches of Naomi's cottonwood kin that had once flanked a wide river were falling to suburban homes.

Downstream of Naomi, a grove of old cottonwoods had, by the 1990s, long ago given way to a suburban neighborhood known as Dietz Farm, named after Robert Dietz, a gentleman farmer from the east who lived on a country estate there from 1910 to 1940. By the 1990s the Dietz Farm neighborhood was still bisected by the old Duranes Acequia, but it was primarily kept leafy and green by irrigation water pumped from a massive City of Albuquerque groundwater well that had been drilled in the 1950s a quarter mile from Naomi, then pumped through the city's municipal water system, or shallow domestic wells drilled when the subdivision was built in the 1970s.

By the 1990s the river posed a new and different challenge. As population sloshed up Albuquerque's mesas to the east and west, the river through the heart of the metropolitan area posed a six-mile-long barrier. River crossings have always represented one of the fundamental collective action challenges facing river cities. By the 1990s it was growing increasingly difficult to get from the suburbs on the river's booming west side to the heart of Albuquerque.

Work toward a series of bridges across that barrier began in the early 1960s, more than a decade into Albuquerque's post–World War II boom. First came a freeway bridge, part of New Mexico's piece of the US Interstate Highway System. The bridge, built with federal money, was funded as a link in a national network. At a local level, it was seen as a swift roadway connection across the Rio Grande.[5] But it was not enough. Planning for the Montaño Bridge, the bridge that would eventually doom Naomi three decades later, began in 1963.[6] One after another, bridges to Naomi's north went in, some dogged by difficult political fights. But no fight was as tricky as the Montaño Bridge and the symbolic struggle over the fate of Naomi.

Community values and governance had changed since the 1920s, when Albuquerque began remaking the river. Few had balked in the 1920s at draining the wetlands across the valley floor; they were "swamps." What opposition there had been then had little to do with disagreement about the community's relationship with the river. The 1920s opposition was entirely about questions of governance and financing. The word "wetland" did not surpass "swamp" in the vernacular until the era of rising environmental values of the 1970s.[7]

To the extent that there were political fights over bridges, it was among people who wanted bridges to bring commercial value to their land rather than opposing bridges seen as bringing harm. This is seen in debates in the early 1930s around the rerouting of the original Route 66 highway, designated in 1926. The famous route was redrawn in 1937 from its path across the Barelas Bridge to its more northerly revised course across the Central Avenue Bridge, which passed Old Town, the developing country club area, and adjacent businesses and neighborhoods.[8]

By the late twentieth century the environmental values that raised so much controversy about the Montaño Bridge remained a minority viewpoint relative to the same city-building ethos that had powered the Conservancy District juggernaut in the 1920s. A 1995 poll found supporters of building the Montaño Bridge outnumbering opponents 77 percent to 13 percent. But a second thing had changed. Even if in the minority, the environmental viewpoint had gained a governance foothold that allowed bridge opponents to delay the project by more than a decade before they exhausted their remedies in the courts. The juggernaut eventually prevailed, but not without a struggle.

Bridges

Bridges are a central feature of the community structure of river cities. Consider London, which has nineteen bridges over the Thames in the dozen miles between Hammersmith and the old docks of Canary Wharf. Prague, "the city of bridges," with eighteen bridges over the Vlatava, was built where people could easily cross. Twenty-five bridges cross the iconic eight-mile meander of the Seine through the heart of Paris.

The core of Albuquerque's metropolitan area in the 2020s had eight automobile bridges over the Rio Grande and one for pedestrians and bicycles in the roughly twenty-mile stretch of the Rio Grande spanning the metropolitan area's core. Beyond the urban core, another eleven river crossings connected communities spanning the Middle Rio Grande from its upstream end at Cochiti Dam to its downstream end at Elephant Butte Reservoir.

Often, a community's first urban form emerges from the places where a river might be crossed, beginning with ferries or fords preceding the solidity of a bridge. This pattern defined Albuquerque's early structure, with Old Town on high ground near one crossing and Barelas near another.

Albuquerque's first bridge was a pontoon affair, built near the village center (soon to become Old Town) in 1876 at what would become a prime crossing in the following century. It was replaced in 1882 with a permanent bridge.[9] "Of all the improvements that have been made in and about this city, during the last six months, perhaps the most important, looking at the future of Albuquerque, is the bridge now being constructed across the Rio Grande," the *Albuquerque Journal* wrote in September 1882. The bridge, the newspaper enthused, would open connections between Albuquerque and vast areas of economic activity to the west.[10]

In 1910 two steel bridges less than two miles apart were built across the Rio Grande in the heart of Albuquerque, one adjacent to what had unambiguously become Old Town and the second at Barelas. Over time, the Old Town Bridge became the dominant crossing. But in those early days of the growing metropolis, the Barelas Bridge mattered the most, linking the employment center at the railyard with early suburbs across the river.

While the challenge was most noticeable in the heart of the growing city, one of the most important early bridges was built at Isleta Pueblo downstream from Albuquerque. To get from the village to farm fields across the Rio Grande, Isletans had used a *barco*—a barge. Every bridge they tried to build would quickly wash away. Katishtya (San Felipe) Pueblo, upstream from Albuquerque, struggled with similar problems. In 1911, as New Mexico was on the brink of statehood, Isleta leader Pablo

Figure 32. Old Town Bridge across the Rio Grande at Albuquerque, circa 1890. Courtesy of the Albuquerque Museum, PA1973.012.010.

Abeita successfully lobbied the US Congress for federal funding for two Pueblo bridges.[11]

Similar crossings were needed up and down the river. In the 1920s at least nine bridges crossed the Rio Grande in the entire Middle Rio Grande Valley, the 120 miles between Cochiti Pueblo upstream and Socorro downstream. River communities need bridges.[12]

Late Twentieth-Century Bridges

Bridge construction stalled in the decades following the interstate completion across the Rio Grande in the 1960s, but growth did not. By the 1980s, pressure to expand the bridge network had become a major political force, not unlike the political force that had pushed for flood control and drainage six decades before. Once again, finding a way to adapt a growing city to the Rio Grande flowing through its midst—or to adapt the river to the city—played a defining role in the politics of Albuquerque's evolving urban structure.

The political battle was engaged in early 1983 when Gov. Toney Anaya proposed widening existing bridges and building one new one. In a replay of sorts of the 1920s "who has a say" arguments over the development of river management infrastructure, Anaya believed he had the legal authority to impose the bridges on recalcitrant local governments for what he viewed as the greater good. It was again a question of the scale of the action needed to manage the growing metropolitan area's relationship with the Rio Grande. The interests of individual local governments were unable, or unwilling, to act in the interests of the greater Albuquerque metropolitan area.[13]

Much of Anaya's 1983 plan survived the decade of political fights that followed, except for the Montaño Bridge, which finally doomed Naomi. Anaya opposed the bridge, throwing his political muscle behind affluent river valley residents, who had been trying since the 1960s to block it more than any others.

It was a clash of modern urbanity with a rural, environmental, country estate sensibility. The City of Albuquerque, led at the time by Mayor Harry Kinney, vowed to keep pushing for the bridge. State interests (as represented by Gov. Anaya) opposed him and, in so doing, were tangling with the complex polycentric local governance clash of a village established to protect the rural ambience and country estates that had formed to protect against the growing metropolis of Albuquerque. The resulting political battle followed the contours of Albuquerque's newly evolved relationship with the river, with all the conflicts and compromises that entailed.

Those conflicts and the comprises were foreshadowed in the 1983 state legislation turning the forested strip of Rio Grande bosque through Albuquerque, the portion of the river channel contained within the river's levees, into the Rio Grande State Park. Working the deal through the New Mexico legislature required two key compromises that signaled the tension among the community's values around the river. First, the legislation was written to explicitly acknowledge that flood control, drainage, and irrigation had primacy over recreation and environmental benefits. Second, land for two new bridges, including the Montaño Bridge along the southern edge of the Village of Los Ranchos, was excluded from the park's footprint.

In other words, the needs of the metropolis—for flood control, drainage, irrigation, and now transportation—were more important to the community than environmental and recreational values. To Rex Funk, who had by that time made the transition from Oxbow-protecting environmental activist to city open-space planner, a compromise was needed to preserve the broader environmental values: "This was a great blow to North Valley bridge opponents, many of whom had supported saving the River and Bosque as a strategy to block bridges they felt would impact their community. Funk empathized with their position but felt that protecting the Rio Grande River and bosque was far more important than fighting a protracted battle against bridges without the Park."[14]

North Valley communities, led by the deep-pocketed residents of the Village of Los Ranchos, tied the Montaño Bridge up in court for more than a decade, attempting strategies that included preservation of archaeological sites and the first litigation over risks to the endangered Rio Grande silvery minnow. The presence of the little fish would shape river management in the twenty-first century, and the legal battles over the Montaño Bridge represented its first appearance on the public stage. The City of Albuquerque countered the threat of the minnow and other environmental concerns by structuring the project so that it could be built entirely with money from the city's budget, removing the straitjacket of political and legal constraints that came via the Endangered Species Act and other state and federal laws when *other people's money*—funding from the state and federal government—is used for a project.

It was not until 1995 that the courts finally ruled in Albuquerque's favor after several decades of court cases, clearing the way for bridge construction. By December, the bulldozers were grinding through the narrow strip of bosque set aside for the bridge corridor, and Naomi, the cottonwood, was gone.

Environmental and Cultural Lessons

The contradiction at the heart of the relationship between the Village of Los Ranchos and the river flowing down its western edge was not lost on supporters of the Montaño Bridge. Before the Middle Rio Grande Conservancy District brought the first waves of levees and drainage works that made it possible for the affluent community to exist, large areas of what had become Los Ranchos were riverside woods and salt-grass marshes—"swamps" in the old vernacular but "wetlands" in the environmentalist language of the 1990s—interlaced with ditches and small subsistence farming plots.

"It's strange but there wasn't any sobbing or candlelight vigils when the thousands of other trees were bulldozed to make way for those expensive Los Ranchos homes, pools, fields, tennis courts, and driveways," one valley resident complained, pointing to the contradiction at the heart of the

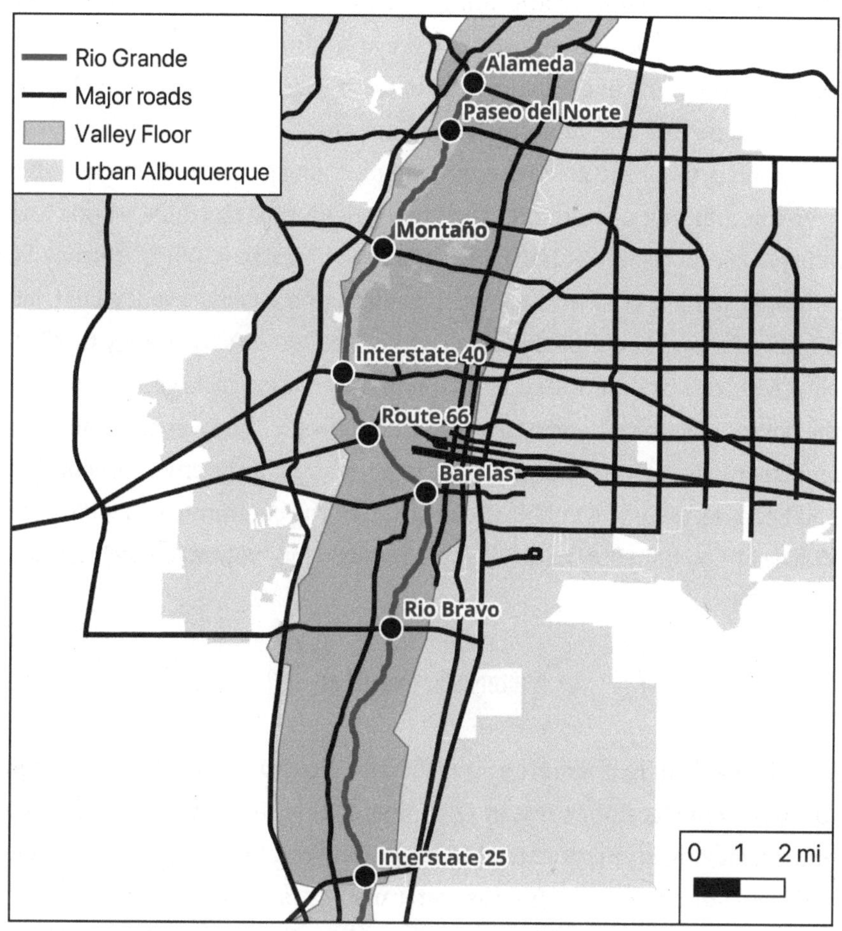

Map 11. Bridges of Albuquerque, circa 2025. Map by John Fleck.

Montaño Bridge fight. In appealing to the preservation of Naomi and the silvery minnow, bridge opponents were appealing to a vision of "nature" and the river's role in the valley that had long ago been abandoned by the very structure of the community in which they lived.[15]

Naomi symbolized an environmental past long gone as she stood watch over the draining of wetlands and the transition of riverside woods and subsistence farms into subdivisions and country estates. When attorney W. A. Sutherland in 1930 praised the formation of the Conservancy District, the use of levees and drains to remake the Rio Grande's hydrology through New Mexico's Middle Valley, as enabling the creation of "a garden spot for the homes of a united, successful, contented people,"[16] he was endorsing the movement away from a natural river to a human-altered environment that had been necessary to enable the creation of the community in which the Village of Los Ranchos' nature-defending residents now made their homes.

Interlude: December

Under a natural hydrograph, a river like the Rio Grande would be expected to run low in December. But in December 2023 the rules were overriding nature, leaving an institutional hydrograph with flows higher than they had been since the end of June as water managers moved the Rio Grande's water past the Middle Valley to communities in southern New Mexico, Texas, and Mexico.

At the Conservancy District's December 2023 meeting, water manager Anne Marken was optimistic that the sacrifices the District had made, reducing diversions to Middle Rio Grande Valley farmers in order to send more water downstream to pay down New Mexico's Compact debt, would help. Until the debt was paid off, the rules would continue to mean little irrigation water for the valley's ditches in late summer and fall.

Marken showed her board members a map projecting chances of above-average precipitation for December-February 2023–2024. "With that," she concluded, "I will encourage everyone to pray for snow."

Figure 33. Birds feed on a Rio Grande sandbar as the first layer of next year's snow begins accumulating on the Sandias. Photograph by John Fleck.

CONCLUSION

"But let us cultivate our garden."
Candide[1]

Through the summer and fall of 2024, the board of directors of the Middle Rio Grande Conservancy District took an odd detour down a path that illustrates the evolving tensions over Albuquerque's relationship with the Rio Grande and the landscape of the valley floor: the challenge of e-bike regulation. This ended up on the policy plate of what is ostensibly a water agency because managing Albuquerque's relationship with the Rio Grande is more than a water-management task. It is about people's relationship with places they hold dear and things they have reason to value.

When Aldo Leopold in 1917 described "people hanging over the rail of the Barelas bridge, and tramping under the cottonwoods along the Rio Grande,"[2] he was describing what the French sociologist and philosopher Henri Lefebvre described as the social production of space. Lefebvre argues that places are more than just physical; they are the product of our interactions with them. The government can slap a label on a landscape, but that label does not always coincide with the lived experiences of the community's members.[3]

Thus, for example, the Conservancy District's spatial logic in carrying out its water delivery task categorized the Oxbow, the wetlands left behind by water managers in their 1950 "rectification" of the river, as inefficient. Rex Funk and Eco Warrior disagreed. Their lived experience with the space reflected something different: a place of environmental value separate from the water-management function of river management. From that tension in the 1970s, a new relationship between the Rio Grande and its community emerged.

The e-bike meetings of 2024 were the latest iteration of such debates. Paths down the side of ditches, including major dirt roads along the district's larger drains, are nominally built and maintained as water-management infrastructure so Conservancy District crews can get to the waterways to do their work. But they also represent remarkable automobile-free corridors through the Middle Valley, sometimes providing convenient access to a piece of property, often providing a lovely, shady, safe place to walk or ride a bike. Or to ride an electric motor-assisted bicycle—an e-bike. In response to the new technology, the Conservancy District's board initially prohibited e-bikes on the district's property, which includes popular paved trails through the green spaces of Albuquerque's Rio Grande Valley.

E-bike enthusiasts were outraged, and e-bike critics were delighted. Speaker after speaker at the 2024 e-bike meetings argued their preferred understanding of how the space should be viewed. Are the district's ditches transportation corridors? Recreational amenities? Environmental sanctuaries? Or, as the district staff was at pains to point out, infrastructure for managing an irrigation system—service roads for Conservancy District pickups?

For our purposes, the outcome—a tangle of careful legal language effectively permitting e-bikes on paved trails along Conservancy District right-of-way—is less important than the terms and process of the debate. There would have been a time, during the first half century of the Conservancy District's existence, when such a discussion would have been unthinkable. As we have seen, the district was managed until the 1970s by a board of appointed experts, beyond the reach of the sort of community input that we saw in the 2024 e-bike debates. State legislator Raymond Garcia's complaints in the 1970s about ditch safety and community parks had nowhere to go other than the pursuit of an entirely new governance structure. The shift that followed toward a more direct form of democratic governance created a community decision-making framework that matches one of the things Elinor Ostrom saw again and again in her studies of successful institutions created for the collective management of natural resources: "Individuals affected by the operational rules can participate in modifying the operational rules."[4] The evolving governance framework of the Middle Rio Grande Conservancy District had created the space for members of the Albuquerque community to have their say about e-bikes and to adapt the nature of their institution to the values of a changing community.

Democracy in a Hotter World

As a terrifying pandemic fog enveloped the world in the spring of 2020, the Duranes Ditch in Albuquerque's North Valley was transformed. Tree-lined and cool, the Duranes has the quasi-geologic structure of a traditional New Mexico acequia. The berms on either side emerged slowly, layers of earth created by centuries of la limpia, the spring cleanings needed to keep the slow, cool water flowing. They are an artifact of a cultural geology, humans clearing sediment from this little branch of the Rio Grande's path one year at a time.

In the twenty-first century, the ditch banks spiderwebbed across the Middle Rio Grande Valley have become walking paths through the neighborhoods of the Albuquerque metropolitan area's valley floor, tree-lined and cool against the summer heat. In the spring and summer of 2020, the Duranes became a pandemic lifeline. The usual flow of ditch walkers turned into a flood.[5]

Dug in 1706, the Duranes cuts a quiet path through Albuquerque's history. It once carried irrigation water four miles south from its brush and log heading on the Rio Grande;

- across the lands of Ambrosio Zamora, who sued, claiming he should not have to pay taxes on Middle Rio Grande Conservancy District benefits he never received;
- past riverside timber, including Naomi the cottonwood, and the farmlands of Los Griegos, where Max Gutierrez and his brothers lived in the 1920s when Albuquerque was creating the Middle Rio Grande Conservancy District;
- through a tangled ditch junction with the old Albuquerque Ditch, which carried water to Old Town;
- through timber and swamp land that by the turn of the twentieth century had become Matthew Dairy, producing milk for a slowly growing city;
- past Palmer's Slough, the old Albuquerque swimming hole;
- following the ever-so-slightly higher ground to carry out its duty, irrigating the farm plots of the village of Los Duranes;
- down through the farmlands between Old Town and the Rio Grande to its final destination, a return to the Rio Grande near what today is Albuquerque's Central Avenue Bridge.

Adjacent to the roughly three-hundred-year-old Los Duranes neighborhood, the former Matthew dairy lands are home—for nearly ninety years now—to the Alvarado Gardens neighborhood. It is a city story and a subdivision story that captures the transition from rural subsistence agriculture to a growing city. Its developers, the owner of an old dairy and his real estate partners, built it in the *immediate wake* of the creation of the Conservancy District, highlighted in local papers as one example of a "rapidly growing group" of small farm and subdivision projects being developed north and south of Albuquerque as the Conservancy District built the first drains and levees in the early 1930s.[6]

Once the Conservancy District drains had turned the swampy bottomland into a development opportunity, the dairy's owners sued to quiet title

Figure 34. Socially distanced, the ditch walkers in the summer of 2020 turned the Duranes ditch into a pandemic lifeline. Photograph by John Fleck.

to various tracts in 1932, simultaneous with the creation of the Alvarado Gardens addition.[7] Within a year, the developers were advertising small two-acre plots: "You may have the security a suburban home affords . . . a rich, well-irrigated farm within three miles of the heart of a growing city."[8] It is a story quickly replicated in other housing developments. Today, the neighborhood, adjacent to the Rio Grande, notably contains the heavily visited, state-owned Rio Grande Nature Center.

Through this neighborhood and others nearby, the Duranes still carries water in the twenty-first century, irrigating 159 properties. The irrigated parcels it now reaches could hardly be called farms. On the largest parcel, the 167-acre city-owned Candelaria Nature Preserve, land once farmed in alfalfa was by 2024 being landscaped into a meticulously gardened replica of the natural landscape described in the 1930s by Marjorie Van Cleave as it was lost when the Conservancy District levees and ditches went in nearly a century before. The land the Duranes crosses today still harkens back to an agri-*cultural* history, even if the landscape it traverses is dramatically changed.[9]

On an early April day in 2011, Joey Trujillo watched as his crew of Middle Rio Grande Conservancy District ditch riders ushered the first water of spring down the Duranes, scooping out tumbleweeds with pitchforks as they backed up water at each successive culvert, following the ditch's wandering path downstream through the neighborhood today known as Dietz Farms. The pickup trucks and backhoe were distinctly modern, as is the fact that a crew of government employees was doing the work paid with property tax revenue rather than the labor of the Duranes community members themselves. But the underlying ritual of the spring ditch cleaning—the work of la limpia—is essentially unchanged from how community members would have done it three centuries ago.

As Trujillo followed his crew south, he pointed off to the west, to a line of trees snaking through the neighborhood, shading twenty-first-century homes. That line of trees, he explained, follows the path of an old irrigation ditch. The ghosts of water are ever with us.[10]

Institutions and the Spandrels of San Marco

Understanding community, as we have seen, requires understanding the institutions of collective action. But they are never completed, evolving in layers, like the dirt along the Duranes ditch bank. The Conservancy District's irrigation canal evolved from a tool for subsistence farming to a community greenbelt, becoming a favorite place for walking amidst nature, riding e-bikes, or serving as an existential lifeline for a modern suburb during a pandemic crisis. These aspects were far removed from the intentions of the fledgling group of public entrepreneurs—Pablo Abeita, Aldo Leopold, and Max Gutierrez—when they gathered at Albuquerque's Commercial Club in 1919 to plan the city's future.

The evolutionary biologists Stephen Jay Gould and Richard C. Lewontin famously laid out an argument in 1979 worth considering as we ponder the modern Duranes ditch. Their metaphor was architectural—the "spandrels of San Marco," gorgeous mosaics found in the ceilings of St. Mark's Cathedral in Venice. Tucked in corners left above the point where two arches meet, they appear purposeful. But the spaces in which the artists place them, curved corners filling spaces between architectural arches, are not.

"The design is so elaborate, harmonious, and purposeful that we are tempted to view it as the starting point of any analysis," they wrote. "But this would invert the proper path of analysis. The system begins with an architectural constraint: the necessary four spandrels and their tapering triangular form. They provide a space in which the mosaicists worked." To focus on the mosaics without understanding the happenstance of the architectural opportunity they exploit leads us astray, Gould and Lewontin wrote. Rather than form following function, it is a never-ending succession of evolving functions atop the old forms.[11]

The Duranes, laid down in the 1700s and preserved as the community chose to create a Conservancy District to build levees, drain the swampy valley floor around Duranes, and consolidate the Middle Rio Grande Valley's irrigation ditches, is one of our spandrels. Consider Philip Harroun's

1895 description of the Duranes: "Duranes ditch heads 3 miles above the old town of Albuquerque, passes below the town, and tails about 1 mile further down. . . . It has a common brush dam diverting about 11 cubic feet per second when at full capacity."[12]

Hidden behind the simple hydrologic description from Harroun, a US Geologic Survey scientist who surveyed the valley's irrigation works in the 1890s, is a rich, complex, and enduring water institution. Harroun's "11 cubic feet per second" was enough water to irrigate perhaps three hundred acres. Creating and maintaining such an irrigation system was beyond the scope and scale of an individual farmer. It required community effort—collective action. Groups of individuals had to come together each year to open their irrigation ditches, maintain them over the spring and summer irrigation seasons, and rebuild their river diversions when the inevitable high flows blew them out. That required rules and cultural norms of shared labor and water. It needed, in short, an institution.

Writes acequia scholar José Rivera:

> In places where the temporary dams were destroyed, rebuilding took investments of labor, a renewable community asset, and we surmise that abandonment was not an option. Subsistence agriculture was the mainstay economy for most rural New Mexicans since the time of the first settlement and lasted well into the twentieth century.[13]

There is physical technology here—Harroun's dismissive "common brush dam," a colonialist's misunderstanding of a sophisticated cultural and physical technology that had served communities well for more than two centuries before the US Geological Survey's science arrived on the scene. But the institution—the group coming together to write rules, a mix of formal and informal, about how to share the water and the responsibility of ensuring its arrival each year—is the more important technology.

Physical technologies and institutions evolve like the biological systems represented by Gould and Lewontin's spandrel metaphor. Institutions that contribute to the success of those using them survive. Those that don't, perish. In the case of the irrigation ditch network on the Middle Rio Grande Valley floor, the institutions in their premodern form—the Pueblo social structures that enabled successful agriculture to support enduring communities—have existed "from time immemorial." With the arrival of the Spanish, the institutions adapted to the complex and changing circumstances of conquest and colonization, emerging in a new form that persisted for another two hundred years.

Between Cochiti Pueblo, at the mouth of White Rock Canyon, and the heart of modern Albuquerque, twenty-six such irrigation systems endured into the twentieth century—physical dams and ditches, but more importantly, the human communities gathered around them in the collective action needed to maintain them year after year—or go hungry.[14]

We no longer use them to feed the metro community today, but they endure—in a very different form—carrying history with them into what became modern Albuquerque.

When Harroun surveyed the valley in 1895, the Duranes had already carried water three miles from its "common brush dam" to the community whose fields it had irrigated for the better part of two centuries. The landscape and communities are far different today, but the ditch is the constant.

Tools for the Future

We know time out of doors in a landscape of water and green—"exposure to . . . blue-green spaces," to borrow the language of researcher Sarai Pouso,[15] benefits mental health and well-being. Pouso and colleagues used COVID-19 lockdowns as a natural experiment to study the role of access to plants and water ("blue-green spaces"). Contact with nature, they found, helped people cope with the depression and anxiety linked to the lockdowns.

COVID-19 emphasized this reality, but the benefits of "blue-green spaces" had been there all along, played out in the desires of a growing community to maintain the rich tapestry of ditches flowing through the city's midst. The language of the boosters in 1927, making the final push for the creation of the Middle Rio Grande Conservancy District, was economic—the creation of a metropolis on the valley floor. But in evoking something more profound, it envisioned something deeper, beyond monetary value: creating a garden.

By the early 1930s, with the economic agony of the Great Depression eating America from the inside out, the push to expand "reclamation" had moved from merely bringing irrigation water to dry lands to the broader goal of drainage—whole river management. But it also meant something more: turning desert river valleys into gardens.

Testifying before the House Committee on Irrigation and Reclamation in December 1930, San Francisco banker and irrigation booster J. Rupert Mason sang the praises of reclamation in economic terms. But Mason's language evoked something more than agricultural profit:

> These epoch-making achievements have gone steadily forward, under fair and foul economic conditions during periods of high mortality for railways, industries, banks, and commercial institutions, and today irrigated agriculture stands in the front ranks in annual earnings and total assets on the capital investment which changed the old deserts into gardens of the new West.[16]

Mason quoted the enthusiastic words of a group of boosters from Southern California, who, with the abundant waters and easy irrigation possible from the region's foothills, were decades ahead of the rest of the West down the evolutionary path of "reclamation." What started there as a push for commercial agriculture had, as happened in Albuquerque, become something more.

> Its broad avenues are embowered in luxuriant foliage and the adjacent orange groves and fine fruit gardens present a marked contrast to the vast barren unirrigated regions thereabout not yet touched by the magic wand—water.[17]

The modern institution that supports the life of the Duranes is rooted in the 1923 state legislation that enabled the creation of conservancy districts. In those early years, whether the institution was robust enough to survive its evolutionary test was unclear. The details mattered as the community struggled to agree on the rules. But the institution survived.

When the Conservancy District floundered over the next half century over a mechanism to finance the benefits it was providing, its enduring argument over "who has a say, and who has to pay" was an argument over the rules. When the community struggled over who would have a say over where to build bridges, it was an argument over the rules. When the community wrestled with the environmental value of a tiny fish, it was an argument over the rules.

We can expect more such discussions, debates, and deliberations to come. Albuquerque's relationship with the Rio Grande is in a perpetual state of becoming, something never completed. For greater Albuquerque and the Middle Rio Grande Valley, like so many other places under climate change, it will be about democracy in a hotter world. When we think about building resilient communities, developing the ability to adapt to such significant change,[18] our first reaction might be to think about designing physical infrastructure. But we suggest that looking closely at the tending to the mix of institutional arrangements is a more important place to begin.

If our point is merely to test evolutionary success, we can stop here. The Duranes and the Middle Rio Grande Conservancy District in which it is embedded have passed the evolutionary test. It continues to exist. But that falls short of the goal if we want to explain *why* it still exists—why it was there for the COVID-19 ditch walkers when they needed it in that dark spring and summer of 2020, for the newly emergent technology of e-bikes. We also must understand how, whether, and why it might provide us with the tools the community needs to negotiate its path through a future with more people and less water.

For this task, the metaphor offered by the evolutionary biologists Gould and Lewontin is helpful. There is a danger, they argue, in narrowly defining "traits"—single-focus objects of evolutionary analysis. What is an eye for? Obviously, to see! But Gould and Lewontin warn us of the risk of defining narrowly. "Organisms are integrated entities," they write, "not collections of discrete objects."

The Middle Rio Grande Conservancy District's elected board meets in the Diego Abeita Board Room, named after a leader from Isleta Pueblo—from a generation after Pablo Abeita—who helped ensure Pueblo water while also bridging divides between the Native and non-Native communities.[19] To visit the board room on the second Monday afternoon of each month is to hear a string of discussions about single traits. The most common single trait discussed is irrigation water delivery to farmers. But the pageant of democracy playing out there each week is full of other traits—culverts over ditches, floods washing across the Conservancy District canals and into nearby neighborhoods, predation from elk on farmlands irrigated with the district water, endless debates about locked gates and community access to the Conservancy District's ditches, and the pros and cons of e-bikes.

The sum of all those traits and the organism they embody must be the unit of analysis here.

If we look at the original goals for which the community established the District—flood control, drainage, and irrigation—the report card is mixed. The Conservancy District and the governmental superstructure in which it is embedded—the federal Army Corps of Engineers and Bureau of Reclamation, the valley's various flood-control agencies—have largely eliminated the risk of Rio Grande floods, though it is an enduring task that will never be finished. As with many metropolitan areas, most of the monetary costs for urban flood protection were, in the end, paid with federal dollars from the mid-1900s onward. Locally, the Middle Valley and local agencies like the Conservancy District continue to cover only a matching fraction (commonly around 25 percent for many decades) for federal entities like the US Army Corps of Engineers.

The completion of the drainage task has been so successful that it is hard to notice. There are no more swamps.

Regarding irrigation, the report card is mixed. The District continues to deliver irrigation water to some 60,000 acres of farmland in the Middle Rio Grande Valley. This is far less than the more than 120,000 acres envisioned. The fact that net cash farm income in the valley is marginal and for some counties negative suggests the institution has failed in meeting its goal of delivering a commercially prosperous belt of agriculture surrounding a growing Albuquerque. Some might even calculate, from the singular restrictive frame of commercial agriculture, that it would be efficient to trade away Middle Valley Conservancy District water to larger and more profitable farms elsewhere.[20] To shrink the ribbons of green from a large, high desert metropolitan area?

But, as argued by the Canadian political economist Brian Lee Crowley, institutional evaluation is often best accomplished from a "gardening" rather than a strictly engineering or mechanical perspective:

> The traditionalist gardener, in contrast, thinks human action does not proceed from abstract first principles, but from messy and very un-theoretical practical experience of what works and has passed the test of time and is acquiesced in by the population regardless of how "quaint" or "inefficient" it appears to those who value only abstractions and not practical success.[21]

A similar perspective can be seen in the words of Elinor Ostrom in her doctoral thesis when she described what she was doing as creating a "natural history of the evolution of a program in public administration." Joseph Burkholder and the other designers of the original Conservancy

District acting in the 1920s were acting as Crowley's engineers, attempting to create and adhere to a design. But we ended up with a century of evolution, of what Crowley would describe as "gardening"—of attempting to tend a patch for human flourishing and capabilities. If we grant that the deeper goal behind the mantra of "flood control, drainage, and irrigation" was to enable the growth of a modern city, the Middle Rio Grande Conservancy District must be considered a stunning practical success.

As Albuquerque enters the middle decades of the twenty-first century, the challenge is how the institutions might respond to the declining Rio Grande due to climate change.

How might the competing values of water for human use outside the levees—the ditches like the Duranes threading through peri-urban neighborhoods—be weighed against the value of the old river itself, snaking down its artificially narrowed path between the levees?

What of societal equity, a challenge that has dogged the institutions in the century since Pablo Abeita and Frank A. Hubbell insisted that the burdens of modernity not be unfairly placed on their communities? How might we avoid the risk as we advance that the garden on the valley floor becomes the province of the city's most affluent? How can our institutions, so robust in adapting to the changes of the last century, adapt to the next century's challenges?

Institutions and Community

To start, we must recognize that the greater Albuquerque community built, borrowed, and modified the various institutional arrangements—defects and all—that continue to define our collective relationship with the river. These arrangements, which have affected us so significantly over the last one hundred years, were created from the valley floodplain up and altered more than once.

The community can alter them again if need be.

Our premise has been that understanding a community requires understanding its relationship with its water. And we must understand the institutions the people of this community created to manage that relationship. To paraphrase Aldo Leopold, we are interested in the relationship of people with people and of the people of greater Albuquerque with their river, the Rio Grande.[22]

This requires analyzing what animated the community's will to act on the scale and in the way we have described and searching for the reasons behind it.[23] Albuquerque as a city emerged from a drained and irrigated river valley floor, where the hydrological system was upended, and the river disconnected from its natural floodplain nearly a century ago. That disconnection created the enabling conditions for the growth of what fellow Burqueños consider a great metropolis.

The Conservancy Act, a set of rules establishing the community's relationship with its river and enabling the creation of the Middle Rio Grande Conservancy District to carry out the work, was the cause. The question is, why? What were the community's reasons for doing it?

The plausible reasons were that the civic boosters wanted to build a city. They wanted it to be a garden spot that was

- well drained.
- well irrigated.
- flood protected.

It would

- bring their businesses and interests economic gain.
- provide jobs to the throngs.
- feed growing home markets.

After all, it was hard to develop economically in a swamp.

We see evidence of their commitment to this in their actions. They invested their wealth, time, and energy in Tobacco Farms, Bosque Farms, in Alvarado Gardens, and similarly the Los Alamos Addition and Merritt Acres, in the Conservancy Beach park, country club, and Huning addition, and a dozen early suburbs that would irrigate their yards and gardens directly from Conservancy District ditches. They began investing in business expansions with the growing city protected by better flood control and drainage. A favorite historical example from January 1, 1931, is the Hutchinson Fruit Company celebrating a new building in downtown Albuquerque, including expansion to six banana rooms to regularly handle expanded rail import of bananas to Albuquerque consumers, which they anticipated was "certain to follow with completion of the conservancy project." [24]

The boosters won the argument over Albuquerque's future. Against sometimes significant opposition, they gathered political support and crafted a winning narrative. Albuquerque was once a garden of Eden, and reclamation writ large would bring its return, only better.

Their 1920s financial model and underlying political structure were deeply flawed, and the flood protection technology was incomplete. Finishing those projects over the ensuing decades would be a struggle and incur steep costs. But the steepest costs and our most significant debts, as borne in the example of the community of Cochiti Pueblo—and the lifelong home of Jose Alcario Montoya—weren't solely financial.

But the valley *was* drained, protected from flooding, and left with a magnificent network of green irrigation ditches to carry out the river's annual spring rite of distribution across the valley floor. Albuquerque became the metropolis the boosters intended. The valley's three cultures—Indigenous Pueblo, Hispanic, and Anglo—coevolved in a combination of conflict, collaboration, and change. This is where we find the relationship of people with people and people with their river.

As the city grew, urban issues came with it: ditch safety, changing environmental values, traffic, bridges, municipal water supply, wastewater, and recreation. The relationship between the community and the river was constantly evolving; never completed, always becoming.

Joey Trujillo, manager of a team of Conservancy District ditch riders, a product of Albuquerque's South Valley who grew up playing in ditches and now managed them, stood next to a newly flowing Albuquerque Main canal one March day in the early 2000s, describing the joy of watching the arrival of the first water of spring. The swamps and the flood menace were gone that warm spring day. The trees bore the promise of spring, buds not yet green, as the dry ditch took its first drink.

It's like you can feel the valley breathing in, he said.

Acknowledgments

The authors are deeply grateful to the students in their Water Resources 571 classes who, over more than a dozen years, have brought their best questions to help us think about water in the Middle Rio Grande Valley. Beyond the coursework, we offer special thanks to Annalise Porter and Brennan Davis, who in their transition from students to water resource professionals, brought energy and curiosity to the task of helping us sort through our muddled thinking. Special thanks to the staff at the Middle Rio Grande Conservancy District, especially Doug Strech for helping us unearth crucial cartographic resources to make sense of the history of the Rio Grande Valley floor, and Anne Marken for helping us understand how water moves through the valley. John Fleck offers special thanks to Scot Key, who first rescued Max Gutierrez from the dustbin of history, and who spent countless hours in the years since bicycling across the book's landscape, both conceptually and quite literally.

We thank the University of New Mexico Department of Economics, the university's Water Resources Program, and the Utton Center at the University of New Mexico School of Law for providing us an academic home for the work.

We also thank Mary Harner, Adrian Oglesby, and two anonymous reviewers for helping us clarify our arguments, and to Sonia Dickey and Baker Morrow at the University of New Mexico Press for helping us take on this project.

For Robert Berrens: This book is dedicated to my family—Mary, Bobby, and Maggie.

For John Fleck: This book is dedicated to Lissa, who has read every word and helped through every struggle.

Notes

Preface

1. NOAA Northeast Regional Climate Center, xmACIS2, https://xmacis.rcc-acis.org/.

2. The Commercial Club, Albuquerque Museum, PA1990.013.057.A, is variously referred to as the Commercial Club Building, the Commercial Building, and the Commerce Building, the latter being how it was listed in the 1919 Albuquerque City Directory as the home of the Chamber of Commerce: See Hudspeth's Albuquerque City Directory, 1919, 69.

3. See Adair, "Reconstructing the Historical Albuquerque Reach of the Middle Rio Grande to Evaluate the Influence of River Engineering on Floodplain Inundation." By the time of the 1919 Commercial Club meeting on drainage, the growing city was appropriating funds paving Fourth Street four miles northward towards the Alameda area and the river bend which was the head of the older river channel. See "Albuquerque," *Albuquerque Morning Journal*, June 19, 1919, 3.

4. Commercial Club, *Albuquerque Journal*, Jan. 18, 1891, 4.

5. Meine, *Aldo Leopold*.

6. Ebright and Hendricks, *Pablo Abeita*.

7. Horgan, *Great River*, x, preface to the fourth edition.

8. Glaeser, *Triumph of the City*.

9. Sen, *Development as Freedom*.

10. Sen, *Home in the World*, 20.

11. Anaya, *Querencia*.

12. Ostrom, "Public Entrepreneurship."

13. Hobbes, *Leviathan*.

14. Ostrom, *Governing the Commons*.

15. Ostrom, "A Long Polycentric Journey."

16. Ostrom, *Why Do We Need to Protect Institutional Diversity?*

17. Beginning in *Governing the Commons*, Elinor Ostrom offered various versions of the design principles used to assess common property resource institutional arrangements. We focus here on two, which were critical in the evolution of Albuquerque's relationship with the Rio Grande—1) rules governing who is entitled to how much of the benefits of the resources, and who pays the costs associated with that use, and 2) rules empowering resource users in the development and modification of the rules.

18. As hydrologic engineers Mark Stone and Ryan Morrison write (Stone and Morrison, *Human Impacts*): "The desert cities of Albuquerque and Reno provide two examples of sprawling communities that occupy historical floodplains, and which depend almost entirely on surface-water diversions or groundwater pumping from hydrologically connected aquifers."

19. Ostrom, "Why Do We Need to Protect Institutional Diversity?"

20. John Fleck, "The Institutional Hydrograph," *Inkstain* (blog), Dec. 9, 2015; https://www.inkstain.net/2015/12/institutional-hydrology-new-mexicos-rio-grande-in-december/.

Introduction

1. US Geological Survey, National Water Information System, Peak Streamflow for New Mexico, gage 08319000, https://nwis.waterdata.usgs.gov/nm/nwis/peak?site_n0=08319000&agency_cd=USGS&format=html.

2. "Conservancy Park is Included in Limits of City: 43 Acres," *Albuquerque Journal*, July 22, 1931, 1.

3. Wood, "Dynamic Fallowing in the Middle Rio Grande," 17.

4. Greenness estimates via OpenET Project, https://openetdata.org/; Melton et al., *OpenET*, 2.

5. Welcome to San Felipe Pueblo, accessed Nov. 17, 2023, https://sfpueblo.com/.

6. "Pueblo" is a Spanish word, and also a category imposed by colonization. Individual members of Pueblo communities most often identify with their home village or, in some cases, their clan. Some also identify with the linguistic family to which their village belongs—Tewa, Tiwa, Keres, Hopi. See Liebmann, *Revolt*, 230.

7. Patrick Lohmann, "Historic Rainfall: Rivers Rise, Damage Mounts as Water Pushes Out N.M. Residents," *Albuquerque Journal*, Sept. 14, 2013, 1.

8. Frost, *The Railroad and the Pueblo Indians*.

9. Cronon, *Nature's Metropolis*.

10. Van Dyke, *The Desert*.

11. Rivera, *Acequia Culture*.

12. In modern terminology, a "hydrologist."

13. Follett, *A Study of the Use of Water for Irrigation on the Rio Grande del Norte Above Fort Quitman, Texas*, 129.

14. Alburquerque Correspondence, *Santa Fe New Mexican*, Aug. 5, 1868, 1 (Note that "Alburquerque," with an additional "r," was the original spelling of the community's name and still in use in the 1860s).

15. Scurlock, *From the Rio to the Sierra*, 35.

16. *Santa Fe New Mexican*, June 9, 1874, 1.

17. *Albuquerque Journal*, April 13, 1889, 4.

18. Scurlock, *From the Rio to the Sierra*, table 17, 33 et seq.

19. "garden," OED Online. Oxford University Press, December 2021; John Fleck, "Ribbons of Green: The Hubbell Oxbow," *Inkstain* (blog), posted Jan. 24, 2023, https://www.inkstain.net/2023/01/ribbons-of-green-the-hubbell-oxbow/.

20. John Fleck, "Collective Action and the Ribbons of Green," *Inkstain* (blog), posted Sept. 19, 2022, https://www.inkstain.net/2022/09/collective-action-and-the-ribbons-of-green/.

21. Fleck, "Going Down to the Water."

22. Schechter, *From the German of Doctor Ralph*, 635–37.

23. Meyer, *Water in the Hispanic Southwest*.

24. Hays, *Conservation and the Gospel of Efficiency*.

25. Ch. 73, art. 18 NMSA 1978. Originally passed in 1923, then amended after a crucial political battle in 1927, the Conservancy Act set out the goals and rules for the remaking of the Middle Rio Grande Valley. See Chapter 2.

26. Ostrom, "Institutions and the Environment."

27. As defined by the economist Daniel Bromley, institutional arrangements refer to the rules of the game, both formal and informal (i.e., social conventions and norms), that both liberate and constrain individual choice behaviors, in settings of repeated interactions among people. See Bromley, *Economic Interests and Institutions*.

28. Ostrom, "Public Entrepreneurship."

29. Bromley, *Sufficient Reason*.

30. Russell, *Racial Groups in the New Mexico Legislature*, pp. 62–71.

31. In the entire creation period of the Conservancy District, roughly 1918 to 1935, members of the six Middle Rio Grande Pueblos did not have the right to vote. While the federal government granted citizenship to Native Americans in 1924, they were barred from the right to vote in New Mexico by interpretation of the state constitution until 1948. For a brief history of the 1948 state district court case involving Isleta Pueblo educator Miguel Trujillo Jr., see: Andrew Oxford, "It's Been 70 Years Since the Court Ruled Native Americans Could Vote in New Mexico," *Santa Fe New Mexican*, Aug. 2, 2018.

32. Westphall, *Albuquerque in the 1870's*, 2.

33. For a broader view of Progressive Era resource management see Hays, *Conservation and the Gospel of Efficiency*.

34. Middle Rio Grande Conservancy District, Fiscal Year 2025 Budget.

35. United States Department of Agriculture, National Agricultural Statistics Service, "New Mexico State and County Data, Vol. 1, Geographic Area Series, Park 31," 2017 Census of Agriculture, https://www.nass.usda.gov/Publications/AgCensus/2017/Full_Report/Volume_1,_Chapter_2_County_Level/New_Mexico/nmv1.pdf; US Department of Commerce Regional GDP & Personal Income, CAINC45 Farm income and expenses, https://www.bea.gov/itable/regional-gdp-and-personal-income.

36. Clark, *Water in New Mexico*, 387.

37. Griego, "When High-Water-Use Neighbors Move In."

38. Notably, in the late 1920s ownership of the Bosque de los Pinos lands was unsuccessfully contested by the Isleta Pueblo before the Pueblo Lands Board. As formed under the Pueblo Lands Act of 1924, the Board essentially upheld the title for the Spanish Land Grant to Antonio Gutierrez and Joaquin Sedillo, which had been previously upheld by the US Supreme Court in 1899. See "Pueblo Land Board Rejects Isleta Claims," *Albuquerque Journal*, Aug. 26, 1928, 9; "New Demand for Firing Hagerman Comes From Isleta, Land Complaint," *Albuquerque Journal*, May 8, 1931, 1; United States v. Chavez, 175 US 509 (1899), US Supreme Court.

39. Otero appears to have acquired the lands via various purchases in the first several decades of the 1900s; this includes purchasing part of the "Nicholas Duran de Chavez" land grant (as purchased by Duran de Chavez, and originally known as the Antonio Gutierrez and Joaquin Sedillo Land Grant of 1716), by settling the delinquent taxes to Valencia County in 1927, shortly after the passing of the Conservancy Act of 1927 that he helped broker. See "Back Taxes Settled on De Chavez Grant," *Albuquerque Journal*, June 10, 1927, 5; "Bosque Farms, New Mexico," http://www.sangres.com/newmexico/valencia/bosquefarms.htm#.YhNMfy1h3fY. As the MRGCD moved into the construction phase, Otero incorporated Bosque Farms Inc. in New Mexico with his partners in February 1931 (see "Legal Notices," *Albuquerque Journal*, Feb. 13, 1931, 8), and incorporated the New Mexico Canning Company in New Mexico with his wife and son in April 1932 (see "Commission Doing Rushing Business," *Albuquerque Journal*, April 5, 1932, 6).

40. "Cannery Will be Established Near Albuquerque to Handle Products of Rio Grande Farms," *Albuquerque Journal*, Dec. 18, 1931, 1.

41. While a savvy businessman and developer, Otero was also described as the "patron" of Valencia County, New Mexico. He was a complicated political figure, navigating a period of modernization. For editorial eulogies of Otero in New Mexico's two largest papers at the time, see Eduardo M. Otero, *Albuquerque Journal*, April 10, 1932, 4; Eduardo Otero, *The Santa Fe New Mexican*, April 11, 1932, 4.

42. Melzer, “New Deal Success or ‘Noble Failure?’”

43. Bosque Farms incorporated as a municipality in 1974.

44. For example, according to USA.com, Albuquerque is ranked as the 417th densest metropolitan area out of 917 areas in the US in population per square mile, but none of the lower-ranked areas have even three-fourths the population of Albuquerque (i.e., they tend to be much smaller cities). See http://www.usa.com/rank/us—population-density—metro-area-rank.htm, accessed Oct. 11, 2023. While measuring urban density is fraught because of judgments about where a metropolitan area’s outer boundaries are drawn, a review of census tracts radiating out from Albuquerque’s urban core suggests it is one of the least dense such areas in the western United States. “Number of people per square mile in 2020,” PolicyMap, map based on data from Census: US Bureau of the Census, 2000 Longform, retrieved Nov. 6, 2023, http://www.policymap.com.

45. See Wu and Oueslati, *Open Space in US Urban Areas*. From their empirical investigation of factors like geography, municipal services provision, price elasticity of housing demand and supply, and the amount of open space, they argue: “[W]e find that most US metropolitan areas—97.39% according to our preferred model—have insufficient open space in their developed areas and additional open-space conservation in those areas will improve social welfare.” When people have preferences for proximity to open space, optimal urban development will result in a mix of undeveloped land and residential development. See Turner, *Landscape Preferences and Patterns of Residential Development*.

46. Albuquerque Planning Department, Visualizing Density: Albuquerque’s Housing Types and Density, May 2015, https://documents.cabq.gov/planning/longrange-plan-revisions/Final_VisualizingDensity-2022.pdf; Albuquerque is generally judged to do well in terms of provision of open space, albeit not always green. Aldo Leopold is viewed as one of our first environmental planners during his time here (1914–1923). See Fleming and Schmader, *Aldo Leopold*.

47. Duranton and Puga, “The Economics of Urban Density.” For a description of the many benefits realized by large cities, see Glaeser, *Triumph of the City*.

48. In their recent review article, “The Economics of Urban Density,” Duranton and Puga describe the “Unhappy Welfare Economics” and the “Unhappy

Politics" of attempting to assess optimal metropolitan density; neither market nor political mechanisms can easily weigh the benefits and costs of density, given externalities, data and measurement problems, tensions between incumbents and newcomers, inequalities between groups. The phrase "demons of density" is drawn from Glaeser, *Triumph of the City*.

49. David, "Why Are Institutions the 'Carriers of History?'"

Chapter 1

1. The biography of Frank A. Hubbell is still to be written. He was a complicated figure. For a historical review of his career, including his resilient recovery from serious political setbacks, see Callary, "A Political Biography of Frank A. Hubbell, 1862–1929."

2. Ostrom, *Governing the Commons*.

3. "Legislative Line-up for Coming Season," *The Santa Fe New Mexican*, Jan. 5, 1927, 3; "Revised House Committees," *The Santa Fe New Mexican*, Feb. 3, 1927, 4; "New Mexico Legislature," Wikipedia, https://en.wikipedia.org/wiki/New_Mexico_Legislature, accessed November 2, 2023.

4. "The Republican Nominee," *Albuquerque Journal*, Aug. 14, 1926, 4.

5. "Democrats Take the Defensive," *The Santa Fe New Mexican*, Sept. 3, 1926, 6.

6. *Rico* translates from the Spanish as "rich" and was applied to the wealthy Hispanic sheep families that dominated the valley's political, economic, and cultural life through much of the 1800s. In the second half of the nineteenth century, the old sheep dynasties were competing with new mercantilist entities, often led by Anglo immigrants, as the sheep industry became more complex and capitalized. Wallace, Jon M. "Livestock, Land, and Dollars: The Sheep Industry of Territorial New Mexico" (master's thesis, University of New Mexico, 2014).

7. "Anderson Defends Land Holdings," *Albuquerque Tribune*, Dec. 6, 1947, 1.

8. "First National Pays $1.00 for Conservancy," *Santa Fe New Mexican*, Feb. 11, 1927, 5.

9. Callary, "A Political Biography of Frank A. Hubbell, 1862–1929."

10. US Census Bureau, undated, Urban and Rural Areas, https://www.census.gov/history/www/programs/geography/urban_and_rural_areas.html, accessed Oct. 12, 2023.

11. Rajan and Ramcharan, *The Anatomy of a Credit Crisis*.

12. For more detailed historical discussion of the changing relationship between the Hispanic villages and "new town" Albuquerque, see Lucero, *Old Towns Challenged by the Boom Town*.

13. For a detailed history of the heavily Anglo immigration into Albuquerque in the decades after the arrival of the railroad, whose participants achieved significant economic mobility in the aggregate, see DeMark, "The Immigrant Experience in Albuquerque, 1880–1920."

14. Hays, *Conservation and the Gospel of Efficiency*.

15. For the conceptual framework, see Polanyi, *The Great Transformation*.

16. For the Progressive Era context in New Mexico, building over the prior decades, see Larson, *The Profile of a New Mexico Progressive*.

17. A brief obituary for Melquiades Turrietta—spelled with two trailing t's—can be found at: *Albuquerque Journal*, March 20, 1950, 2.

18. "Local Campaigning," *Albuquerque Journal*, Oct. 30, 1982, 4.

19. Advertisement, Zillow.com, retrieved Jan. 2, 2023. https://www.zillow.com/homedetails/Turrietta-Ln-SW-Albuquerque-NM-87105/2061503835_zpid/.

20. US Census Bureau, "Urban and Rural," accessed Sept. 13, 2023, Census.gov.

21. Middle Rio Grande Conservancy District, 1927 property maps, sheet 53; Middle Rio Grande Conservancy District, Plane Table Maps, sheet F6–123.

22. Follett, *A Study of the Use of Water for Irrigation on the Rio Grande del Norte Above Fort Quitman, Texas*.

23. Sánchez, *Don Fernando Durán y Chaves's Land and Legacy*.

24. Lucero, *Old Towns Challenged by the Boom Town*.

25. Karttunen, *An Analytical Dictionary of Nahuatl*.

26. Middle Rio Grande Conservancy District, 1927 Property Maps, Sheets 56 and 57.

27. See Orona, "River of Culture, River of Power." With a focus on the greater Albuquerque area, and especially Mexican American protests of the creation and implementation of the MRGCD from 1923–1947, Orona's work is an exploration of how race, class, and power dynamics altered patterns of human relationships with the landscape. Initial petition for creation of the Middle Rio Grande Conservancy District was filed in New Mexico's Second Judicial District Court in September 1923. Several amended petitions better specified the affected area and provided names of additional supporting landowners. Opposition was immediately organized in late 1923 by Frank A. Hubbell, including recruiting in former New Mexico Governor Octaviano Larrazolo. "Delegates From Four Counties Oppose Project of Reclamation," *Albuquerque Journal*, Nov. 12, 1923, 1. Opposition petitions were submitted in March 1924, under the name of Larrazolo, with more than 3,000 signatures (with more than 2,000 recognized by the Court), with predominantly Hispanic surnames (Orona, "River of Culture, River of Power"). After public hearings, the Second Judicial District Court approved the amended petition (as filed under the name Marion L. Fox and others), creating the MRGCD (In Rio Grande Conservancy Dist., No. 14,157 [N.M. Dist. Ct. Aug. 26,1925]). See Orona, "River of Culture, River of Power"; McDonald et al., *An Evolutionary History of the Middle Rio Grande Conservancy District*; 3–29; Brown, "The Middle Rio Grande Conservancy District's Protected Water Rights."

28. The New Mexico Conservancy Act of 1923 allowed for the creation of Conservancy Districts with a judicially appointed board with three members. The superseding New Mexico Conservancy Act of 1927 called for a five-member judicially appointed board and grandfathered in the MRGCD created under the 1923 Act, but with the need for a new Board.

29. Orona, "River of Culture, River of Power," 23.

Chapter 2

1. Frost, *The Railroad and the Pueblo Indians*, 17.

2. Lucero, *Old Towns Challenged by the Boom Town*; US Territorial Economy, 1846–1912, Albuquerque Tricentennial, Albuquerque Historical Society, https://albuqhistsoc.org/SecondSite/pkfiles/pk189territoreconom.htm.

3. Orona, "River of Culture, River of Power."

4. Autobee, *The Salt River Project*.

5. In the thirty years from 1870 to 1900, Bernalillo County's population grew 277 percent (from 7,591 to 28,630), and then only grew another 4 percent (to 29,955) in the next twenty years to 1920.

6. "The First Step First," *Albuquerque Journal*, Dec. 21, 1921, 10. Albuquerque civic boosters were aware and referencing Phoenix's Salt River Project, as reflected in the archives of the Middle Rio Grande Valley (Reclamation) Association circa 1922, which include a 1922 copy of US Congressional Hearings detailing trade successes. US Congressional Record, June 9, 1922, 9278–87. See Middle Rio Grande Valley Association Records, University of New Mexico Center for Southwest Research and Special Collections, Collection Identifier MSSC-62-SC.

7. "As the People View It," *Albuquerque Morning Journal*, July 23, 1923, 6.

8. For a 1912 story on McMillen and others hurrying along a stretch of the El Camino Real (and later to be the pre-1937 Route 66) to beat a flooding arroyo when returning from visiting dances at Santa Domingo Pueblo, see "Thrills and Spills on Sunday," *Albuquerque Journal*, Aug. 11, 1912, 9.

9. As an example of the range of their collaboration in public entrepreneurship, Hubbell and McMillen partnered in 1920 to help raise money to build Sara Raynolds Hall on the then-tiny University of New Mexico campus.

10. For critical discussion of McMillen's disturbing work on the Alameda Land Grant, see Houghton, *The Blighted History of the Alameda Land Grant*.

11. "Plan of C of C Enterprise Under His Leadership," *Albuquerque Journal*, Jan. 23, 1918, 4.

12. See Rio Grande Drainage Survey, New Mexico, by State Engineer, laws of 1917, chapter 71, began Nov. 1917, completed Dec. 1918, Geo. M. Neal, Engineer in

Charge, James A. French, State Engineer; "French Points Out Solution of Valley Problem," *Albuquerque Journal*, Nov. 17, 1917, 4.

13. Aldo Leopold, "Pulling Together for Drainage," *Albuquerque Evening Herald*, May 13, 1918, 11.

14. New Mexico Office of the State Engineer, Rio Grande Drainage Survey, 1917–1918, map sheets 9 and 10.

15. "River Park From Barelas to Bridge, Plan," *Albuquerque Morning Journal*, Jan. 12, 1917, 8.

16. "C. of C. Board Selects Leopold for Secretary," *Albuquerque Morning Journal*, Jan. 9, 1918, 8.

17. See the June 6, 1919, example, as Leopold writes to his mother, discussing cauliflower in his home garden while awaiting arrivals for an Albuquerque drainage conference. Aldo Leopold to Clara Leopold, June 13, 1919, Aldo Leopold Papers, University of Wisconsin Library.

18. This fledgling drainage association is the civic precursor to the association variously referred to as the Middle Rio Grande (Valley) (Reclamation) Association, which was active circa 1922–1923 and also grew out of the efforts of the Albuquerque Chamber of Commerce. A key organizer was the publicity man Marion L. Fox, the former influential editor of the *Albuquerque Journal* (1912–1920); Fox served as the manager-director of the reorganized Albuquerque Chamber of Commerce, 1922–1923, and secretary of the Reclamation Association. "River Project to be Pushed in Legislature," *Albuquerque Journal*, Jan. 6, 1923, 3. Notably, the amended petition (1924) for establishing the MRGCD, which was eventually approved by the court (1925), was filed under M. L. Fox as the lead name. "Notice of Hearing on Amended Petition and Additional Petitions in Support Thereof," *The Santa Fe Mexican*, May 14, 1925, 3.

19. "Drainage Meet Results in a Permanent Body," *Albuquerque Morning Journal*, May 17, 1918, 2.

20. Hays, *Conservation and the Gospel of Efficiency*, 2

21. Leopold, *A Sand County Almanac*. While prominent in his own time, Leopold's rise in broad public consciousness can be traced to the rise of the environmental movement in the 1960s and after. See Google Ngrams: https://

books.google.com/ngrams/graph?content=Aldo+Leopold&year_start=1800&year_end=2019&corpus=en-2019&smoothing=3, retrieved Oct. 17, 2023.

22. Meine, *Aldo Leopold: His Life and Work*. Meine writes, "By 1922, Leopold had to outgrow the Roosevelt-era conservation mold. He was now opposed, for instance, to the unnecessary drainage of river basins." But as of late 1923, after passage of the Conservancy Act, and filing for the District, Leopold clearly remained a booster for Albuquerque and drainage. As a development venture, he partnered in the incorporation of the Home Building and Loan Association of Albuquerque (*The Santa Fe New Mexican*, Dec. 31, 1923, 3). In a 1923 speech on problems with boosterism's focus on bigger rather than better, Leopold wrote: "Moreover, just why do we wish to grow by unearned increment instead of an earned increment derived from our own basic resources. Does it ever occur to the booster that . . . we have potential agriculture in the valley, crippled by seepage and threatened by silting, that is declining by neglect while he is playing with conventions and brass bands? That the lack of public interest in these real resources is causing them to deteriorate instead of develop? "A Criticism of the Booster Spirit," speech prepared for Ten Dons Club, dated Oct. 6, 1923, University of Wisconsin Library, Aldo Leopold Papers: 9/25/10-6—Writings #16 Unpublished Manuscripts, Typescript copies, section 5: Philosophic and Literary, to 1940, 355–67.

23. Burkholder, *Report of The Chief Engineer*, 34.

24. For a critical perspective on the role of Eurocentric Progressive Era science during this period, see K. Maria D. Lane, *Fluid Geographies: Water, Science, and Settler Colonialism in New Mexico*, University of Chicago Press, 2024.

25. Wahl, "Redividing the Waters."

26. "US Reclamation Service is Interested in a Project for Valley, says Director Davis," *Albuquerque Journal*, Dec. 20, 1921, 1.

27. Similarly, earlier in 1919, a consulting drainage engineer from the Reclamation Service, Joseph Burkholder, had assured Aldo Leopold, Alonzo McMillen, the Chamber of Commerce and others in the civic crowd that their irrigated agriculture would naturally match with their desired drainage efforts. After the MRGCD's legal creation, combined with the 1925 Gault Report plan

on drainage, irrigation and flood control for the valley, Burkholder would return in 1926 to become the first chief project engineer of the MRGCD (with Arthur E. Morgan as one of the consulting engineers). "Burkholder Appointed Head Engineer of Big Conservation District." *Albuquerque Journal*, Feb. 17, 1926, 1.

28. "U.S. Reclamation Service is Interested in a Project for Valley," says Director Davis, *Albuquerque Journal*, Dec. 20, 1921, 1.

29. See "Houston Opposed to Giving Lands to States: Secretary of Agriculture Has Plan to Make Money for the Federal Government by Leasing Grazing Lands to Stockmen," *Albuquerque Morning Journal*, June 24, 1919, 7; "Drainage Plans Are Not Likely to Get U.S. Aid," *Albuquerque Morning Journal*, Feb. 25, 1921, 2.

30. Smith, Hearing, published July 7, 1921, citation HRG-1921-IAH-0008, 24; Orona, "River of Culture, River of Power."

31. Associated Press, "Harding's Aid to Be Enlisted in Reclamation," *Albuquerque Journal*, May 12, 1921, 5.

32. "Most Western States Already Provided with Laws Enabling Action Under M'Nary Bill," *Albuquerque Journal*, Aug. 13, 1922, 6.

33. Orona, "River of Culture, River of Power."

34. "Mechem States Valley Drainage is a Possibility," *Albuquerque Morning Journal,* Dec. 3, 1921, 7.

35. "Mechem States Valley Drainage is a Possibility," *Albuquerque Morning Journal*, Dec. 3, 1921, 7.

36. "Reclamation Association Elects Officers; Directors from Each County Picked," *Albuquerque Morning Journal*, May 19, 1922, quoted in Orona, "River of Culture, River of Power."

37. "Movement to Reclaim 200,000 acres of Rio Grande Valley Bottoms Gets United Support," *Albuquerque Journal*, June 27, 1922, 3.

38. At its 1902 creation, the Reclamation Act called for interest-free financing on its projects, with local irrigators given ten years to pay the money back, which amounted to a 14 percent payback. By the 1920s, when Albuquerque was pursuing Smith-McNary money, the interest-free payback period had been extended to twenty years, effectively increasing the size of the subsidy. By 1926, it had been raised to forty years, and to fifty years in 1939—an effective federal subsidy of 50 percent. Wahl, "Redividing the Waters."

39. "Reclamation is Put Under Full Sail at Meeting," *The Albuquerque Evening Herald*, June 27, 1922, 5.

40. "Reclamation is Put Under Full Sail at Meeting," *The Albuquerque Evening Herald*, June 27, 1922, 5.

41. Laws of 1923, Chapter 140. An Act to provide for the Organization of Conservancy Districts for the Purposes of Cooperating with the Government of the United States Under the Terms of the Federal Reclamation Act law and Other Federal Laws, and to Define the Purposes and Powers Thereof. New Mexico—6th Legislature, Regular Session : 211–78.

42. Orona, "River of Culture, River of Power."

43. Such efforts are not unusual for urban centers. For a Chicago history of connecting rural lands to an urban center, see Cronon, *Nature's Metropolis*.

44. The enabling court order, stating the District's purpose, is quoted from Brown, "The Middle Rio Grande Conservancy District's Protected Water Rights." Note that the original approved District was projected to cover seven counties before being quickly trimmed to the current four (Sandoval, Bernalillo, Valencia, and Socorro).

45. See "Harding's Aid to be Enlisted in Reclamation," *Albuquerque Morning Journal*, May 12, 1921, 5; "700 People at Hoover Dinner in Albuquerque," *Albuquerque Journal*, Nov. 17, 1922, 4.

46. "McNary Denies Repudiation of Reclamation Bill," *The Arizona Republican*, Dec. 13, 1923, 8.

47. "Smith-M'Nary Bill Modified by Framers," *The Capitol Journal*, Dec. 18, 1923, 6.

48. The prominent water engineer and lawyer, Jay Turley, had been arguing for over a year in New Mexico circles that this private bonding path could always be pursued, rather than waiting for federal bureaucracy. But the context was for a proposed Santa Fe area collaboration with Albuquerque and the Middle Valley. See "Turley Proposes Plan for More City Water," *The Santa Fe New Mexican*, Aug. 3, 1922, 5.

49. See Bock, *History of the Miami Flood Control Project*; Giertz, "An Experiment in Public Choice"; Holmes and Wolman, *Early Development of Systems Analysis in Natural Resources Management from Man and Nature to the Miami Conservancy District*. For discussion of Morgan's later New Deal role in leading the Tennessee Valley Authority (TVA), see Dunkelman, *Why Nothing Works*.

50. "First Photographs of Pueblo Floods," *Albuquerque Morning Journal*, June 21, 1921, 3.

51. "House and Senate Committees at Joint Hearing Result in Agreement Between Interested Parties," *Albuquerque Journal*, Feb. 11, 1925, 3.

52. "Conservancy Act Is Like Mustang Without Bridle," *Santa Fe New Mexican*, Feb. 3, 1925, 3.

53. "File Demurrer to Amended Petition for Conservancy District," *Albuquerque Journal*, Oct. 7, 1924, 5. See discussion in Orona, "River of Culture, River of Power," 130.

54. See "New Conservancy Bill Goes Through," *The Santa Fe New Mexican*, March 5, 1925, 2; and *The Santa Fe New Mexican*, March 16, 1925, 2.

55. "Criticism of River Suit is Made by Reid," *Albuquerque Journal*, Sept. 18, 1925, 7.

56. "Court Grants Conservancy As Petitioned," *The Santa Fe New Mexican*, Aug. 1, 1925, 1.

57. Turley, 1925. "Public Corporation District is Plan for Public Purpose." Paper submitted to the New Mexico State Bar Association, with conclusions excerpted in *The Santa Fe New Mexican*, Sept. 5, 1925, 5.

58. "Conservancy District Held Constitutional, Reclamation Assured," *Albuquerque Journal*, Dec. 13, 1925, 1.

59. Anna V. Huey, "85,000 Acres of Farms Lost in Middle Rio Grande Valley Since Year 1850," *Santa Fe New Mexican*, Jan. 31, 1927, 4.

60. See for example, Resolution of the Board of Directors of the Middle Rio Grande Conservancy District, M-09-24-18-157, Sept. 24, 2018, on file with the authors.

61. There were other more directly targeted economic appeals, such as the 1922 publicity campaign to property owners by Albuquerque Chamber of Commerce manager-director Marion L. Fox, of "Don't Drown—Dam It," *Albuquerque Journal*, May 12, 1922, 1.

62. "Straightening of Rio Grande Channel More Important Than Fighting Colorado—M'Millen," *Albuquerque Journal*, July 3, 1925, 1.

63. "Kiwanis Hears of Necessity of River Work," *Albuquerque Journal*, Sept. 23, 1926, 3.

64. Hedke, C. R., *A Report on the Irrigation Development and Water Supply of the Middle Rio Grande Valley as It Relates to the Rio Grande Compact*, Rio Grande Valley Survey Commission, 1925.

65. For a late twentieth-century review of the claim, see Wozniak, *Irrigation in the Rio Grande Valley, New Mexico*.

66. Wyoming v. Colorado, 259 US 419, 42 S. Ct. 552, 66 L. Ed. 999 (1922).

67. "Watch Our Water," *Albuquerque Journal*, Sept. 22, 1934, 8.

68. See "Turley Proposes Plan for More City Water," *The Santa Fe New Mexican*, Aug. 3, 1922, 5; "To Hold Special Meeting on Conservancy District," *The Santa Fe New Mexican*, July 23, 1924, 8; "Conservancy Petition is Filed by Turley," *The Santa Fe New Mexican*, April 7, 1924, 1.

69. See, "Turley Offers to Sell Water to Los Angeles," *Albuquerque Journal*, Nov. 23, 1925, 3; "Los Angeles Sends Surveyors to Check Up Jay Turley Rights," *The Santa Fe New Mexican*, Nov. 28, 1925, 7; "State Will Fight Claims of Turley to Water Rights; Filings of Albuquerque Claimant on San Juan Outlawed, Engineer Neel Says in Controversy," *Albuquerque Journal*, Nov. 28, 1925, 1. In these tensions lay the seeds of the 1960s San Juan-Chama Project. In 1932 Turley would state that after a 1924 legal setback restricting his use of large 1903 Territorial water rights claims in the San Juan, he pursued moving his rights claims (later denied) into the Rio Grande basin: "I served notice of intention to transfer the water to other lands. This plan included the transfer of 1,000 cfs of water over into the basin of the Chama for use down the valley of the Rio Grande in New Mexico." See "Turley Warns State to Guard Its Water Rights Claims from California," *The Santa Fe New Mexican*, Nov. 17, 1932, 2.

70. Jay Turley, "As the People View It," *Albuquerque Journal*, July 23, 1923, 6. Notably, Mrs. Jay Turley was also active with a Bernalillo County Republican

Club resolution supporting "declaration officially of the Middle Rio Grande Conservancy District as soon as possible." "Republicans of County Meet to Get Organized," *Albuquerque Journal*, Dec. 14, 1923, 7.

71. Burkholder repeatedly made the public claim that as early as 1850, and extending to 1880, there had been 125,000 irrigated acres in the Middle Rio Grande Valley. For examples, see "Conservancy Remedy to Farm Problems," *Albuquerque Journal*, Oct. 28, 1928, 32; Joseph F. Burkholder, "A Few Facts You Should Know Regarding the Middle Rio Grande Conservancy District," *Albuquerque Journal*, May 6, 1929, 3.

72. Lepore, *The Story of America*.

73. "Committee Not to Act on Bill for Several Days—Lay Down Six Hours' Barrage of Speeches on Conservancy," *Santa Fe New Mexican*, Feb. 11, 1927, 5.

74. "Committee Not to Act on Bill for Several Days—Lay Down Six Hours' Barrage of Speeches on Conservancy," *Santa Fe New Mexican*, Feb. 11, 1927, 5.

75. Against the arc of his remarkable political career, the MRGCD issues were perhaps not a prominent thread, but reflect his advocacy for Hispano/Latino rights. Octaviano Ambrosia Larrazolo was born in Mexico in 1859 and died in Albuquerque in 1930. He was admitted to the Texas state bar in 1888 before moving to New Mexico in 1895. Larrazolo did not become a Republican until 1912 but also pushed back against the historical political machine (e.g., the Frank A. Hubbell machine in Bernalillo County), where many Hispanics were traditionally part of the Republican party in New Mexico Territory in the late nineteenth and early twentieth century. Larrazolo served as New Mexico Governor from 1919 to 1921, where he was a supporter of drainage efforts for the Middle Valley, conditional on federal financing. After the 1925 case, where he unsuccessfully challenged the constitutionality of the MRGCD and Conservancy Act (NM Supreme Court: In re Proposed Middle Rio Grande Conservancy Dist., 242 P. 683 [N.M. 1925]) and the 1927 Conservancy Act debates at the state legislature, Larrazolo would go on serve in the US Senate from 1929 to 1930, as the first Hispanic United States senator. See Vigil and Lujan, *Parallels in the Career of Two Hispanic US Senators*; Walter, *Octaviano Ambrosio Larrazolo*.

76. "Politics, Bad Faith, Charged at Hearing on Larrazolo Bill," *Albuquerque Journal*, Feb. 11, 1927, 1.

77. "Republican Floor Leader Errett Will Fight Larrazolo Amendment to Conservancy Bill," *Albuquerque Journal,* Feb. 8, 1927, 3.

78. "Duke Citians Storm City for Conservancy Bill Hearing," *Santa Fe New Mexican*, Feb. 10, 1927, 2.

79. "Caravan of Protest Will Carry 500 Albuquerqueans to Santa Fe Today to Fight for Conservancy," *Albuquerque Journal*, Feb. 10, 1927, 1.

80. "Republican Floor Leader Errett Will Fight Larrazolo Bill for Amending Conservancy Statutes," *Albuquerque Journal*, Feb. 8, 1927, 1.

81. Meine, *Aldo Leopold*.

82. The organic nature of this collective tension is seen in current 2020s debates over the New Mexico Game Commission Board appointment process, and the New Mexico State Engineer appointment credential requirements.

83. "Chief Beneficiaries Must Carry Heaviest Taxation Load if River Project Succeeds," Expert Opinion, *Albuquerque Journal*, Feb. 27, 1927, 1.

84. "Drainage May Be Had Immediately, Says Burkholder," *The (Albuquerque) Evening Herald*, Sept. 2, 1919, 6.

85. "Lay Down 6 Hours' Barrage of Speeches on Conservancy," *Santa Fe New Mexican*, Feb. 11, 1927.

86. See "Names for New Conservancy Board, Submitted to Judge Helmick, Have His Approval," *Albuquerque Journal*, March 6, 1927, 1; "Conservancy Bill Passes," *Albuquerque Journal*, March 8, 1927, 7.

87. "Names for New Conservancy Board, Submitted to Judge Helmick, Have His Approval," *Albuquerque Journal*, March 6, 1927, 1.

88. "Larrazolo Resigns from Legislature," *Santa Fe New Mexican*, March 10, 1927, 4.

89. "Apache Grant Files Protest to Conservancy," *Albuquerque Journal*, June 22, 1928, 8.

90. "Plan Would Cut Marcial from Improved Area," *Albuquerque Journal*, July 14, 1928, 6; "Conservancy Plan Protest," *Albuquerque Journal*, July 17, 1928, 4.

91. "Score of Bird Refuges in this State," *The Albuquerque Tribune*, Jan. 17, 1934, 1; See "Good Chance of Refuge in Middle Valley," *The Albuquerque Tribune*, Feb. 6, 1934, 4.

92. Comparison is for 2017: $15.5m direct revenues to the region attributed to Bosque del Apache National Wildlife Refuge, versus $9.2m market values of all crop sales (including nursery and greenhouses), with 239 farms and 16,203 irrigated acres, for Socorro County. See US Fish and Wildlife Service, *The Economic Contributions of Recreational Visitation at Bosque del Apache National Wildlife Refuge*; Division of Economics, US Fish and Wildlife Service, 2019, https://ecos.fws.gov/ServCat/DownloadFile/165199; and USDA Census of Agriculture, 2017.

Chapter 3

1. Advertisement, *Albuquerque Journal*, March 11, 1928, 4.

2. John Fleck, "Tobacco Farming and Swamps in Early 20th century Albuquerque," *Inkstain* (blog), posted June 7, 2022, https://www.inkstain.net/2022/06/tobacco-farming-and-swamps-in-early-20th-century-albuquerque/.

3. Gale et al., *Tobacco and the Economy*.

4. Advertisement, *Albuquerque Journal*, March 11, 1928, 4.

5. Advertisement, *Albuquerque Journal*, March 11, 1928, 4.

6. Wood, "Dynamic Fallowing in the Middle Rio Grande."

7. "Cultivators of the earth are the most virtuous and independant [sic] citizens." Thomas Jefferson, "Notes on Virginia," in Jefferson, *The Works of Thomas Jefferson*.

8. Follett, *A Study of the Use of Water for Irrigation on the Rio Grande del Norte Above Fort Quitman, Texas.*

9. Follett, 129; Phillips et al., *Reining in the Rio Grande*.

10. "Irrigation," *Weekly New Mexican*, March 17, 1868, 2.

11. McCall, *1850 Report of the Secretary of War Communicating Colonel McCall's Report in Relation to New Mexico*.

12. Kennedy, *Agriculture of the United States in 1860*.

13. *The Daily New Mexican*, March 31, 1875, 1.

14. "Down the Rio Grande," *The Las Vegas Gazette*, Sept. 26, 1880, 4.

15. Von Thünen, *The Isolated State in Relation to Agriculture and Political Economy*.

16. Atencio, "Social Change and Community Conflict in Old Albuquerque, New Mexico."

17. Advertisement, *Albuquerque Citizen*, Sept. 27, 1899, 3.

18. United States Bureau of the Census, *United States Census of Agriculture, 1950*.

19. Beginning in the 1970s in the United States, milk use shifted from beverage toward cheese and other dairy products. This combined with an increasing focus on exports and consolidation of production into ever larger operations. Together, this all contributed to altering the geography of dairy operations brought by refrigeration, with operations increasingly located away from urban centers. See MacDonald et al., *Changing Structure, Financial Risks, and Government Policy for the U.S. Dairy Industry*.

20. Flint and Flint, *Overhaul: A Social History of the Albuquerque Locomotive Repair Shops*.

21. Berthier-Foglar, "Early Tourism in New Mexico."

22. National Register of Historic Places Inventory—Nomination Form, Historic *Resources of Albuquerque's North Valley*, undated.

23. Anderson Defends Land Holdings, *Albuquerque Tribune*, Dec. 6, 1947, 1

24. "Syndicate buys F. A. Hubbell Farm as First Move in Development of Tobacco Industry in River Valley," *Albuquerque Journal*, Dec. 6, 1925, 1. The local syndicate leaders were L. C. Bennett and A. R. Hebenstreit.

25. "Tobacco Industry Development in Valley Has Great Future, Mewborne Tells Lions Club," *Albuquerque Journal*, Dec. 1, 1926, 1.

26. See for example, Conservancy District, Plane Table Maps, sheet F6-P114.

27. USDA Census of Agriculture Historical Archive, various years; https://agcensus.library.cornell.edu/.

28. Middle Rio Grande Conservancy District, 1927 Property Maps, sheet 49; Middle Rio Grande Conservancy District, Plan Table Maps, sheet F6-p116.

29. *Albuquerque Journal*, Sept. 16, 1934, 4.

30. “Back Taxes Settled On De Chavez Grant,” *Albuquerque Journal*, June 20, 1927, 5.

31. “Eduardo M. Otero,” *Albuquerque Journal*, April 10, 1932, 4.

32. *Albuquerque Journal*, March 22, 1932, 2.

33. Rural Rehabilitation Corp bought Bosque Farms for $72,000 from estate of Eduardo Otero (2,420 acres or $29,75 an acre). The plan was to settle 200 families, many of which were Dust Bowl refugees from Oklahoma. “200 Families to be Transferred,” *The Albuquerque Tribune*, April 23, 1935, 1.

34. See Reeves, *History of New Mexico*, 334; “Country Club Officers Named for the New Year,” *Albuquerque Journal*, Jan. 12, 1927, 8; “Country Club Members!” (advertisement), *Albuquerque Journal*, Oct. 29, 1927, 6.

35. Herkenhoff, Gordon (Corky), personal communication, 2011; Herkenhoff, Gordon (Corky), author interview, March 24, 2022.

36. Middle Rio Grande Conservancy District, Plane Table Maps, sheets F2-P1, F2-P2, and F2-P12.

37. “New Mexico Towns,” *The Albuquerque Daily Citizen*, Jan. 26, 1903; 7.

38. Philip Zimmer to Letter to Lee J. Raynolds, “Middle Rio Grande Valley Association Records, 1992,” Center for Southwest Research Center, University Libraries, University of New Mexico.

39. Herkenhoff, Gordon (Corky), author interview, March 24, 2022.

40. Herkenhoff, Gordon (Corky), personal communication, 2011.

41. Wood, *Dynamic Fallowing*, 17.

42. US Department of Agriculture, Census of Agriculture, County Summary Highlights, Table 1, various years.

43. Hämäläinen, *The Comanche Empire*.

44. Carlson, “New Mexico’s Sheep Industry, 1850–1900.”

45. Moyer, “The Frank A. Hubbell Company, Sheep and Cattle”; “50,000 by 1920, Slogan of Boosters at Great Banquet,” *Albuquerque Journal*, Nov. 11, 1915, 5.

46. Porter et al., *New Mexico’s Greenbelt Law*.

47. Bernalillo County Assessor’s Office, Public Parcel Data Map, accessed Sept. 24, 2024, https://www.bernco.gov/assessor/find-a-property/assessor-map-search/.

48. City of Albuquerque, “Open Space Farmlands,” https://www.cabq.gov/parksandrecreation/open-space/lands/open-space-farmlands.

49. During his time living in Albuquerque between 1914 and 1924, Aldo Leopold belonged to one of the South Valley private hunting clubs, and his journals contain various references to it, and pictures with family members. But Leopold was also worrying that commercial clubs would become the only way individuals of limited means would be able to hunt ducks. In 1919 he wrote of the need to preserve accessible public hunting lands for the populace. See Aldo Leopold, “A Plea for State-Owned Ducking Grounds,” in Brown and Carmony, *Aldo Leopold's Southwest*. As elsewhere, Leopold's plea was ratified in the Middle Valley. If the original focus was waterfowl hunting, today a string of wetland sites through the southern half of the Middle Valley provide access to variety of outdoor recreation activities, including bird watching and hunting. These include the state-managed Ladd S. Gordon Waterfowl Complex, in Valencia and Socorro Counties, and the federally managed Bosque del Apache National Wildlife Area just below the southern boundary of the MRGCD. All public lands were designated after the creation of the MRGCD.

50. Zillow, Las Estancias Dr. SW, https://www.zillow.com/homedetails/Las-Estancias-Dr-SW-Albuquerque-NM-87105/2056373155_zpid/, retrieved Oct. 15, 2023.

Chapter 4

1. See Orona, “River of Culture, River of Power.”

2. Wallace, *Livestock, Land and Dollars*; Charles, “Development of the Partido System in the New Mexico Sheep Industry.”

3. See “Honorable Emiliano L. Gutierrez: Member of the House of Representatives of the 33rd Legislative Assembly from Bernalillo County,” *Santa Fe New Mexican*, Feb. 23, 1901, 2.

4. See discussions in Wallace, “Livestock, Land, and Dollars”; Carlson, “New Mexico's Sheep Industry, 1850–1900.”

5. Wallace, *Livestock,* 208–9.

6. "Injunction Fence is Prohibited by Supreme Court," *Albuquerque Journal*, Feb. 18, 1918, 8.

7. "Order," *Albuquerque Journal*, Feb. 1, 1922, 4.

8. The 1920s maps created by the MRGCD of land ownership on the valley floor, used in initial assessments, show extensive sprinkling of both and small and larger land holdings by the known mercantile families of the prior decades (e.g., Hubbell, Huning, and Ilfeld), and also corporate entities whose directors were known to have participated extensively in tax deed sales and dispossession (e.g., James W. Norment, and the Mutual Investment and Agency Company [MIAC] incorporated in New Mexico in 1918, and the Security Investment and Development Company [SIDC] incorporated in in New Mexico in 1913), or land grant break-ups (e.g., the Alonzo B. McMillen family and the San Mateo Land Company, incorporated in New Mexico in 1907).

9. See "May Secure Huge Area for a Song," *Albuquerque Journal*, Feb. 3, 1913, 8; "Suit Involving Title to Land Begun in Court," *Albuquerque Journal*, Dec. 9, 1918, 3.

10. *Albuquerque Citizen*, April 20, 1907, 1.

11. "Hubbell Harmony Hums Happily at Bolters Junta," *Albuquerque Journal*, Sept. 24, 1911, 1.

12. "Rustlers Have a Strong Band, Officers Think," *Albuquerque Morning Journal*, March 26, 1918, 8.

13. "Defense Council Names Units for Rural Districts," *Albuquerque Journal*, July 12, 1918, pl. 3; for general history of defense councils, see Mathews, *State Councils of Defense*.

14. Geertz, *The Interpretation of Cultures*.

15. One of the authors made a practice, on many visits during the research for this book, of engaging walkers in idle conversation about the place. They generally loved the green and water but knew little or nothing about the ditches' history or modern function.

16. Middle Rio Grande Conservancy District, ISO Logs, 2022.

17. "Estimated median income of a family, between 2017–2021," PolicyMap, based on data from Census: US Bureau of the Census, American Community

Survey, accessed September 11, 2023, http://www.policymap.com; OpenET Project, https://openetdata.org/.

18. Lamadrid and Rivera, *Water for the People*; Smith et al., *La Cultura de la Acequia Madre*.

19. Together the father and one son represented about 1.3 percent of the sheep owned in the county in 1902, and separately each had herds smaller than the average owned herd of about 1,200. See "Albuquerque Assessment Roll," *Albuquerque Morning Journal*, April 14, 1903, 4. Several points of note: First, the number of sheep in Bernalillo County appears to have been significantly dropping relative to prior decades. See Carlson, "New Mexico's Sheep Industry, 1850–1900." Historically, large sheep-stock companies would be several orders of magnitude larger than Maximiano Sr.'s (1,000), and have their herds spread over as many as four or five counties. See Moyer, "The Frank A. Hubbell Company, Sheep and Cattle."

20. National Register of Historic Places Inventory Nomination Form, Historic Resources of Albuquerque's North Valley, Los Griegos Historic District, 8.

21. Follett, *A Study of the Use of Water for Irrigation on the Rio Grande del Norte Above Fort Quitman, Texas*.

22. Historic Resources of Albuquerque's North Valley, Los Griegos Historic District, National Register of Historic Places Inventory—Nomination Form.

23. Joseph Burkholder is a prominent functionary in the history of the MRGCD, in his role as initial chief engineer and lead author of the District Plan from 1928. Like Arthur E. Morgan, primary architect of the Miami (OH) Conservancy District that the MRGCD is modeled after, Burkholder is a product of the Progressive Era. Serving as chief engineer for the MRGCD was only one of many achievements in Burkholder's long career in water resources and civil engineering. After leaving the MRGCD in 1932, he went to work for the Metropolitan Water District (MWD) of Southern California and oversaw construction work on the Colorado River Aqueduct. He would later serve on the MWD board, when he was general manager and chief engineer for the San Diego County Water Authority from 1944–1953; his work there included overseeing construction of San Diego Aqueduct. For a testimonial to his MWD career, see Minutes, Regular Meeting of the Board of Directors, The Metropolitan Water District of Southern California April 14, 1953. As a Reclamation Service engineer, Burkholder's initial work in New Mexico involved solving agricultural drainage issues in the Lower Rio Grande Valley that emerged (1917) after construction of the Elephant Butte Dam and Reservoir. See "Drainage for Lower Valley: Work is to Start Immediately to Relieve Land of Water Damage," *El Paso Herald*, July 11, 1917, 2. Burkholder provided initial consultation on Middle Rio Grande Valley drainage in Albuquerque in 1918/1919, with the efforts organized by Aldo Leopold and the Albuquerque Chamber of Commerce. "Drainage May be Had Immediately Says Burkholder," *Albuquerque Tribune,* Sept. 2, 1919, 6. Burkholder had further consultations in his role with the Reclamation Service with the Albuquerque booster group in 1922. He would leave to other international duties before he was to take up the role of first chief engineer of the MRGCD in Feb. 1926. See J. L. Burkholder is "Glad to Be in the West Again," *Albuquerque Journal*, March 10, 1926, 8. Simultaneously, Arthur E. Morgan, of the Dayton-Morgan Engineering Company, was signed as consulting engineer. See "Two Conservancy Board Engineers Sign Contracts," *Albuquerque Journal*, March 9, 1926, 1. Burkholder resigned from the MRGCD in Dec. 1932, shortly after the RFC bond purchase rescue.

24. Middle Rio Grande Conservancy District, ISO Logs, 2021.

25. Data from tree ring constructions done by the TreeFlow project. See Woodhouse et al., "Rio Grande and Rio Conchos Water Supply Variability from Instrumental and Paleoclimatic Records," 9.

26. Sargeant and Davis, *Shining River, Precious Land*, 4.

27. Sargeant and Davis, *Shining River, Precious Land*, 104.

28. Murphy, *Destructive Floods in the United States in 1904*, 148.

29. "Realtors Urge Mass Meeting on Conservancy," *Albuquerque Journal*, Feb. 2, 1927, 3; "Rotary Joins Fight Against Changing Law," *Albuquerque Journal*, Feb. 4, 1927, 8.

30. For an early 1900s Bernalillo County discussion of their roles and responsibilities, see "Strayed or Stolen," *Albuquerque Journal*, June 20, 1903, 2.

31. Ostrom, "Why Do We Need to Protect Institutional Diversity?"

32. "Rushing Rio Grande—The Conditions at Barelas, Atrisco and Other Places—Watching Alameda Dyke," *Albuquerque Journal*, June 13, 1903, 8; "River Discussions—City Council Grants Full Power to Mayor to Act—Flood Districts Visited," *Albuquerque Journal*, June 18, 1903, 1; "Up to the City," *Albuquerque Journal*, June 26, 1903, 2; "The Dyke Question," *Albuquerque Journal*, June 27, 1903, 1; "Flood Water Committee Makes Able Report for the Safety of the City—To Rebuild Alameda Dyke," *The Albuquerque Weekly Citizen*, June 27, 1903, 8; "Will Protect City," *The Albuquerque Weekly Citizen*, July 11, 1903, 7; "Mayor's Statement—Falsehoods Were Fully Answered—Dyke Expenses Were Audited," *The Albuquerque Weekly Citizen*, July 18, 1903, 7; "Important Session of City Council last Night—Repairing Alameda Dyke," *Albuquerque Journal*, April 27, 1904, 5; "Rio Grande Goes on Rip-Roaring Wild Rampage," *Albuquerque Journal*, Oct. 1, 1904, 2; "Grunsfeld Answers," *Albuquerque Journal*, July 13, 1903, 1; "Favors Building Levee System Along Rio Grande," *Albuquerque Journal*, Nov. 3, 1904, 5; "The Late Floods," *Albuquerque Journal*, June 20, 1905, 4; "Bernalillo County Faces Bankruptcy," *Albuquerque Journal*, April 3, 1904, 7; "County Taxes Take Jump of Six and a Half Mills," *Albuquerque Journal*, July 8, 1905, 5.

33. "Crest of the Rise Expected Here in Next Two Days," *Albuquerque Journal*, May 27, 1905, 5.

34. "County Commissioners' Proceedings," *Albuquerque Morning Journal*, April 26, 1920, 5.

35. "County Commissioners' Proceedings," *Albuquerque Morning Journal*, July 29, 1920, 5.

36. "County Commissioners' Proceedings," *Albuquerque Morning Journal*, July 30, 1920, 5.

37. "Commissioners Urge Drainage as of First Importance to Central Rio Grande Valley," *The Evening Herald*, Aug. 11, 1921, 1.

38. "Commissioners Urge Drainage as of First Importance to Central Rio Grande Valley," *The Evening Herald*, Aug. 11, 1921, 1. The agent was Lee Reynolds.

39. "New Water Users Association Formed; Officers Elected," *Albuquerque Journal*, May 6, 1929, 8.

40. "Conservancy Injunction Suit Fails, Bids on Bonds Will Be Received Today," *Albuquerque Journal*, May 18, 1929, 1.

41. "Bids on Bonds Are Reported Put in Monday," *Albuquerque Journal*, May 21, 1929, 1.

42. "Avert the Floods," *Albuquerque Journal*, Aug. 15, 1929, 4.

43. Gutierrez v. Middle Rio Grande Conservancy Dist., 282 P. 1, 34 N.M. 346 (1929).

44. Gutierrez v. Middle Rio Grande Conservancy District.

45. Gutierrez v. Middle Rio Grande Conservancy District.

46. See discussion in Orona, "River of Culture, River of Power,"164–66.

47. "Damaging Rains Continue to Sweep Over the City and Suburbs, Streets Flooded," *Albuquerque Journal*, Sept. 23, 1929, 1 and 3.

48. "1–2 Percent Will Be Interest Rate for First Security Issue," *Albuquerque Journal*, May 30, 1929, 1; and "$2 Million Conservancy Bonds Sold," *The Santa Fe New Mexican*, May 30, 1929, 5.

49. "Conservancy Case Will Go to US Supreme Court," *Albuquerque Journal*, Dec. 4, 1929, 1

50. "Reach Conservancy Arrangement," *Albuquerque Journal*, Jan. 24, 1930, 1.

51. Hartley, *The Reclamation of the Missouri Bootheel*.

52. "Staccato Exhaust of Dragline Ditch Digger Continues after Conservancy Celebration Closes," *Albuquerque Journal*, March 21, 1930, 1.

53. "Staccato Exhaust of Machine Continues as Celebration Closes," *Albuquerque Journal*, March 21, 1930, 7.

54. "Gutierrez, Rodey Make Statements Concerning Trouble at Los Lunas," *Albuquerque Journal*, April 21, 1930, 1.

55. On the stand in District Court hearings over the charges against Max Gutierrez and the Farmers' Association, Burkholder directly denied accusations of making any negative remarks against Spanish American people. See "Burkholder Not Armed at Ditch War, He Says in Ouster Action: Denies Expressing Hate for Mexicans," *Albuquerque Journal*, June 12, 1930, 1. Burkholder's 1930 testimony also expressed that the delay in the MRGCD bond sale was due to the litigation by Max and the farmers' association. On this point, under Max's name as president, public advertisements were run in local papers discouraging bond purchases. See "Notice to Prospective Purchasers of Middle Rio Grande Conservancy District Bonds" paid advertisement, *Albuquerque Journal,* May 20, 1929, 8.

56. The *Albuquerque Journal* later described accounts of the day as "brimming with contradictions"—"Ouster Hearing Ends, Decisions is Expected About Midweek," *Albuquerque Journal*, June 15, 1930, 1.

57. "Gutierrez and Rodey Tell of Los Lunas Affair," *Albuquerque Journal*, April 21, 1930, 3.

58. "Dillon Coming to Investigate the Los Chavez Mixup Tuesday," *Albuquerque Journal*, April 22, 1930, 1.

59. "Farmers Blame Project Board for Troubles; Ask for Ouster," *Albuquerque Journal*, May 14, 1930, 1.

60. "Conservancy Hearing Set," *Santa Fe New Mexican*, May 24, 1930, 5.

61. "Hearing Set for July 2 on Charges Against Farmers Group," *Albuquerque Journal*, June 4, 1930, 1; John Fleck, "The Circuitous Path to Max Guteirrez's Grave," *Inkstain* (blog), posted Dec. 19, 2020, https://www.inkstain.net/2020/12/the-circuitous-path-to-max-gutierrezs-grave/.

62. This adaptability through changing times is seen in Max's fluid political career in Bernalillo County, where he is first seen active in the Republican party, later participating in Fusionist party and Independent party efforts, and then creating a Liberty Club (which could only endorse candidates with two-thirds approval). Finally, Max spent the last several decades of his life active in the Democratic party. See "Maximiano Gutierrez Funeral Is Thursday," *Albuquerque Journal*, June 11, 1952, 2.

63. "Socorro Ditch Board Fights Conservancy," *Albuquerque Journal*, Feb. 24, 1938.

64. "Report on Families in San Marcial Is In," *Albuquerque Journal*, June 18, 1938, 3.

65. "Rice Plans 175 Houses," *Albuquerque Tribune*, March 23, 1962, 1.

Chapter 5

1. Gutzler et al., "An Extreme Annual Precipitation Anomaly in the Preradiosonde Era."

2. Associated Press, "Plentiful Rains Benefit State," *Albuquerque Journal*, March 23, 1941.

3. "In New Mexico," *Albuquerque Journal*, May 1, 1941, 6; "Rio Grande Full Here as Spring Run-Off Begins in Mountains," *Albuquerque Journal*, April 30, 1941, 1.

4. "Order Guard to Prepare for Emergency Flood Duty," *Albuquerque Tribune*, May 10, 1941, 1; "Engineer Warns Breaks Expected in River Dikes," *Albuquerque Tribune*, May 12, 1941, 1.

5. "Dramatic Battle Against Rio Grande Seen From Air," *Albuquerque Journal*, May 14, 1941, 1.

6. Data from USGS gage 08313000, Rio Grande at Otowi Bridge.

7. Scurlock, *From the Rio to the Sierra.*

8. Scurlock. *From the Rio to the Sierra*, 38.

9. "Anti-Nepotism Measure Put Before House," *Albuquerque Tribune*, Feb. 4, 1941, 1.

10. "County May Get Drainage Expert Without Expense," *Albuquerque Journal*, May 7, 1916, 1.

11. "A Needed Project," *Albuquerque Journal*, July 23, 1941, 6.

12. "Sutherland Promises to Try to Get Government to Take Over Conservancy," *Albuquerque Journal*, Aug. 27, 1942, 12.

13. Clark, *Water in New Mexico*.

14. US Bureau of Reclamation, *Plan for Development of the Middle Rio Grande Project*, Aug. 30, 1947. in 81. Cong., 2 sess., H. Doc. 653, 153 et seq.

15. Reclamation, *Plan for Development of the Middle Rio Grande Project*, 157.

16. Reclamation, *Plan for Development of the Middle Rio Grande Project*, 159.

17. Reclamation, *Plan for Development of the Middle Rio Grande Project*, 158.

18. The association included prominent involvement of both the MRGCD and Albuquerque Chamber of Commerce, as well as representatives from south

valley communities like Los Lunas and Belen. Hubert Ball, MRGCD manager, is quoted as saying: "The main purpose of this organization is to turn the heat on Congress to reinstate the funds appropriated for this district." "Organize Group for Rio Fight," *Albuquerque Journal*, April 29, 1947, 1.

19. The Los Alamos Atomic Laboratories the newly established (1942–1943). Los Alamos bomb research and development laboratory, as part of the larger Manhattan Project. See Gosling, *The Manhattan Project*, 35, 37–38.

20. David E. Lilienthal, United States Atomic Energy Commission, to the Honorable Dennis Chavez (D-NM), United States Senate, April 7, 1949, in Middle Rio Grande Flood Control Association, *The Facts About the Flood Control and Reclamation Project in the Middle Rio Grande Valley and Its Importance in the National Defense Program*, Valiant Printing Company. Across his long political career, Senator Chavez was an ardent supporter of securing the federal Middle Rio Grande Project. Of note, Dionisio "Dennis" Chavez (1888–1962) was born in the Middle Valley in the village of Los Chavez, while New Mexico was still a territory. "Dennis Chavez," Wikipedia, accessed Nov. 17, 2024. Thus, the "battle at Los Chavez" in 1930 involving Max Gutierrez, Pearce C. Rodey, and Joseph Burkholder occurred in the same small farming village where Dennis Chavez's family had lived for several generations.

21. "Rio Project to President," *Albuquerque Tribune*, June 17, 1948; "Looking Up," *Albuquerque Tribune*, July 1, 1948, 10; Gahan, *Middle Rio Grande Project*.

22. $5.8 million (or roughly $67 million in 2024 dollars), was appropriated by the US Congress to pay off 86 percent of the remaining $6.7 million bond debt owed by the MRGCD. $1.4 million ($16 million in 2024 dollars) was paid by the MRGCD from their guarantee fund, accrued from a small ad valorem property tax implemented when the federal RFC entered the frame in the 1930s when the MRGCD was trying to sell the original bonds. In 1956 the two large remaining bondholders were the state of New Mexico and Harvard University. "$6.7 Million Bonds are Retired Here," *Albuquerque Journal*, Feb. 02, 1956, 11.

23. US Department of Agriculture NRCS, April 1, 2023.

Chapter 6

1. *Proposed Dam Sites Located on Indian Lands Within New Mexico*, House Committee on Indian Affairs, May 26, 1943; John Fleck, "On Cochiti Dam and the Notion of 'Flooding,'" *Inkstain* (blog), posted May 19, 2023, https://www.inkstain.net/2023/05/on-cochiti-dam-and-the-notion-of-flooding.

2. Daniel Arquero, Cochiti Pueblo, personal communication.

3. Sando, *Pueblo Profiles*.

4. Sando, *Pueblo Profiles*, 54.

5. Starr, *A Study of the Census of the Pueblo of Cochiti*.

6. Sando, *Pueblo Profiles.*

7. Griswold, S., 2021. "Boarding School History Underpins Yazzie Martinez Findings on Native Education," *New Mexico in Depth*. Sept. 3, 2021.

8. Boetel, Ryan, "A New Beginning for Education at Isleta Pueblo," *Albuquerque Journal*, Aug. 2, 2015.

9. See Malcolm Ebright and Rick Hendricks, *Pablo Abeita: The Life and Times of a Native Statesman of Isleta Pueblo, 1871–1940*, University of New Mexico Press, 2023.

10. "Indian Reads Remarkable Address on Attitude of Pueblos to Legislation," *Albuquerque Morning Journal*, May 18, 1920, 4.

11. Frost, *The Railroad and the Pueblo Indians.*

12. United States v. Sandoval, 231 US 28, 34 S. Ct. 1, 58 L. Ed. 107 (1913); Long, *Senator Bursum and Pueblo Indians Land Act*.

13. Weir, "Time Immemorial."

14. Bayer, Laura, and Floyd Montoya, *Santa Ana: The People, the Pueblo, and the History of Tamaya*, University of New Mexico Press, 1994.

15. Pueblo Lands Board Report, April 30, 1930, quoted in Hodges, *Report on Irrigation and Water Supply of the Pueblos.*

16. Hodges, 274.

17. Hodges, 304–7.

18. Ostrom, "Why Do We Need to Protect Institutional Diversity?"

19. *Rio Grande Drainage Survey*, New Mexico Office of the State Engineer, 1918.

20. Mann, "A Reservoir Runs Through It."

21. H. F. Robinson, "Failure to Drain Costs Albuquerque and Valley Enormous Sum Annually," *Albuquerque Morning Journal*, April 28, 1920, 3.

22. "50,000 by 1920, Slogan of Boosters at Great Banquet," *Albuquerque Journal*, Nov. 11, 1915, 5.

23. "Can Drain Rio without Federal Aid," *Albuquerque Journal*, Sept. 28, 1915, 3.

24. "Bernalillo Road to Build," *Albuquerque Morning Journal*, May 14, 1920, 1.

25. United States v. Joseph, 94 U.S. 614, 24 L. Ed. 295 (1877).

26. Teeters, "'A Simple Act of Justice.'"

27. Teeters, "'A Simple Act of Justice.'"

28. Horn, "The Cause of Every American Artist: The Fight over the Bursum Bill and the Making of New Mexico as a Cultural Center," *El Palacios: Art, History and Culture of the Southwest*. Summer Issue, 2021.

29. During the 1920s the political confederation of the nineteen autonomous Pueblos commonly went by the name "Council of All of the New Mexico Pueblos." The more common long-term name was the All Pueblo Council (APC), which became the All Indian Pueblo Council (AIPC) in 1965, with the signing of an organizational constitution (see Walden, "The Pueblo Confederation's Political Wing"). While the early 1920s are seen as formative for this political confederation, its cooperative roots extend far longer and are recognized as one of the oldest political confederations in North America. See Sando (1992), 263. Only more recently the AIPC was renamed as the All Pueblo Council of Governors (APCG). The current APCG includes the nineteen Pueblos of New Mexico and Texas, with the addition of Pueblo of Ysleta del Sur (near El Paso, Texas), whose ancestral people moved southward down the Rio Grande during the period of the Pueblo Revolt in the late 1600s.

30. Wenger, *Land, Culture, and Sovereignty*. Historical summaries of the Nov. 5, 1922, inter-Pueblo meeting at Santo Domingo Pueblo (Kewa Pueblo) over the Bursum bill do not definitely place either Pablo Abeita (Isleta) or Jose Alcario Montoya (Cochiti) as being there, although they were known Pueblo leaders and interpreters at the time. There were various Anglo supporters who helped organize (e.g., John Collier) and were present for parts of the meeting, and various accounts exist. For example, Elizabeth Shepley Sergeant's first-person account only names Charlie Kie (Laguna Pueblo) as chair and notes the activities of several interpreters among the representatives present for twenty New Mexico Pueblos. Elizabeth Shepley Sergeant, "Big Powwow of Pueblos," *The New York Times*, Nov. 26, 1922, 88, 96. Weeks after the meeting, Pablo Abeita wrote a letter, along with Francis C. Wilson, rebutting Holm Bursum's defense of his bill. See "Pablo Abeita and F.C. Wilson Discuss Bursum's Indian Bill," *Albuquerque Journal*, Nov. 26, 1922, 9. Further, growing out of that November 5, 1922, council meeting, both Abeita and Montoya were connected with a Pueblo delegation that subsequently visited Washington, DC, to argue against the Bursum Bill in the early months of 1923. Pablo Abeita is regularly listed in national papers as orator and spokesperson for the group, and Jose Alcario Montoya is listed by Horn in a 1923 picture of the delegation with President Calvin Coolidge. Horn, *The Cause of Every American Artist.*

31. Lawrence, D. H., "Certain Americans and an Englishman," *New York Times Magazine*, Dec. 24, 1922, 8.

32. "Meeting Refutes Charge 'Paid Agents' Stirred up Indians Against the Bursum Bill," *Santa Fe New Mexican*, Nov. 25, 5.

33. "Pablo Abeita and F.C. Wilson Discuss Bursum's Indian Bill," *Albuquerque Journal*, Nov. 26, 1922, 9; Native Americans were not considered United States citizens until 1924, with the Indian Citizenship Act (also known as Snyder Act). The Act granted citizenship to all Native Americans born in the US but left voting rights to the states. As noted by Bird, "World War II veteran Miguel Trujillo, an Isleta Pueblo citizen, successfully sued to obtain Native Americans' right to vote." Bird, "Leaving the Ladder Down." See also discussion in Walden, "The Pueblo Confederation's Political Wing."

34. For examples, see: (i) "New Mexicans in Washington: Conflict of Authority," *Albuquerque Morning Journal*, June 22, 1921, 3; (ii) Wenger, *We Have a Religion*; and (iii) Sando, *Pueblo Profiles*.

35. "Rotary Club Takes Swat at Bad Bills," *Santa Fe New Mexican*, Nov. 24, 1922, 3.

36. For an example of such arguments in the Middle Valley, see: "An Empire Rotting in the Hands of the Pueblos: Thousands of Acres of Rich Valley Land Lie Idle," *Albuquerque Morning Journal*, Jan. 6, 1905, 5.

37. "Collier's Council of Indians Wants Water Rights Safeguarded," *Santa Fe New Mexican*, Dec. 2, 1927, 7.

38. "Conservation Measure Gets Official O.K.," *Albuquerque Journal*, Jan. 22, 1928, 1.

39. "Liberal Policy for Indians in Bratton's Bill," *Albuquerque Journal*, Feb. 10, 1928, 1.

40. "Indian Advisor Against Further Opposition to Reclamation Measure," *Albuquerque Journal*, Feb. 18, 1928, 1.

41. The total "prior and paramount" acreage was later increased by the US Secretary of Interior to 8,847 acres. Mann, "A Reservoir Runs Through It."

42. Worster, *A River Running West*.

43. Randell and Curley, "Dams and Tribal Land Loss in the United States."

44. *Report of the Special Committee of the U.S. Senate on the Irrigation and Reclamation of Arid Lands*, United States Senate, 1890, 25.

45. *Report of the Special Committee*, 1890.

46. "Big News for Albuquerque," *Albuquerque Journal*, Sept. 10, 1889, 2.

47. Walcott, *Twenty-First Annual Report of the Director of the United States Geological Survey*.

48. Robinson, Report of Aug. 13, 1913, quoted in Hodges, *Report on Irrigation and Water Supply*.

49. Whitehead, *Science and the Modern World*.

50. Pecos, *The History of Cochiti Lake from the Pueblo Perspective*.

51. Phillips et al., *Reining in the Rio Grande*; Welsh, "The United States Army Corps of Engineers in the Middle Rio Grande Valley, 1935–1955"; Pecos, *The History of Cochiti Lake*; Pinel, "Stopping the Flood of damages from Cochiti Dam."

52. Pecos, *The History of Cochiti Lake*.

53. Pecos, *The History of Cochiti Lake*.

54. Bird, "Leaving the Ladder Down."

55. Bird, "Leaving the Ladder Down."

Chapter 7

1. Cliff, W. Wilson, 1972. "Financing Plagued Conservancy District," *Albuquerque Journal*, April 12, 1972, A1, A10.

2. The final modified plan in Burkholder's *Report of the Chief Engineer* estimated 126,571 acres within the District to be benefitted (see Table 5, 43), with a projection of 123,267 irrigable acres. As noted, "The assessed valuation of the middle Rio Grande valley, including land and improvements, is about $40,000,000 on a basis of 50 percent of actual value, of which about $20,000,000 is in the city of Albuquerque." Burkholder, *Report of the Chief Engineer*, 40. The report identified a total population of 55,000: 35,000 in Albuquerque (presumably including proximal unincorporated areas), 8,0000 in other primary towns (Belen, Bernalillo, Los Lunas, and Socorro), 3,000 in Pueblos, with a remainder of 9,000.

3. A summary of US Senate Hearings testimony by the Assistant Secretary of the Interior on the breakout of assessment burdens, including the federal portion for the six Pueblos in the Middle Valley, can be found at: "Indians Pay $45 Per Acre for Conservancy, Says Edwards," *The Santa Fe New Mexican*, Jan. 26, 1929, 7.

4. Walker and Cockerill, *Farm Organization Practices and Costs of Producing Crops in the Middle Rio Grande Conservancy District of New Mexico*. Based on MRGCD initial assessment records, Calkins states: "About 45 per cent of the project is carried by the agricultural land; about 15 per cent by the private urban property; about 23 per cent by the public utilities; the remaining 17 per cent by the State and other public corporations." Calkins, *Reconnaissance Survey of Human Dependency on Resources in the Rio Grande Watershed*, 60.

5. For example, a producing, medium-age orchard could be assessed as low as $20 an acre. In contrast, swamp or lake land was assessed at $52 an acre, as were uplands with considerable leveling needed and not currently irrigable. Initial assessments averaged $44 an acre with annual payments of $3 an acre. See Walker and Cockerill, *Farm Organization Practices and Costs of Producing Crops in the Middle Rio Grande Conservancy District of New Mexico*, 10.

6. Under the Farm Credit Administration, the Federal Farm Bank of Wichita refused to make loans in the Middle Rio Grande Valley from 1919 through the 1930s. See "Federal Loans Skip This Area," *Albuquerque Journal*, July 20, 1935, 8; "Valley Land Loan Discrimination," *Albuquerque Journal*, Feb. 1, 1936, 8; "Valley Loans Blocked Again," *Albuquerque Journal*, July 18, 1936, 8; "Sidestep," *The Albuquerque Tribune*, Jan. 20, 1937, 10.

7. "To Correct a Situation," *Albuquerque Journal*, July 12, 1925, 12; "Producers of Valley Will Seek Market—Failure to Pack and Grade According to Specifications Blamed," *Albuquerque Journal*, July 11, 1935, 1.

8. "Great News," *Albuquerque Journal*, Oct. 7, 1934, 4; and Cliff, W. Wilson, "Financing Plagued Conservancy District," *Albuquerque Journal*, April 12, 1972, A1, A10.

9. "Whole City Will Join Celebration Tonight of Conservancy Bond Sale," *Albuquerque Journal*, Oct. 14, 1932, 1.

10. Calkins, *Reconnaissance Survey of Human Dependency on Resources in the Rio Grande Watershed*, 2.

11. Calkins *Reconnaissance Survey of Human Dependency on Resources in the Rio Grande Watershed*, 39.

12. Calkins, *Reconnaissance Survey of Human Dependency on Resources in the Rio Grande Watershed.*

13. "Valley Farmers Promised Delay in Tax Sale," *Albuquerque Journal*, Nov. 27, 1937, 1.

14. *Albuquerque Journal*, Dec. 4, 1937, 1.

15. "Postponement of Tax Sales is Considered," *Albuquerque Journal*, Dec. 3, 1937, 1.

16. "Court Declares Conservancy Tax Sales Illegal," *Albuquerque Journal*, Aug. 4, 1939, 1.

17. McDonald et al., *An Evolutionary History of the Middle Rio Grande Conservancy District.*

18. See, "Memorial of Legislature of New Mexico," US Congressional Record-Senate, Oct. 15, 1940, 13576.

19. With respect to the N.M. Relief Act of 1940, the court found: "The Relief Act offends the due process, the equal protection, and the contract clauses of the United States Constitution, and is therefore void." Relating to the MRGCD's bond obligations (to both private parties and the RFC), the Act essentially attempted to eliminate all further assessments against agricultural lands in the District not under cultivation and make current liens payable in equal installments through 1955. Durand v. Middle Rio Grande Conservancy Dist, 46 N.M. 138, 123 P.2d 389 (N.M. 1942).

20. "Conservancy Gets Tax Concession, Ready to Redeem; Governor Agrees to 50 percent and Up Basis for Repurchase; See "No Delay; District Officials Say Rehabilitation Can Start at Once," *Albuquerque Journal*, July 26, 1939, 1.

21. "Total of 3125 Landowners Have Applied for Rehabilitation Aid: Conservancy Approves 2,829 Loans for $752,520, Nearly 30,000 Acres Redeemed." *Albuquerque Journal*, Dec. 6, 1944, 2. The redemption program was to continue, with the RFC leaving the District in 1946 and the MRGCD continuing the program in modified form into the 1950s. There was an initial delay in Socorro County landowners participating, as the county had not collected tax deeds due to delinquency: "Socorro Farmers Barred From Rehabilitation Plan," *Albuquerque Journal*, Feb. 27, 1940, 1; For context on the 30,000 acres initially redeemed, Clark, *Water in New Mexico,* notes that 34,000 acres of the 97,300 irrigable non-Pueblo lands in the District had been under tax-sold status to the state (i.e., State Tax Commission) due to delinquencies.

22. By 1950 Conservancy District tax delinquency was low, driven by a greater than 98 percent payment rate in Bernalillo County, as revenue collections tilted to the urban core even before the formal federal takeover. "Conservancy District's Tax Delinquency Low," *Albuquerque Journal*, Feb. 5, 1950, 11.

23. See, "District Looks to Reclamation, But Tax Matter First, Says Butt," *Albuquerque Journal*, May 4, 1939, 6; "District Asks Bureau Survey," *Albuquerque Journal*, April 24, 1940, 14.

24. United States House of Representatives, Middle Rio Grande Project: Letter from the Secretary of the Interior, transmitting a Report and Findings on the Middle Rio Grande Project, H. Doc. 653, 81st Cong., 2nd Sess., United States

Government Printing Office, 1950; Welsh, "The United States Army Corps of Engineers in the Middle Rio Grande Valley, 1935–1955.".

25. *The Facts About the Flood Control and Reclamation Project in the Middle Rio Grande Valley and Its Importance in the National Defense Program, 1950*. Middle Rio Grande Flood Control Association Records, MSS 410-SC, University of New Mexico Center for Southwest Research and Special Collections.

26. "$6.7 Million in Bonds Retired Here," *Albuquerque Journal*, Feb. 2, 1956, 11; Gagan, *Middle Rio Grande Project*; DuMars and Nunn, *Middle Rio Grande Conservancy District Water Policies Plan*.

27. Cliff, W. Wilson, "Conservancy Tax Spurs Conflict," *Albuquerque Journal*, April 14, 1972, A1.

28. *The Rio Grande in the Albuquerque Metropolis: Plan Recommendations for a "City Edges" Study*, City Edges Study, City of Albuquerque, 1975.

29. Tom Harmon, "A Walk on the Wild Side," *Albuquerque Journal*, Jan. 19, 1983, 17.

30. Tom Harmon, "A Walk on the Wild Side," *Albuquerque Journal*, Jan. 19, 1983, 17.

31. Tom Harmon, "A Change at Last," *Albuquerque Journal*, May 3, 1983, 17.

32. Heron Marquez, "Ditch Precautions Remain in Limbo After Five Months," *Albuquerque Journal*, Sept. 11, 1983.

33. McDonald et al., *An Evolutionary History of the Middle Rio Grande Conservancy District*.

34. "Ditch Fencing South in Suit Against District," *Albuquerque Journal*, July 9, 1972, 67.

35. "Ditch Fencing South in Suit Against District," *Albuquerque Journal*, July 9, 1972, 67.

36. "Drainage Meet Results in Permanent Body," *Albuquerque Morning Journal*, May 17, 1918, 2.

37. "Real Estate Transfers," *Albuquerque Journal*, Dec. 12, 1934, 8 (re Tract 11 of MRGCD Map 46).

38. Platting of the subdivision was approved in 1951 (*Albuquerque Journal*, June 14, 1951, 16), followed by a suit to quiet title, with lots being sold by 1958

(*Albuquerque Journal*, April 24, 1958, 17). By Census and other public records, both Procopio Armijo and his wife Barbarita appear to have lived their entire lives in Albuquerque's Atrisco/Del Rio area (from the 1880s into the 1970s and 1960s, respectively), witnessing the growth of the metropolitan area, and its changing relationship with the river.

39. "State Park Asked for South Valley," *Albuquerque Journal*, June 4, 1967, 27.

40. "Garcia to Oppose Vincent Brunacini," *The Albuquerque Tribune*, Feb. 28, 1966, 25; "Garcia Will Seek to Keep House Seat: Prime Mover for River Park," *Albuquerque Journal*, June 19, 1968, 2; "Three Seek Party Nod," *Albuquerque Journal*, May 25, 1970, 5.

41. "Legislators Back Vast River Park," *Albuquerque Journal*, Jan. 12, 1968, 52.

42. "A Rio Grande Park is Given House Nod," *The Santa Fe New Mexican*, Feb. 7, 1968, 5.

43. Rose Marie Walker and V. B. Price, "Child Drowns While Playing Near Ditch," *Albuquerque Tribune*, April 20, 1967, 1.

44. "Fence Authority Sought in Ditch Safety Proposal," *Albuquerque Journal*, Sept. 13, 1967, 44.

45. Jim Boyer, "Elected Mid Rio Board Is Goal of Legislators," *Albuquerque Tribune*, Jan. 23, 1968, 20.

46. "Panel Approves Mid Rio Board Election Bill," *Albuquerque Journal*, Feb. 6, 1968, 2; Coll later moved to Santa Fe and was elected to the State House there, eventually switching from the Republican to Democratic parties.

47. C. A. Hundertmark, "Major Park Along the River is Proposed," *Albuquerque Tribune*, Jan. 9, 1968, 1.

48. "Legislators Back Vast River Park," *Albuquerque Tribune*, Jan. 12, 1968, D-4.

49. "Garcia Will Seek to Keep House Seat," *Albuquerque Journal*, June 19, 1968, 2.

50. "Mid-Rio Measure Sent to Committee," *Albuquerque Journal*, Feb. 9, 1974, 7.

51. John A. Webster, United Press, "'Feed Bill' Waits King's Signature," *Santa Fe New Mexican*, Jan. 22, 1974, 23.

52. "Rio Board Election Bill Past House," *Santa Fe New Mexican*, Feb. 5, 1974.

53. "Is a 'liberal,' aspirant says," *Albuquerque Tribune*, March 12, 1974, 16.

54. Bill Hume, "MRGCD Bill Proposed," *Albuquerque Journal*, Feb. 21, 1973, 4.

55. Robert V. Beier, "Fight Looms Over Mid Rio Board," *Albuquerque Journal*, Nov. 21, 1974, 66.

56. Wayne S. Scott, 1959. "'59 Conservancy Tax Revision is Climax of 20 Years Planning and Working," *Albuquerque Journal*, Nov. 29, 1959, pp. 1, 4.

57. Harrison Burrall Jr., "Benefits Largely Illusionary," *Albuquerque Journal*, Oct. 31, 1974, 5.

58. Wayne S. Scott, "Amendment Seeks Election Of Mid Rio District Board," *Albuquerque Journal*, Oct. 25, 1974, D-4.

59. Agar and Taylor, "Human Eddies and Flows."

60. Wayne Scott, "Flood District, Knocked Out By Court, to Close Office Sept. 1," *Albuquerque Journal*, Aug. 9, 1958, 1.

61. Agar and Taylor, "Human Eddies and Flows." The need for flood control of waters coming off the increasingly developed uplands didn't go away. Nor did the desire for elected representation. Quickly, the New Mexico legislature created the Albuquerque Metropolitan Arroyo Flood Control Authority (AMAFCA). The enabling legislation allowed for the acquisition, maintenance, and operation of flood-control systems to protect residents in the urban area. Located within Bernalillo County, today AMAFCA serves a population of approximately 679,000 and protects nearly $20 billion of net taxable property value. Notably, relative to this historical discussion, the Authority is governed by elected directors with similar taxing powers as the MRGCD but restricted to one county.

62. "Vote Against Amendment 2," *Albuquerque Journal*, Oct. 20, 1974, 4.

63. Eppie Armijo, "Editorial Position Attacked," *Albuquerque Journal*, Oct. 27, 1974, 7.

64. Susskind, *Water and Democracy*.

65. Reynolds v. Sims, 377 US 533 (1964).

66. Marousek, "Orr v. Kneip."

67. The question of proportion is based on the authors' assessment of District activities and history. The District's broad powers under the Conservancy Act of 1927, as amended, allow the agency to serve multiple purposes. While arguably there are some joint costs, the established practice has never been to provide disaggregation of the expenditures among purposes publicly.

68. Robert V. Beier, "Fight Looms Over Mid Rio Board," *Albuquerque Journal*, Nov. 21, 1974, 66.

69. "Senate OKs Seven-Person Mid Rio Board," *Albuquerque Journal*, March 13, 1975, 2; Associated Press, "Apodaca Signs 21 Bills," *Las Vegas Optic*, April 11, 1975, 5.

70. Mike Tumolillo, "Floating Doll Warns: Don't be a Ditch Dummy," *Albuquerque Tribune*, March 2, 2005, A7.

71. Thompson, "Urbanization and the Middle Rio Grande Conservancy District."

72. Baca's time with the MRGCD occurred between his two terms as the New Mexico Commissioner of Public Lands (1983 to 1987 and 1991 to 1993). He also served as the mayor of Albuquerque from 1997 to 2001.

73. Robert Rodriguez, "Beware of Undertow," *Albuquerque Journal*, Aug. 16, 1989, 29.

74. Tony Davis, "Conservancy District Criticized," *Albuquerque Tribune*, Nov. 24, 1987, 6.

75. Dennis Domrzalski, "Conservancy Official's Farm Work was Done at District Expense, 2 claim," *Albuquerque Tribune*, Nov. 24, 1987, 6.

76. Robert Rodriguez, "Beware of Undertow," *Albuquerque Journal*, Aug. 16, 1989, 29.

77. Rodriguez, "Beware of Undertow."

78. After a 1985 New Mexico Attorney General ruling based on state law from the mid-1950s requiring a water toll for special water districts, the MRGCD implemented a flat per-acre water service charge with a five-acre minimum charge and the same Class A and Class B system. Irrigators opposed the toll, and interest groups disagreed over the A/B system and relative rates in the late 1980s. These challenges eroded the financial health of the district. See "Too Little Too Late," *Albuquerque Journal*, Sept. 22, 1986, 4; "Urban Ditches Face Cloudy Future," *Albuquerque Journal*, March 8, 1987, 3; "Residents Protest Proposed Conservancy District Tax Hike," *Albuquerque Journal*, July 20, 1989, 36; and DuMars and Nunn, *Middle Rio Grande Conservancy District Water Policies Plan*.

79. Under a 1993 amendment to the state Conservancy Act, Conservancy District irrigators pay a flat per acre water service charge (WSC), and all parcels in the District (with exemptions) pay an ad valorem tax proportional to property values, with separate mill rates for Residential/Agricultural and Non-residential/Commercial. In effect since 1995, this remains the modern system of district financing. For current New Mexico state laws governing Conservancy Districts, see 2021 New Mexico Statues, Chapter 73—Special Districts, and specifically Articles 14 through 18: N.M. Stat § 73-14-1 (2021) to N.M. Stat § 73-18-43 (2021).

80. Rodriguez, "Beware the Undertow," *Albuquerque Journal*, Aug. 16, 1989, 29.

Chapter 8

1. Janelle Stamper, "Water Accord Reached," *Albuquerque Journal*, July 14, 1976, 24.

2. Aldo Leopold, "A Plea for State-owned Ducking Grounds," In Brown and Carmony, *Aldo Leopold's Southwest*.

3. OpenET, accessed Sept. 6, 2023, https://openetdata.org/.

4. See Marris, *Rambunctious Garden*.

5. Crawford et al., *Middle Rio Grande Ecosystem: Bosque Biological Management Plan*.

6. Crawford et al., *Middle Rio Grande Ecosystem: Bosque Biological Management Plan*.

7. Van Cleave, "Vegetative Changes in the Middle Rio Grande Conservancy District."

8. From public records (Census etc.,): Majorie J. Van Cleave was born in 1914 and passed away in 1975, after moving away from Albuquerque in the 1940s with her husband and family. She graduated from Albuquerque High School in 1931 and earned a Bachelor of Science in Education in 1934, when she was twenty years old, completing her master's thesis when she was twenty-one. Her father E. Van Cleave partnered with Leopold and five others in 1923 in incorporating the Home Building and Loan Association of Albuquerque

("Loan Association Incorporated," *The Santa Fe New Mexican*, Dec. 31, 1923, 3). Whether this friendly connection had any influence on the ecological interests of a young Marjorie, we can only speculate.

9. "Society," *Albuquerque Journal*, Oct. 12, 1932; "City Principals, Teachers Await Opening of School," *Albuquerque Tribune*, Aug. 30, 1935; "Many Parties are Given for Miss Vancleave," *Albuquerque Tribune*, May 11, 1936, 6.

10. Van Cleave, "Vegetative Changes in the Middle Rio Grande Conservancy District"; Crawford et al., *Middle Rio Grande Ecosystem*.

11. "rectify, v." OED Online, March 2023, accessed June 27, 2023, Oxford University Press.

12. Bob Brashear, "Engineers 'Train' Rio Into Straight Channel," *Albuquerque Tribune*, March 26, 1959, 13.

13. Grassel, "Taking Out the Jacks."

14. Mary Harner et al., *Loss of Open Areas and a Changing Albuquerque Bosque and River*, Middle Rio Grande Endangered Species Collaborative Program 2020 Science Symposium.

15. Crawford et al., *Middle Rio Grande Ecosystem*.

16. "Work on Channelization of Middle Rio Grande Saving Valuable Water," *Albuquerque Journal*, June 22, 1956, 19.

17. Heberlein, *Navigating Environmental Attitudes*.

18. "River Park from Old Albuquerque to Bridge, Plan," *Albuquerque Morning Journal*, Jan. 12, 1917, 8.

19. "River Park from Old Albuquerque to Bridge, Plan," *Albuquerque Morning Journal*, Jan. 12, 1917, 8.

20. "Rio Grande Park Virtually Certain to Be Established; County Will Share Expense," *Albuquerque Morning Journal*, March 28, 2018, 8.

21. "Girl Drowned While Wading Near Old Town," *Albuquerque Journal*, May 31, 1923.

22. "Homes are Going Up on Site of Palmer's Slough, Drained as Malaria Control Project," *Albuquerque Journal*, March 20, 1936, 9.

23. "Some Facts About Rio Grande Park," *Albuquerque Forward*, No. 1, Aug. 1918, 1.

24. "Help Rio Grande Park," *The Evening Herald*, Sept. 9, 1918, 6.

25. "The Rio Grande Park Plan," *The Evening Herald*, April 10, 1920, 14.

26. "Immense Crowd at Dedication of Rio Grande Park, Country Club and Huning Castle Addition," *Albuquerque Journal*, July 1, 1929, 3.

27. "Homes are Going Up on Site of Palmer's Slough, Drained as Malaria Control Project," *Albuquerque Journal*, March 20, 1936, 9.

28. Rex Funk, "Birth of New Paradigm," in City of Albuquerque, *History of Albuquerque's Major Public Open Space.*

29. See discussions in Thompson, "Urbanization and the Middle Rio Grande Conservancy District"; and McDonald et al., *An Evolutionary History of the Middle Rio Grande Conservancy District*.

30. For recent discussion, see chapter 2 in Banzhaf, *Pricing the Priceless*.

31. Other national legislative examples include the Wilderness Act of 1965, rooted in Aldo Leopold's early expressions of wilderness preservation, which developed in his last few years in Albuquerque. With extensive discussion of New Mexico and the Southwest, see: Leopold, "A Plea for Wilderness Hunting Grounds."

32. "Outdoor Notes," *Albuquerque Journal*, Aug. 19, 1994, C6.

33. US Fish and Wildlife Service, "Endangered and Threatened Wildlife and Plants; Final Rule to List the Rio Grande Silvery Minnow as an Endangered Species," Federal Register 59, no. 138 (July 20, 1994): 36988–36995, https://www.govinfo.gov/content/pkg/FR-1994-07-20/html/94-17576.htm.

34. See Berrens et al., "Valuing the Protection of Minimum Instream Flows in New Mexico"; Berrens and Grijalva, "Valuation of Species Preservation." As one evaluative criterion, Moore et al., *Noah's Ark in a Warming World*, provide evidence that sustained federal efforts to protect the silvery minnow pass an economic benefit-cost test.

35. "FWS Issues No Jeopardy Biological Opinion Covering Middle Rio Grande Water Management Activities," *Journal of Water*, Sept. 19, 2017.

Chapter 9

1. Fergusson, Erna, *Albuquerque Herald*, Dec. 18, 1922, quoted in the City of Albuquerque Water Resources Department's *Noticias del Agua*, June 1985.

2. City of Philadelphia, *History of the Water Works*, 1860, quoted in Smith, *City Water, City Life*.

3. Smith, *City Water, City Life*, 5.

4. "Water Works," *Albuquerque Journal*, Aug. 18, 1882, 3.

5. "Water Works," *Albuquerque Journal*, Dec. 8, 1882, 2.

6. "Incorporation," *Albuquerque Journal*, July 19, 1884, 2.; "Albuquerque Grows from Frontier Town to Metropolis," *Albuquerque Journal*, Sept. 12, 1937, 23. Albuquerque was formally incorporated as a town in 1885, and then as a city in 1891. Old Town remained separate until it was annexed in 1949. See "Albuquerque History," Albuquerque Public Library, https://abqlibrary.org/abqhistory.

7. "No. 27, an ordinance for the erection, construction and maintenance of water works in the town of Albuquerque, and to regulate the same," *Albuquerque Journal*, Sept. 24, 1885, 3.

8. "Notice," *Albuquerque Journal*, March 28, 1886, 4.

9. *Albuquerque Journal*, April 27, 1886, 1.

10. Sanborn Fire Insurance Map from Albuquerque, Bernalillo County, New Mexico; Sanborn Map Company, 1891, Library of Congress Geography and Map Division, accessed Aug. 15, 2023, http://hdl.loc.gov/loc.gmd/g4324am.g4324am_g056701891.

11. "State College and Varsity to Meet on Forum," *Albuquerque Journal*, March 6, 1915, 8.

12. Howe, *The Modern City and Its Problems*, 168.

13. Obeng-Odoom, "The Meaning, Prospects, and Future of the Commons."

14. Clyde Tingley, "Water Users, Attention," *The Evening Herald*, May 20, 1915, 6.

15. "M.O. Advocates Organize Water Users League," *Albuquerque Morning Journal*, March 21, 1916, 6. Metcalf was the founder of the Socialist Party in New Mexico and was the party candidate for the US Senate in 1916. See "Socialists of New Mexico Expecting Big Vote This Year," *Albuquerque Journal*, Sept. 24, 1916, 11. He also was prominent as one of framers of the Albuquerque city charter adopted in 1918, see: Metcalf, William P., "One of Duke City's Grand Old Men, Dies At His Home After Thirty Years of Useful Residence Here," *Albuquerque Journal*, Oct. 22, 1920, 1.

16. "The Water Problem," *Albuquerque Journal*, June 20, 1915, 12.

17. Houghton, *The Blighted History of the Alameda Land Grant*.

18. "Plans C. of C. Enterprise Under His Leadership," *Albuquerque Journal*, Jan. 23, 1918, 4.

19. Expansion into the east mesa area up from the river valley floor was beginning, with proposed connection the city water supply. See "University Heights," *Albuquerque Journal*, Feb. 16, 2016, 10.

20. "McMillen's Letter," *Albuquerque Journal*, April 18, 1916, 8.

21. "Albuquerque Water Bond Issue Approved by Court," *New Mexico State Record*, July 12, 1918; inflation adjustment calculated using Bureau of Labor Statistics CPI calculator, https://www.bls.gov/data/inflation_calculator.htm.

22. "Report of the Committee on Sewers," *Albuquerque Journal*, March 7, 1883, 4.

23. "The Question of Sewerage," *Albuquerque Journal*, Jan. 11, 1884, 2.

24. City of Albuquerque, *Water and Sewer History*, undated.

25. "House Drains," *Albuquerque Journal*, March 29, 1890, 3.

26. "City Council," *Albuquerque Journal*, Feb. 26, 1891, 1.

27. "Council Will Do Something Quick About Sewers," *Albuquerque Journal*, Feb. 6, 1906, 5.

28. "Urges That Sewers Be Fixed Now," *Albuquerque Journal*, June 10, 1906, 2.

29. "Enormous Amount of Work on New Sewer Plans," *Albuquerque Journal*, Feb. 28, 1908, 5; "James Gladding Succumbs at 70," *Albuquerque Tribune*, Feb. 2, 1955, 4.

30. "Last Meeting of the Old Regime Yesterday," *Albuquerque Journal*, April 18, 1908, 2.

31. "Sewer Committee's Report," *Albuquerque Journal*, March 16, 1909, 7.

32. "Sewer Expert Submits Report on Proposed System for Albuquerque," *Albuquerque Journal*, Nov. 10, 1908, 1.

33. "City Must Expand Water Plant This Year, Engineer F. Kimball States in His Annual Report," *Albuquerque Journal*, Jan. 14, 1922, 3. The park referred to is the proposal originated by Aldo Leopold in 1918, which eventually came to fruition in the 1930s, and lies downstream along the Rio Grande of what is known today as Tingley Beach. At the time of the report, James N. Gladding was city manager and Clyde Tingley was the chair of the city commission.

34. Williamson-Teller, "Protecting Water Quality and Religious Freedom at Isleta Pueblo."

35. "Water Quality Woes," *Albuquerque Journal*, Sept. 17, 1992, 18.

36. Williamson-Teller, *Protecting Water Quality and Religious Freedom.*

37. City of Albuquerque v. Browner, 97 F.3d 415 (10th Cir. 1996).

38. City of Albuquerque v. Browner, 97 F.3d 415 (10th Cir. 1996).

39. Theis, *The Relation between the Lowering of the Piezometric Surface and the Rate and Duration of Discharge of a Well Using Ground-Water Storage*.

40. "City May Handle Engineers' Work on 13 Projects," *Albuquerque Tribune*, June 30, 1954, 29.

41. "State Engineer Denies Basin to End Farming," *Albuquerque Tribune*, Dec. 20, 1956, 39.

42. Hall, "Steve Reynolds—Portrait of a State Engineer as a Young Artist."

43. City of Albuquerque v. Reynolds, 379 P.2d 73, 71 N.M. 428 (1962).

44. New Mexico Office of the State Engineer Water Rights Database, Water Rights ID SD 03089 247429 607318

45. Glaser, *The San Juan-Chama Project*.

46. The eventual San Juan-Chama Project has contracts for allocation of 96,200 acre-feet per year of water across more than a dozen entities, with about three-fourths allocated to municipal and industrial users and the remainder to agricultural irrigation. The two largest recipients are Albuquerque's municipal system at 48,5000 AFY for municipal and industrial sectors and the MRGCD at 20,900 for agricultural irrigation. US Bureau of Reclamation, *San Juan-Chama Project*, https://usbr.gov/projects/index.php?id=521.

47. Albuquerque Bernalillo County Utility Authority, *San Juan-Chama Project*, accessed Aug. 27, 2023, https://www.abcwua.org/your-drinking-water-san-juan-chama-project/.

48. However, an early economic analysis of various San Juan-Chama Project options was conducted by an interdisciplinary group out of University of New Mexico (UNM) and New Mexico State University (NMSU) and first circulated in 1959, as led by the UNM economist Nathaniel Wollman. Wollman, *The Value of Water in Alternative Uses.* That study included consideration of options for water left in the river for fish and wildlife habitat. The modeling analysis for 1955–1975 included the following: (i) use of proposed transfer of project water at levels of either 235,000 AFY or 110,000 AFY; (ii) calculated only market effects (e.g., changes employment, income, in expected profits), but both primary and secondary, for twelve counties in both the San Juan and Rio Grande basins of New Mexico; and (iii) investigated a variety of allocations across three sectors: Municipal and Industrial (M&I), Agriculture, and Recreation. The recreation sector essentially allocated water to the river for fish and wildlife habitat, with the assumption that this would induce increased effects in the recreation-related economy. The recreation water would by assumption be sourced by reductions in irrigation water allocations in the upper regions of the Rio Grande. Economic effects on Gross State Product were evaluated for model simulations with different allocations to different sectors. In all simulations, Benefit/Cost (B/C) ratios for allocations of project water to a set of irrigation projects on the Rio Grande were unfavorable (<1). In contrast, all model simulations for the M&I and Recreational sectors were highly favorable (>1) (Table 33, 85). Estimated gross product per acre foot of water after adjustment (primary value added plus valued added by purchases) in 1954 dollars were in the range of $14 to $18 for Agriculture, $198 to $293 for Recreation, and $1,237 to $3,304 for M&I (Table 17, 39). One can speculate that had the proposed allocations to the Rio Grande for fish and wildlife habitat been made (and protected moving downstream) in the 1960s, then they might well have mitigated the later needed endangered species protection allocations. The economic information supporting allocation of water to the Rio Grande for protecting fish and habitat was available prior to the project being constructed.

49. Veihl, *Securing Environmental Flows for the Rio Grande Silvery Minnow.*

Chapter 10

1. See James A. French, *First Report of the State Engineer of New Mexico*, 1914. This report covered 1912–1914 and included discussion of improving El Camino Real and New Mexico bridge building laws, 10–15; James A. French, *Report of the State Highway Engineer and State Engineer of New Mexico for the Fifth and Sixth Fiscal Years, Dec. 1, 1916, to Nov. 30, 1918*, 1918, which contains the *Report of the Rio Grande Drainage Commission* (145–62) and lays out the drainage plan with a focus on the importance of Albuquerque to the state.

2. Aldo Leopold, *New Mexico Journal, 1917–1924*. Entry for August 24, 1918. University of Wisconsin-Madison Libraries, https://digital.library.wisc.edu/1711.dl/4H7W7SOLVJ6YI8I. Among the numerous hunting trips in his journals, Leopold reported four short visits (mostly by himself) to the Los Griegos area in late summer 1918, during the period he would have been working on drainage issues for the Chamber. He carefully reported bagging two dozen doves over those trips (31–34).

3. "Honorable Emiliano L. Gutierrez: Member of the House of Representatives of the 33rd Legislative Assembly from Bernalillo County," *Santa Fe New Mexican*, Feb. 23, 1901, 2: "Mr. Gutierrez' principal mission and his chief ambition, as a member of the house, is to aid in the passage of such laws that will protect the interests of the taxpayers, advance the territory in educational and material ways, and it is largely due to his efforts that the bill known as H.B. No. 21, providing for the construction of bridges was passed."

4. See "Commissioners Urge Drainage As of First Importance to Central Rio Grande Valley: Max Gutierrez Tells Rotarians Alkali Eats up Profits of Farmers While Irrigation System Encourages Waste of Water," *The Evening Herald*, Aug. 11, 1921, 1; "Gutierrez to Carry on Road Work as Agent: County Board Authorizes Commissioner to Supervise Road Work Without Pay," *Albuquerque Journal*, Aug. 22, 1922, 3; "County to Give $5,000 to Central Paving," *Albuquerque Journal*, Aug. 24, 1922, 3.

5. "Last I-40 City Link Will Open Monday," *Albuquerque Journal*, Oct. 17, 1969.

6. "Petitioners Will Seek Montaño-Montgomery Bridge, Road Backing," *Albuquerque Journal,* May 19, 1963, C-6.

7. Google NGrams, retrieved Aug. 8. 2023, https://books.google.com/ngrams/graph?content=wetlands%2Cswamps&year_start=1800&year_end=2019&corpus=en-2019&smoothing=3.

8. See "Governor Says People Should Settle Battle," *Albuquerque Journal*, June 6, 1930, 6; J. T. Rodgers, "Public Opinion: New Bridge Road," *Albuquerque Journal*, June 22, 1930, 4; Frank Zoretich, "Trying to Bridge a Gap on Old Route 66," *Albuquerque Journal*, April 25, 1992, 13.

9. Van Citters and Roxlau, *A Characterization of Historic Resources along Bridge Boulevard from Eighth Street to Coors Boulevard.*

10. "The Bridge," *Albuquerque Journal*, Sept. 28, 1882, 4.

11. Ebright and Hendricks, *Pablo Abeita*.

12. "Order Changing the Boundaries of Game Refuges," *Santa Fe New Mexican*, Jan. 21, 1928, 6.

13. Robertson, John, "Bridge Plan Excludes Montaño," *Albuquerque Journal*, Feb. 8, 1983, 1.

14. City of Albuquerque, *History of Albuquerque's Major Public Open Space.*

15. "Montaño Chasm Difficult to Bridge," *Albuquerque Journal*, Jan. 15, 1996, 7.

16. "Reach Conservancy Arrangement," *Albuquerque Journal*, Jan. 24, 1930, 1.

Conclusion

1. Voltaire, *Candide*, Boni and Liveright, 1918. We choose here the "Modern Library of the World's Best Books" edition, the classic school text version.

2. "River Park from Old Albuquerque to Bridge, Plan," *Albuquerque Morning Journal*, Jan. 12, 1917, 8.

3. Lefebvre, *The Production of Space*.

4. Ostrom, *Governing the Commons,* 90.

5. John Fleck, "On Gardens," *Inkstain* (blog), posted March 8, 2023, https://www.inkstain.net/2023/03/on-gardens/.

6. "Famous Valley Ranch North of Old Town is Being Subdivided," *Albuquerque Journal*, March 5, 1933, 7; On lands originally part of the Albuquerque Grant, whose title ran back to the Spanish Crown, James Matthew's dairy had served the growing Albuquerque market for several decades before eventually merging into a larger operation. With real estate and financing partners, Matthew created the Matthew Dairy and Supply Company (incorporated in New Mexico in 1912), which acquired additional North Valley land, much of it swampy or alkaline, including the Alvarado Farm, in 1919.

7. *Albuquerque Journal*, Dec. 29, 1932, 7.

8. *Albuquerque Journal*, March 5, 1933, 3.

9. We emphasize the word "culture" here in the root of the word "agriculture" because the thing we today call culture, meaning the breadth of human activities in community, is linguistically rooted in the practice of cultivating the land. Oxford English Dictionary, under "culture (n.), sense I.1.a," Sept. 2024, https://doi.org/10.1093/OED/5591036717.

10. John Fleck, "Precious Water, Ever Elusive, 100 Years of Statehood," *Albuquerque Journal*, Jan. 6, 2012, 32.

11. Gould and Lewontin, *The Spandrels of San Marco*; the phrase "form follows function" comes from the architect Louis Sullivan's essay *The Tall Office Building Artistically Considered*, anthologized in Louis Sullivan, *The Public Papers*, University of Chicago Press, 1988.

12. Quoted in José A. Rivera, *Presas Efimeras of New Mexico*, Working Paper, Landscape Architecture Commons, 2022, https://digitalrepository.unm.edu/cgi/viewcontent.cgi?article=1001&context=arch_fsp.

13. Rivera, *Presas Efimeras.*

14. This represents the ditches between Cochiti and Isleta identified in Burkholder.

15. Pouso et al., "Contact with Blue-Green Spaces."

16. *Loans for Relief of Drainage Districts*, Hearing before the House Committee on Irrigation and Reclamation, Dec. 11–12, 1930; quoted in John Fleck, "On Gardens," *Inkstain* (blog), March 8, 2023.

17. Mason in *Loans for Relief of Drainage Districts.*

18. For recent examples of such discussions, see: Sant, *From the Ground Up*; Kochskämper et al., "Resilience and the Sustainable Development Goals."

19. The room was named for Diego Abeita in 1985: "[H]is knowledge and experience in water matters had bridged an understanding between the District and Indian Pueblos." *The Albuquerque Tribune*, June 7, 1985, 3. Abeita (1904–1984) was an Isleta Pueblo leader and involved in efforts to secure Pueblo prior and paramount water storage in El Vado reservoir. He was head of the Six Middle Rio Grande Pueblos Irrigation Committee 1951–1977. "A Fighter: Isleta Activist's Deeds Will Weather Years," *The Albuquerque Tribune*, Sept. 27, 1984. See also Diego Abeita, "Isleta Indians Fashion Harness for Big River: Begin Construction Work on Diversion Dam at Pueblo," *The Albuquerque Tribune*, Sept. 16, 1933.

20. Trail and Ward, *Uniting Agricultural Water Management, Economics, and Policy for Climate Adaptation*.

21. B. L. Crowley, "Why We Need Gardeners. Law and Liberty," Nov. 6, 2024, 1, https://lawliberty.org/why-we-need-gardeners/. See also: B. L. Crowley, *Gardeners vs. Designers: Understanding the Great Fault Line in Canadian Politics*, Sutherland House Books, 2020.

22. "There are two things that interest me: the relation of people to each other, and the relation of people to land." From *Wherefore Wildlife Ecology*? In Leopold, *The River of the Mother of God and other Essays*, 336.

23. Bromley, *Sufficient Reason*.

24. "Hutchinson Celebrates New Plant on Firm's Fourth Anniversary," *Albuquerque Journal*, Jan. 1, 1931, 10.

Bibliography

Adair, Jourdan, "Reconstructing the Historical Albuquerque Reach of the Middle Rio Grande to Evaluate the Influence of River Engineering on Floodplain Inundation." Master's thesis, University of New Mexico, 2016. https://digitalrepository.unm.edu/ce_etds/121.

Agar, M., Taylor, E., "Human Eddies and Flows: The Mid-Century Floods of Albuquerque." *Water History* 6, (2014): 227–45.

Anaya, Rudolfo A., *Heart of Aztlan*. Editorial Justa Publications, 1976.

Anaya, Rudolfo. *Querencia: Reflections on the New Mexico Homeland*. University of New Mexico Press, 2020.

Atencio, Tomas, "Social Change and Community Conflict in Old Albuquerque, New Mexico." PhD thesis, University of New Mexico, 1985.

Autobee, Robert. *The Salt River Project*. Bureau of Reclamation History Program, 1993.

Banzhaf, H. Spencer. *Pricing the Priceless: A History of Environmental Economics*. Cambridge University Press, 2024.

Bayer, Laura, and Floyd Montoya. *Santa Ana: The People, the Pueblo, and the History of Tamaya*. University of New Mexico Press, 1994.

Berrens, Robert P., Philip Ganderton, and Carol L. Silva. "Valuing the Protection of Minimum Instream Flows in New Mexico," *Journal of Agricultural and Resource Economics* (1996): 294–308.

Berrens, Robert P., and Therese Grijalva. "Valuation of Species Preservation," Oxford Research Encyclopedia of Environmental Science. May 26, 2021.

Berthier-Foglar, Susanne. "Early Tourism in New Mexico: A Primitivist Pastime or a Tool of Integration?" *Angles: New Perspectives on the Anglophone World* 5 (2017).

Bird, Diane. "Leaving the Ladder Down." *El Palacios: Art, History and Culture of the Southwest* (Winter 2019).

Bock, Carl August. *History of the Miami Flood Control Project: Technical Reports: Part II*, Dayton: n.p., 1918.

Bromley, Daniel W. *Economic Interests and Institutions: The Conceptual Foundations of Public Policy*. Basil Blackwell, 1989.

Bromley, Daniel W. *Sufficient Reason: Volitional Pragmatism and the Meaning of Economic Institutions*. Princeton University Press, 2006.

Brown, David Earl, and Neil B. Carmony, eds. *Aldo Leopold's Southwest: Twenty-Six Early Writings by the Author of a Sand County Almanac*. University of New Mexico Press, 1995.

Brown, Lisa D. "The Middle Rio Grande Conservancy District's Protected Water Rights: Legal, Beneficial, or Against the Public Interest in New Mexico," *Natural Resources Journal* 40 (2000): 1.

Burkholder, Joseph L. *Report of the Chief Engineer, Joseph L. Burkholder, Submitting a Plan for Flood Control, Drainage and Irrigation of the Middle Rio Grande Conservancy project*. Middle Rio Grande Conservancy District, 1928.

Calkins, Hugh G. *Reconnaissance Survey of Human Dependency on Resources in the Rio Grande Watershed, Regional Bulletin No. 33, Conservation Economics Series No. 6*. Albuquerque, NM: US Soil Conservation Service, 1936.

Callary, Carol N. "A Political Biography of Frank A. Hubbell, 1862–1929." Master's thesis, University of New Mexico, 1967.

Carlson, Alvar W. "New Mexico's Sheep Industry, 1850–1900: Its Role in the History of the Territory," *New Mexico Historical Review* XLIV (1969).

Charles, Ralph. "Development of the Partido System in the New Mexico Sheep Industry." Master's thesis, University of New Mexico, 1940.

City of Albuquerque. *History of Albuquerque's Major Public Open Space*, 2019. https://www.cabq.gov/parksandrecreation/documents/history-of-albq-major-public-open-space-final.pdf.

Clark, Ira G. *Water in New Mexico: A History of its Management and Use*. University of New Mexico Press, 1987.

Coan, Charles Florus. *A History of New Mexico. Vol. 2*, American Historical Society, Incorporated, 1925.

Crawford, Clifford S., Anne C. Cully, Rob Leutheuser, Mark S. Sifuentes, Larry H. White, and James P. Wilber. *Middle Rio Grande Ecosystem: Bosque Biological Management Plan*, US Fish and Wildlife Service, District 2 (1993).

Cronon, William. *Nature's Metropolis*. W. W. Norton, 1991.

Crowley, B. L. *Gardeners vs. Designers: Understanding the Great Fault Line in Canadian Politics*. Sutherland House Books, 2020.

David, Paul A. "Why are Institutions the 'Carriers of History'? Path Dependence and the Evolution of Conventions, Organizations and Institutions," *Structural Change and Economic Dynamics* 5, no. 2 (1994): 205–20.

Davis, Brennan. "Heat Mitigation Impacts of Agriculture, Greenspace, and Riparian Forest in Albuquerque, New Mexico." Master's professional project, University of New Mexico Water Master of Water Resources and Master of Community and Regional Planning professional project, 2024.

DeMark, Judith Boyce. "The Immigrant Experience in Albuquerque, 1880–1920." PhD thesis, University of New Mexico, 1984.

DuMars, Charles T., and S. C. Nunn. *Middle Rio Grande Conservancy District Water Policies Plan*. Middle Rio Grande Conservancy District, Albuquerque, NM (1993).

Dunbar, N. W., D. S. Gutzler, K. S. Pearthree, et al. *Climate Change in New Mexico over the Next 50 Years: Impacts on Water Resources*. New Mexico Bureau of Geology and Mineral Resources, Bulletin 164, 2022. https://doi.org/10.58799/B-164.

Dunkelman, Marc J. *Why Nothing Works: Who Killed Progress—and How to Bring It Back*. PublicAffairs, 2025.

Duranton, Gilles, and Diego Puga. "The Economics of Urban Density." *Journal of Economic Perspectives* 34, no. 3 (2020): 3–26.

Ebright, Malcolm, and Rick Hendricks. *Pablo Abeita: The Life and Times of a Native Statesman of Isleta Pueblo, 1871–1940*. University of New Mexico Press, 2023.

Fleck, John. "Going Down to the Water," *Natural Resources Journal* 57 (2017): vi–x.

Fleming, W. and M. Schmader. "Aldo Leopold: Albuquerque's First Environmental Planner." *The Western Planner* (2010).

Flint, Richard, and Shirley Cushing Flint. *Overhaul: A Social History of the Albuquerque Locomotive Repair Shops*. University of New Mexico Press, 2021.

Follett, W. W., *A Study of the Use of Water for Irrigation on the Rio Grande del Norte above Fort Quitman, Texas*. International Boundary Commission, 1896.

Forrest, Suzanne. "A Trail of Tangled Titles: Mining, Land Speculation, and the Dismemberment of the San Antonio de las Huertas Land Grant," *New Mexico Historical Review* 71, no. 4 (1996): 4.

French, James A. *First Report of the State Engineer of New Mexico*, 1914.

French, James A. *Report of the State Highway Engineer and State Engineer of New Mexico for the Fifth and Sixth Fiscal Years, December 1, 1916, to November 30, 1918*, 1918.

Frost, Richard H. *The Railroad and the Pueblo Indians: The Impact of the Atchison, Topeka and Santa Fe on the Pueblos of the Rio Grande, 1880–1930*. University of Utah Press, 2015.

Gagan, Andrew. *Middle Rio Grande Project*, Bureau of Reclamation, 2013.

Gale Jr., H. Frederick, Linda F. Foreman, and Thomas C. Capehart Jr. *Tobacco and the Economy: Farms, Jobs, and Communities*. US Department of Agriculture Economic Research Service Report No. 789, 2000.

Geertz, Clifford. *The Interpretation of Cultures*. Basic Books, 1973.

Giertz, J. Fred. "An Experiment in Public Choice: The Miami Conservancy District," 1913–1922, *Public Choice* (1974): 63–75.

Glaser, Leah S. *The San Juan-Chama Project*. Bureau of Reclamation History Program, 1998.

Glaeser, Edward. *Triumph of the City: How Our Greatest Invention Makes Us Richer, Smarter, Greener, Healthier, and Happier*. Penguin Press, 2012.

Gosling, F.G., *The Manhattan Project: Making the Atomic Bomb*. DOE/MA-0001. Washington: History Division, Department of Energy, January 1999.

Gould, Stephen J. and Richard Lewontin. "The Spandrels of San Marco and the Panglossian Paradigm: A Critique of the Panglossian Program," *Proceedings of the Royal Society of London* B 205 (1979): 581–98.

Grassel, Kathy. "Taking Out the Jacks: Issues of Jetty Jack Removal in Bosque and River Restoration Planning." Master's in Water Resources Professional Project Report, University of New Mexico, 2002.

Griego, Tylee M. "When High-Water-Use Neighbors Move In: Farming Pecans in Valencia County, New Mexico," Master's in Water Resources Professional Project Report, University of New Mexico, 2022.

Gutzler, David S., Sharon M. Sullivan, and Deirdre M. Kann. "An Extreme Annual Precipitation Anomaly in the Preradiosonde Era," *Bulletin of the American Meteorological Society* 97, no. 6 (2016): 989–1001

Hall, G. Emlen. "Steve Reynolds—Portrait of a State Engineer as a Young Artist," *Natural Resources Journal* 38 (1998).

Hämäläinen, Pekka. *The Comanche Empire*. Yale University Press, 2008.

Harner, Mary, Emma Brinley Buckley, Mic Rhode, et al. *Loss of Open Areas and a Changing Albuquerque Bosque and River*. Middle Rio Grande Endangered Species Collaborative Program 2020 Science Symposium.

Hartley, J. J., *The Reclamation of the Missouri Bootheel: The Formation of the Little River Drainage District*. Arkansas State University, 2016.

Hays, Samuel P. *Conservation and the Gospel of Efficiency: The Progressive Conservation Movement, 1890–1920*. No. 40. University of Pittsburgh Press, 1999.

Heberlein, Thomas A. *Navigating Environmental Attitudes*. Oxford University Press, 2012.

Hedke, C.R. *A Report on the Irrigation of the Middle Rio Grande Valley, N.M., as it Relates to the Rio Grande Compact*, Rio Grande Valley Survey Commission, 1925.

Hobbes, Thomas. *Leviathan*. Open Road Media, 2020. http://public.eblib.com/choice/PublicFullRecord.aspx?p=6185336.

Hodges, Paul V. *Report on Irrigation and Water Supply of the Pueblos of New Mexico in the Rio Grande Basin*. N.p., 1938.

Holmes, K. John, and M. Gordon Wolman. "Early Development of Systems Analysis in Natural Resources Management from Man and Nature to the Miami Conservancy District," *Environmental Management* 27 (2001): 177–93.

Horgan, Paul. *Great River: The Rio Grande in North American History*. 4th ed. Wesleyan University Press, 1954.

Houghton, Kristopher N. "The Blighted History of the Alameda Land Grant: Montoya v. Unknown Heirs of Vigil," *Natural Resources Journal* (2008): 983–1008.

Howe, Frederic C. *The Modern City and Its Problems*. C. Scribner's Sons, 1915.

Jefferson, Thomas. *The Works of Thomas Jefferson*. Edited by Paul Leicester Ford. G.P. Putnam's Sons, 1904.

Karttunen, Frances E. *An Analytical Dictionary of Nahuatl*. University of Texas Press, 1983.

Kennedy, Joseph Camp Griffith. *Agriculture of the United States in 1860: Compiled from the Original Returns of the Eighth Census. Vol. 2.* US Government Printing Office, 1864.

Kochskämper, E., L. M. Glass, W. Haupt, S. Malekpour, and J. Grainger-Brown. "Resilience and the Sustainable Development Goals: A Scrutiny of Urban Strategies in the 100 Resilient Cities Initiative." *Journal of Environmental Planning and Management* (2025): 1–27.

Lamadrid, Enrique R., and José A. Rivera, eds. *Water for the People: The Global Heritage of New Mexico's Acequias*. University of New Mexico Press, 2023.

Larson, Robert W. "The Profile of a New Mexico Progressive." *New Mexico Historical Review* 45, no. 3 (1970): 5.

Lefebvre, Henri, *The Production of Space*. Translated by Donald Nicholson-Smith. Blackwell Publishing, 1991.

Leopold, Aldo. "A Criticism of the Booster Spirit." Speech prepared for Ten Dons Club, dated October 6, 1923. University of Wisconsin Library, Aldo Leopold Papers: 9/25/10-6—Writings #16 Unpublished Manuscripts, Typescript copies, section 5: Philosophic and Literary, to 1940, 355–67.

Leopold, Aldo. "A Plea for State-Owned Ducking Grounds." In *Aldo Leopold's Southwest*, edited by David E. Brown and Neal B. Carmony. University of New Mexico Press, 1995.

Leopold, Aldo. "A Plea for Wilderness Hunting Grounds," *Outdoor Life*, November 1925.

Leopold, Aldo. *A Sand County Almanac, and Sketches Here and There*. Oxford University Press, 1949.

Leopold, Aldo. *The River of the Mother of God: And Other Essays by Aldo Leopold*. University of Wisconsin Press, 1992.

Leopold, Aldo. "Wherefore Wildlife Ecology?" In *The River of the Mother of God and Other Essays*, edited by Susan L. Flader and J. Baird Callicott. University of Wisconsin Press, 1991.

Lepore, Jill. *The Story of America: Essays on Origins*. Princeton University Press, 2012.

Liebmann, Matthew. *Revolt: An Archaeological History of Pueblo Resistance and Revitalization in 17th Century New Mexico*. University of Arizona Press, 2012.

Long, A. "Senator Bursum and Pueblo Indians Land Act of 1924." Master's thesis, University of New Mexico, 1949.

Lucero, Brian Luna. "Old Towns Challenged by the Boom Town: The Villages of the Middle Rio Grande Valley and the Albuquerque Tricentennial." *New Mexico Historical Review* 82, no. 1 (2007): 3.

MacDonald, J., J. Cessna, and R. Mosheim. *Changing Structure, Financial Risks, and Government Policy for the U.S. Dairy Industry*. ERR-205, US Department of Agriculture, Economic Research Service, 2016.

Mann, Joshua. "A Reservoir Runs Through It: A Legislative and Administrative History of the Six Pueblos' Right to Store Prior and Paramount Water at El Vado." *Natural Resources Journal*, 2007.

Marousek, Linda A. "Orr v. Kneip: Defining the Limits of One Person, One Vote in the OAHE Conservancy Subdistrict." *South Dakota Law Review* 25 (1980): 597.

Marris, Emma. *Rambunctious Garden: Saving Nature in a Post-Wild World*. Bloomsbury Publishing USA, 2013.

Mathews, John Mabry. "State Councils of Defense." *American Political Science Review* 12 (1918): 509–510.

McCall, George A., *1850 Report of the Secretary of War Communicating Colonel McCall's Report in Relation to New Mexico*. 31st Congress, 2nd Session, Senate Executive Document No. 26. Government Printing Office, Washington, DC.

McDonald, Brian, John Tysseling, Michael Browde, and Lee Brown. "An Evolutionary History of the Middle Rio Grande Conservancy District." *New Mexico Business,* April (1980): 3–30.

Meine, Curt. *Aldo Leopold: His Life and Work*. University of Wisconsin Press, 1988.

Melton, Forrest S., Justin Huntington, Robyn Grimm, Jamie Herring, Maurice Hall, Dana Rollison, et al. "OpenET: Filling a Critical Data Gap in Water Management for the Western United States." *Journal of the American Water Resources Association* 58, no. 6 (2022): 971–94.

Melzer, Richard. "New Deal Success or 'Noble Failure?' Bosque Farms' Early Years as a Federal Resettlement Project, 1935–1939." *New Mexico Historical Review* 85, no. 1 (2010): 2.

Meyer, Michael C. *Water in the Hispanic Southwest: A Social and Legal History, 1550–1850*. University of Arizona Press, 1996.

Moore, Frances C. Arianna Stokes, Marc N. Conte, and Xiaoli Dong. "Noah's Ark in a Warming World: Climate Change, Biodiversity Loss, and Public Adaptation Costs in the United States." *Journal of the Association of Environmental and Resource Economists* 9, no. 5 (2022): 981–1015.

Moyer, Curt. "The Frank A. Hubbell Company, Sheep and Cattle." *New Mexico Historical Review* 54, no. 1 (1979): 64.

Murphy, Edward Charles. *Destructive Floods in the United States in 1904*. US Government Printing Office, 1904.

Obeng-Odoom, Franklin. "The Meaning, Prospects, and Future of the Commons: Revisiting the Legacies of Elinor Ostrom and Henry George." *American Journal of Economics and Sociology* 75, no. 2 (2016).

Orona, Kenneth M., "River of Culture, River of Power: Identity, Modernism, and Contest in the Middle Rio Grande Valley, 1848–1947." PhD thesis, Yale University, 1998.

Ostrom, Elinor. “A Long Polycentric Journey.” *Annual Review of Political Science* 13, no. 1 (2010): 1–23.

Ostrom, Elinor. *Governing the Commons: The Evolution of Institutions for Collective Action*. Cambridge University Press, 1990.

Ostrom, Elinor. “Institutions and the Environment.” *Economic Affairs* 28.3 (2008).

Ostrom, Elinor. “Public Entrepreneurship: A Case Study in Ground Water Basin Management.” PhD thesis, University of California, Los Angeles, 1965.

Ostrom, Elinor. “Why Do We Need to Protect Institutional Diversity?” *European Political Science* 11 (2012): 128–47.

Pecos, Regis. “The History of Cochiti Lake from the Pueblo Perspective.” *Natural Resources Journal* 47 (2007).

Phillips, Fred M., G. Emlen Hall, and Mary E. Black. *Reining in the Rio Grande: People, Land, and Water*. University of New Mexico Press, 2015.

Pinel, S. L. “Stopping the Flood of Damages from Cochiti Dam,” *Cultural Survival Quarterly Magazine*, vol 12–2 (1988).

Polanyi, Karl. *The Great Transformation: The Political and Economic Origins of Our Time*. Beacon Press, 2001.

Pouso, S., Á. Borja, L. E. Fleming, E. Gómez-Baggethun, M. P. White, and M. C. Uyarra. “Contact with Blue-Green Spaces During the COVID-19 Pandemic Lockdown is Beneficial for Mental Health.” *The Science of the Total Environment* 756 (2020): 143984.

Rajan, Raghuram, and Rodney Ramcharan. “The Anatomy of a Credit Crisis: The Boom and Bust in Farm Land Prices in the United States in the 1920s.” *American Economic Review* 105, no. 4 (2015).

Randell, Heather, and Andrew Curley. “Dams and Tribal Land Loss in the United States.” *Environmental Research Letters* 18, no. 9 (2023)

Reeves, Frank D. *History of New Mexico*. Center for Southwest Research, University Libraries, University of New Mexico, 1961.

Rivera, José A. *Acequia Culture: Water, Land, and Community in the Southwest*. University of New Mexico Press, 1998.

Rivera, José A. *Presas Efímeras of New Mexico*. Working Paper, Landscape Architecture Commons, 2022.

Russell, John C. "Racial Groups in the New Mexico Legislature." *The Annals of the American Academy of Political and Social Science* 195, no. 1 (1938): 62–71.

Sánchez, Joseph P., and Larry D. Miller. *Martineztown, 1823–1950: Hispanics, Italians, Jesuits & Land Investors in New Town Albuquerque*. Rio Grande Books, 2008.

Sánchez Joseph P, and Spanish Colonial Research Center. *Don Fernando Durán y Chaves's Land and Legacy*. Spanish Colonial Research Center, National Park Service, 1998.

Sando, Joe. *Pueblo Nations: Eight Centuries of Pueblo Indian History*. Clear Light Publishers, 1992.

Sando, J. *Pueblo Profiles: Cultural Identity Through Centuries of Change*. Clear Light Publishers, 1998.

Sant, A. *From the Ground Up: Local Efforts to Build Resilient Cities*. Island Press, 2022.

Sargeant, Kathryn, and Mary Davis. *Shining River, Precious Land: An Oral History of Albuquerque's North Valley*. Albuquerque Museum, 1986.

Schechter, Ronald. "Review of 'From the German of Doctor Ralph': Two New Translations of Voltaire's Candide, by Daniel Gordon and David Wootton," *Eighteenth-Century Studies* 35, no. 4 (2002): 635–37.

Scurlock, Dan. *From the Rio to the Sierra: An Environmental History of the Middle Rio Grande Basin.* US Department of Agriculture, Forest Service, Rocky Mountain Research Station, 1998

Sen, Amartya. *Development as Freedom.* Oxford University Press, 1999.

Sen, Amartya. *Home in the World: A Memoir.* W. W. Norton, 2022.

Smith, Carl. *City Water, City Life: Water and the Infrastructure of Ideas in Urbanizing Philadelphia, Boston, and Chicago*. University of Chicago Press, 2013.

Smith, Jeffrey S., Matthew R. Engel, Douglas A. Hurt, Jeffery E. Roth, and James M. Stevens. "La Cultura de la Acequia Madre: Cleaning a Community Irrigation Ditch." *The North American Geographer* 3, no. 1 (2001).

Starr, F. "A Study of the Census of the Pueblo of Cochiti, New Mexico." *Proceeding of the Davenport Academy of Natural Sciences,* Vol. 7, (1899): 33–44.

Stone, Mark C., and Ryan R. Morrison. "Human Impacts on the Hydrology, Geomorphology, and Restoration Potential of Southwestern Rivers." In *Standing Between Life and Extinction: Ethics and Ecology of Conserving Aquatic Species in North American Deserts*, edited by David L. Propst, Jack E. Williams, Kevin R. Bestgen, and Christopher W. Hoagstrom. University of Chicago Press, 2020.

Susskind, Lawrence. "Water and Democracy: New Roles for Civil Society in Water Governance." *International Journal of Water Resources Development* 29, no. 4 (December 2013): 666–77.

Teeters, Lila M. "'A Simple Act of Justice': The Pueblo Rejection of US Citizenship in the Early Twentieth Century," *The Journal of the Gilded Age and Progressive Era* 21, no. 4 (2022).

Theis, Charles V. "The Relation Between the Lowering of the Piezometric Surface and the Rate and Duration of Discharge of a Well Using Ground-Water Storage," *Eos, Transactions American Geophysical Union* 16.2 (1935).

Thompson, Stephen A. "Urbanization and the Middle Rio Grande Conservancy District," *Geographical Review* (1986).

Trail, Shanelle M., and Frank A. Ward. "Uniting Agricultural Water Management, Economics, and Policy for Climate Adaptation Through a New Assessment of Water Markets for Arid Regions." *Agricultural Water Management* 305 (2024): 109101.

Turner, Matthew A. "Landscape Preferences and Patterns of Residential Development." *Journal of Urban Economics* 57, no. 1 (2005): 19–54.

Twitchell, Ralph Emerson. *The Leading Facts of New Mexican History: Vol. 5.* Torch Press, 1917.

United States Bureau of the Census, and United States Bureau of Agricultural Economics. *United States Census of Agriculture, 1950. Volume 5, Special Reports. Part 9, Economic Class and Type of Farm : A Graphic Summary, Cooperative Report*. Washington, D.C.: US Dept. of Commerce, Bureau of the Census and US Dept. of Agriculture, Bureau of Agricultural Economics.

United States Department of Agriculture, National Agricultural Statistics Service. *2017 Census of Agriculture*. https://www.nass.usda.gov/Publications/AgCensus/2017/index.php.

US Fish and Wildlife Service. *The Economic Contributions of Recreational Visitation at Bosque del Apache National Wildlife Refuge*. Division of Economics, US Fish and Wildlife Service, 2019.

Van Citters, Karen, and Kathy Roxlau. *A Characterization of Historic Resources Along Bridge Boulevard from Eighth Street to Coors Boulevard*. Van Citters Historic Preservation, 2015.

Van Cleave, Marjorie. "Vegetative Changes in the Middle Rio Grande Conservancy District." Master's thesis, University of New Mexico, 1935.

Van Dyke, John C. *The Desert: Further Studies in Natural Appearances*. Johns Hopkins University Press, 1999.

Veihl, Ashley. "Securing Environmental Flows for the Rio Grande Silvery Minnow." Master's in Water Resources Professional Project Report, University of New Mexico, 2023.

Vigil, Maurilio, and Roy Lujan. "Parallels in the Career of Two Hispanic US Senators," *The Journal of Ethnic Studies* 13, no. 4 (1986): 1.

Von Thünen, Johann. *The Isolated State in Relation to Agriculture and Political Economy*. Palgrave Macmillan UK, 2009.

Wahl, Richard W. "Redividing the Waters: The Reclamation Act of 1902." *Natural Resources & Environment* 10, no. 1 (Summer 1995).

Walcott, Charles D., *Twenty-First Annual Report of the Director of the United States Geological Survey, 1899–1900: Part IV—Hydrology*. 1901.

Walden, R., "The Pueblo Confederation's Political Wing: The All Indian Pueblo Council, 1920–1975." Master's thesis, University of New Mexico, 2011.

Walker, A. P., and P. W. Cockerill. *Farm Organization Practices and Costs of Producing Crops in the Middle Rio Grande Conservancy District of New Mexico*. Agricultural Experiment Station, New Mexico College of Agriculture and Mechanic Arts, State College of New Mexico. 1933.

Wallace, Jon M., "Livestock, Land, and Dollars: The Sheep Industry of Territorial New Mexico." Master's thesis, University of New Mexico, 2014.

Walter, Paul A.F., "Octaviano Ambrosio Larrazolo," *New Mexico Historical Review* 7, no. 2 (1932).

Weir, Lorraine. "'Time Immemorial' and Indigenous Rights: A Genealogy and Three Case Studies (Calder, Van Der Peet, Tsilhqot'in) from British Columbia." *Journal of Historical Sociology* 26, no. 3 (2013): 383–411.

Welsh, Michael. "The United States Army Corps of Engineers in the Middle Rio Grande Valley. 1935–1955." *New Mexico Historical Review* 60, 3 (1985).

Wenger, Tisa Joy. "Land, Culture, and Sovereignty in the Pueblo Dance Controversy." *Journal of the Southwest* 46, no. 2 (2004), 381–412.

Wenger, Tisa Joy. *We Have a Religion: The 1920s Pueblo Indian Dance Controversy and American Religious Freedom*. University of North Carolina Press, 2009.

Westphall, Victor. "Albuquerque in the 1870's." *New Mexico Historical Review* 23, no. 4 (1948): 2.

Whitehead, Alfred North. *Science and the Modern World: Lowell Lectures.* Macmillan, 1925.

Wild, Peter, and Neil Carmony. "The Trip Not Taken: John C. Van Dyke, Heroic Doer or Armchair Seer?" *The Journal of Arizona History* 34.1 (1993): 65–80.

Williamson-Teller, Verna. "Protecting Water Quality and Religious Freedom at Isleta Pueblo." In *Original Instructions: Indigenous Teachings for a Sustainable Future*, edited by Melissa K. Nelson. Inner Traditions/Bear, 2008.

Wojan, Timothy R. "Metaphors of Regional Policy: Cities as Engines, Multilevel Governance in Gardens." *Regional Studies* 51, no. 2 (2017): 324–35.

Wollman, Nathaniel. *The Value of Water in Alternative Uses: With Special Application to Water Use in the San Juan and Rio Grande Basins of New Mexico*. University of New Mexico Press, 1962.

Wood, Jared. "Dynamic Fallowing in the Middle Rio Grande: A Look at The Environmental Water Leasing Program." Master's Professional Project Report, University of New Mexico Water Resources, and Community and Regional Planning programs, 2023.

Woodhouse, C.A., D. W. Stahle, and J. Villanueva-Díaz. "Rio Grande and Rio Conchos Water Supply Variability from Instrumental and Paleoclimatic Records," *Climate Research*, 51 (2012): 125–36.

Worster, Donald. *A River Running West: The Life of John Wesley Powell*. Oxford University Press, 2002.

Wozniak, Frank E. *Irrigation in the Rio Grande Valley, New Mexico: A Study and Annotated Bibliography of the Development of Irrigation Systems*. US Forest Service Rocky Mountain Field Station, 1998.

Wu, JunJie, Jialing Yu, and Walid Oueslati. "Open Space in US Urban Areas: Where Might There Be Too Much or Too Little of a Good Thing?" *Journal of the Association of Environmental and Resource Economists* 10, no. 2 (2023): 315–52.

Index

Page numbers in italic text indicate illustrations.